"I liked helping
my mom with the
jelly bean
thumbprints
at Easter."
—Louis, 6

"The triangle
cookies with the
nuts on top
are *good*."
—Jenna, 11

"It was fun
to decorate the
cookies for our
Halloween party."
—Isabel, 7

"These congo
bars rock!"
—Lucas, 9

"Blondies are a
really nice change
from brownies.
I love the walnuts."
—Sophia, 11

"The sugar cookie
flowers are super
delicious!"
—Olivia, 4

Mom's **Big** Book of
COOKIES

200 FAMILY FAVORITES YOU'LL LOVE MAKING AND YOUR KIDS WILL LOVE EATING

LAUREN CHATTMAN

The Harvard Common Press

Boston, Massachusetts

For Rose and Eve
and all of their cookie-loving friends in Sag Harbor

The Harvard Common Press
535 Albany Street
Boston, Massachusetts 02118
www.harvardcommonpress.com

Printed in China

Printed on acid-free paper

Library of Congress Cataloging-in-Publication Data
Chattman, Lauren.
   Mom's big book of cookies : 200 family favorites you'll love making and your kids will love eating / Lauren Chattman.
      p. cm.
   Includes index.
   ISBN 1-55832-300-7 (hardcover : alk. paper)
1. Cookies. I. Title.
   TX772.C383 2006
   641.8'654—dc22

2006002862

ISBN-13: 978-1-55832-300-1
ISBN-10: 1-55832-300-7

Special bulk-order discounts are available on this and other Harvard Common Press books. Companies and organizations may purchase books for premiums or resale, or may arrange a custom edition, by contacting the Marketing Director at the address above.

Cover design by Night & Day Design
Interior design by Marysarah Quinn
Photography by Becky Luigart-Stayner
Food styling by Debby Nakos
Prop styling by Jan Gautro
Illustrations by Laura Tedeschi

10 9 8 7 6 5 4 3 2 1

acknowledgments

Of all things sweet, cookies are my favorite. Thanks so much to everyone at The Harvard Common Press—Bruce Shaw, Valerie Cimino, Christine Alaimo, Liza Beth, Betsy Young, Christine Corcoran Cox, Virginia Downes, Pat Jalbert-Levine, Abby Collier, Amy Etcheson, and Megan Weireter—for helping me write my dream book. Thanks also to copyeditor Robin Catalano for editorial fine-tuning. I am absolutely thrilled that this book contains so many photos by Becky Luigart-Stayner. Without them, it would be like a sugar cookie without the icing. Debby Nakos did a beautiful job of styling the cookies for the photo shoot. Thanks also to Marysarah Quinn for the fun interior book design and to Night & Day Design for the kid-friendly cover.

Thanks to Angela Miller for her always sage advice. Through his example, Roland Mesnier reminded me to seek perfection in every cookie, and he taught me some really great recipes. The students in Mrs. Cosgrove's and Mrs. Daniels's nursery and pre-K classes at the Tuller School, and the students in Mrs. Deyermond's and Mr. Malone's third- and fourth-grade classes at Sag Harbor Elementary, enthusiastically tasted and critiqued my work.

My daughters, Rose and Eve, are experts in baking beyond their years. Their contributions to this book are too numerous to list. My husband, Jack Bishop, knows almost as much as they do, and I thank him with all my heart for helping me through every step of this wonderful project.

contents

cookie basics for moms

As I pull into the Tuller School parking lot, I see 10 little heads turn away from swinging, sliding, and playing in the sandbox and swivel toward my silver station wagon. Their reaction is Pavlovian. Before I can grab my shopping bag of biscotti with M&M's and open the door, the kids are racing toward the fence that separates the cars from the playground, some of them shouting, "Cookies! We want cookies!" They gather around me as I pull the container from my bag, attempting orderliness, because by now they know that I won't dole out today's samples until they've quit pushing each other and are quiet. My daughter Eve glows with pride at her mother, the cookie lady. Mrs. Cosgrove and Mrs. Daniels wait in the background, smiling, because they know that whatever is left over will go to them.

It's a scene I got used to, because for a whole school year I brought cookies to get some feedback from my target audience: kids. Once I got over the fear of being rushed by a gang of hungry four-year-olds, I never felt more popular. That's not to say that this crowd was easy to please. Some kids didn't like nuts, some didn't like oatmeal, some didn't even like chocolate. And the thing about four-year-olds is they don't hold back on the criticism. If one of them thought the day's cookie was yucky, she wouldn't discreetly wrap it in a napkin and throw it away. Instead, she'd hand it right back to me, with a bite taken out. But I can honestly say that during the course of many months, I baked cookies that pleased each one of kids in the Tuller School pre-K.

I also presented cookies to a more sophisticated audience, the third-graders at Sag Harbor Elementary. On Tuesdays, after I handed out pizza to Mrs. Deyermond's class, I'd pass around the cookies I'd made that morning. If my daughter Rose, the most discriminating cookie tester on Long Island, deigned to eat a cookie after eating a slice of pizza, then I knew it was a winner. But even if she turned me down, I found enthusiastic takers for my Bird's Nest Cookies with Easter Eggs or my Black and White Cookies. The older kids were often interested in how certain cookies were made. How did I shape the dough into nests? Was there a trick to spreading the black and white icings so they stayed separate? Their curiosity gave me hope about the future of home baking.

To get the adult perspective on baking for kids, I shared cookies with my friends who are moms. I was expecting only opinions and advice, but I also got a ton of sentimental reminiscences. One friend told me about her own grandma's perfectly pale Scottish shortbread. Another described her entire family's mania for chewy almond macaroons. After all of this baking, eating, and talking, I was more convinced than ever of the importance of cookies in the family diet. For four-year-olds, there is the instant gratification of eating something yummy. For nine-year-olds, making them is a highly enjoyable way to learn that food doesn't only come from a package or a drive-through window. For grownups, baking and eating cookies is a way to please and teach children, as well as a way to remember the pleasures of our own childhoods.

This book contains the 200 or so recipes that passed muster with my children and their friends and schoolmates. It is a scrapbook of several years of baking, and each cookie has a special memory attached to it. I made a Giant Chocolate Chip Cookie for my older daughter's first slumber party; the Candy-Covered Gingerbread House sat proudly on the counter until February one year. I know that I will bake my favorite cookies over and over again, month after month, year after year. Thanksgiving Maple

Leaves will be served alongside the apple pie as long as I am hosting Thanksgiving dinner. Santa's visit will always be preceded by the baking of Stained Glass Star Cookies. Early every morning, I'll be taking out a roll of Slice-and-Bake Chocolate Chippers cookie dough and cutting off a few rounds to bake fresh for the lunch boxes. Homemade cookies help me and my family have fun together in the kitchen and foster traditions to celebrate special days and ordinary days, too.

I hope that you will enjoy all of the recipes included here, but more than that I hope that you will find a handful of favorites that you'll make over and over again until they become your signature recipes. When I was a kid, my great-grandmother Rose (my daughter is named after her) brought her signature Sour Cream Icebox Cookies to our house whenever she visited. My sisters and I (and I think my dad was involved here, too) greedily emptied the coffee tin of cookies within minutes of her arrival. I didn't realize as I gobbled that these light, tangy cookies with a dusting of cinnamon sugar were the stuff of memories. But years later, my sisters, my cousins, and I still talk about them when we see each other at family occasions. The cookies are a touchstone for us. They bind us together as a family as they help us remember our great-grandma and our own childhoods. I was overcome with excitement years ago when I found the recipe, in her handwriting, in my mother's recipe box. My own mom never tried to duplicate them. Instead, she made my great-grandma's beef and vegetable soup and her potato pancakes, and makes them to this day. But she saved the vanilla extract–stained piece of paper, as if she knew that I would want to make them myself and share them with my own children. My own experience tells me that homemade treats will not only please your kids while they're eating them, but they also will give them a sense of family history. Who knows? It may even prompt them to ask you for recipes when they have kids of their own.

From Wedding Cakes to Oatmeal Cookies

If you had told me when I was in cooking school that 10 years down the road my toughest critics would be preschoolers, I would have been confused. Is this why I was spending my nights learning how to make fondant-covered wedding cakes? But looking back, it makes complete sense.

My career as a professional baker and cookbook author coincided with motherhood. I left my job as a teacher when my first daughter, Rose, was born, and began a nighttime course in professional baking and pastry arts in New York City when she was three months old. At 5 P.M. my husband would take over the child care, and I'd walk the 10 blocks to cooking school, where I learned how to bake fancy cakes. This training led to a job at a high-end restaurant in East Hampton, where I'd sometimes make 300 individual desserts a night during the high season. But on my days off, I was cooking simple food and baking simple treats. I left restaurant work to write a series of cookbooks filled with streamlined recipes for family meals and quick, kid-friendly desserts. By

then I had two daughters, and I was thrilled to have a job essentially developing recipes just for them.

When I wrote *Mom's Big Book of Baking* (The Harvard Common Press, 2001), I covered all the baking basics, from pancakes and waffles to pizza and cupcakes. I used my training and restaurant experience, in combination with my experience as a mom, to come up with recipes for the highest-quality baked goods with the least amount of fuss. The cookie chapter was the longest and most fun to write. There I was able to record all my favorite recipes for classic cookies. But there were a lot of recipes and ideas I didn't have room to cover, since I had to save some space for the muffins and popovers.

When it was time to think about another book, I naturally thought of cookies. In an entire book devoted to the subject, I'd be able to present some of my favorites that hadn't made it into the first book and develop new recipes for fun cookies beyond the classics. The candy aisle of the supermarket was a magnet for my kids, so I knew I'd want to develop recipes for a bunch of cookies made with candy. There were so many holidays beyond Christmas that deserved their own cookies—Halloween, Thanksgiving, Chinese New Year, President's Day.... It actually wasn't all that tough to get to 200. In fact, once I got going it was kind of hard to stop.

The same principles of taste and simplicity that guided me in *Mom's Big Book of Baking* guided me with cookies. Because of my passion for pastry and my professional training, I set the same high standards for my chocolate chip cookies that I would for more

I Hosted a Back-to-School Cookie Exchange Party, and You Can, Too

During the writing of this book, I gave away hundreds of cookies to family, friends, neighbors, and total strangers. (I got some weird looks in the schoolyard as I tried to unload that day's work, offering zipper-lock plastic bags of chocolate chip or peanut butter cookies to parents waiting to pick up their kids.) Then one day, just after I had tested my last recipe (Chocolate Moose Cookies, for the record), I started to think it might be fun to ask people over for a cookie party where I wasn't the one doing all of the baking. I set the date for the Sunday before the first day of school and invited all of the girls in my daughters' new classes, along with their mothers. (It's not that I think that cookies are a girl thing, it's just that my small backyard can't accommodate more than 30 people at once.) I asked each mother-daughter pair to bring 30 or so homemade cookies. When the guests RSVP'd, I'd jot down what kind of cookies they were planning on bringing, nixing their first choices if necessary, so we wouldn't end up swapping 15 different kinds of oatmeal cookies.

To prepare for the party, I made finger sandwiches and lemonade and set up the food outside in the yard. Then I set out 15 large paper plates inside on the dining room table. When the guests arrived, I arranged their cookies on one of the plates, along with a little card I had prepared with the name of the cookie, its baker, and a note if it contained nuts because one of the kids at the party was allergic. I was impressed with the variety—oatmeal and peanut butter were represented, but so were Scottish shortbread, Italian biscotti, and all-American molasses cookies. There were some terrific cookies that I hadn't yet considered, like the late-summer zucchini bars and gooey maple-walnut tassies. I filed away some good ideas for my next book!

After we had lunch outside, we all went indoors and filled the cookie tins we had brought with two cookies from each of the plates on the table. Everyone went home with a wonderful selection of treats from bakers all around the town. The kids would be able to take some cookies in their lunch boxes on the first day of school, and their families would be able to enjoy the leftovers for the next few days.

complicated baking projects. I don't want to eat them or serve them if they're not absolutely the best. But as a busy mom, I don't have time for the fanatical measures I used to take, like chopping up imported chocolate bars to make my own chocolate chips. So I try to strike a balance, suggesting Ghirardelli Double Chocolate Chips for European-style richness, instead of Hershey or Nestlé.

It didn't take me long to realize that the keys to kitchen success are the same whether you are baking for demanding restaurant customers or for your own children. In both cases, you have to know your audience and be realistic about how much time you have to bake. I used to love to make beautifully iced cookies, but now I use sprinkles and sanding sugar more often than a pastry bag to decorate. It's quicker, for sure. Just as important, kids find sprinkles appetizing beyond any other decoration, and even little ones can toss them onto cookies. When baking for and with kids, it's not about camera-ready cookies, but about taking into account what they're going to enjoy most, and then getting messy and having fun.

Filling the Cookie Jar

I wanted to get creative with this book, so I didn't set too many ground rules for myself. But I knew there weren't going to be any overly grown-up flavors or fussy styles. So bourbon balls and delicate tuiles that tend to shatter in little hands were out. There weren't going to be cookies so costly or difficult to decorate that they'd make novice bakers cry. So cookies garnished with gold leaf and cookies iced to look like Wedgwood china would not be included. Other than that, I tried to keep an open mind about what kids would like. Sure, I have one child whose preferred food coloring is white. But I have another one whose favorite fruit is the fig. I have considered both types of eater, and there are many cookies here for each of them, and for all kids in between.

Chapter 1 is a tribute to the triumvirate that rules American cookiedom: chocolate chip, oatmeal, and peanut butter. Here you'll find my very best versions of these classics. In addition, you'll find variations that keep you in the comfort zone of these familiar favorites while allowing you to experiment with your kids' preferred flavors. If they're like my kids and love coffee Heath bar crunch ice cream, they'll gobble up Coffee Heath Bar Crunch–Chip Cookies (page 28). If your children are culinary globetrotters, Oatmeal Cookies with Apricots and Pistachios (page 41) add some exotic Mediterranean sweetness and crunch to the classic oatmeal cookie.

Chapter 2 is a collection of slice-and-bake cookies. Most kids are familiar with this concept because they've seen commercials for refrigerated cookie dough hundreds of times. Surprise them by making some from scratch. If you keep a roll of Pecan Sandies (page 67) or Brown Sugar Buttons (page 71) in the freezer, you can slice off as few or as many as you like whenever your kids get the craving, just like they do on TV.

Chapter 3 contains recipes that I've collected over the years to ensure that I'll be able to make cookies even when my pantry is bare. These "desperation" recipes include a four-ingredient shortbread (see page 88) that is absolutely fabulous. If you think the situation is hopeless because you've run out of flour and the market is closed, you are so wrong! There are always Flourless Peanut Butter Cookies (page 81) or Cinnamon Toast Meringues (page 92).

Brownies and bar cookies are a mom's staple, because they're so quick to make and so easy to pack. Not only will you find the recipe for my best brownies in **Chapter 4**, but you'll also find my best blondies, gingerbread, lemon squares, and seven-layer bars.

Chapter 5 is one of my favorites, because it is pure sugar-fueled fun. Every cookie recipe here includes candy as a key ingredient. Just choose your poison—Reese's Pieces, peppermint patties, malted milk balls, Kraft Caramels—and get baking.

For times when two cookies are better than one, turn to **Chapter 6** for different ways to sandwich together cookies with a matching filling. Chocolate cookies with vanilla filling are represented, of course, but so are more unusual combinations, such as molasses with maple and hazelnut with Nutella and raspberry.

Chapter 7 is for sentimental and old-fashioned moms. Here you will find such "heirloom" recipes as Snickerdoodles and Raisin Hermits (pages 174 and 180), as well as newer heirlooms like Ranger Cookies (page 181), made with Special K cereal, and Potato Chip Cookies (page 182). My great-grandma's sour cream cookies (see page 190) are included, too.

For rainy days and snow days, I've compiled a bunch of cookie projects to keep kids busy and satisfied. Check out **Chapter 8** when you hear the bad weather report, and pick up supplies before you are housebound with nothing to do. If your kids are artistic, get them busy painting sugar cookie dough with egg-yolk paint or rubber-stamping the dough with food coloring. If they're animal lovers, let them make Chocolate Chip Kitty Cats or Chocolate Moose Cookies (pages 206 and 207).

Chapter 9 will keep you in cookies during holidays throughout the year. If you have never celebrated Mardi Gras or Chinese New Year, you might think about doing so now, just as a good excuse to make Chinese New Year Fortune Cookies or Mardi Gras Praline Cookies (pages 218 and 220).

This book ends with a selection of "cookies in a jar." These are homemade cookie mixes to make and give as gifts. Sometimes the only gift more thoughtful than a batch of homemade cookies is a jar of homemade cookie mix, which lets the recipient bake some of your delicious cookies from scratch with hardly any work at all.

Common Sense, Uncommon Cookies

Here are some commonsense tips worth keeping in mind when getting ready to bake, even if you've heard them many times before.

Choose your recipe wisely. If you're rushed and hassled, choose a recipe that you can put together while doing five other things. You know your abilities. If you've never whipped egg whites before and the kids are relying on you to bring cookies to tomorrow's PTA bake sale, don't try meringues tonight. Stick with something familiar—maybe chocolate chip or peanut butter cookies, but with a new twist. When you want to try a new type of cookie or one that requires special shaping or decorating, set aside some time just for baking. Especially if you are working with your kids, don't try to answer the phone or empty the dishwasher as you work. I can't tell you how many cookies I've burned because I was on the phone with my own mother while putting away laundry and supervising homework, and didn't hear the timer going off.

Make sure you have all your ingredients before you begin. There's a very good reason why recipes begin with the ingredients list: so that you can go through it and make sure you've got everything. Avoid the sadness of having creamed together the butter and sugar only to realize that you're short a half cup of flour by checking that you have everything before you start.

Shop wisely for ingredients. Cookie baking can be an expensive hobby, but cutting corners can be a mistake. Saving money by sacrificing flavor is not an option for me. I would never substitute margarine for more expensive butter. But I do buy butter in quantity at my local warehouse club, where it actually costs the same or less than margarine at the supermarket. It will keep in the freezer for months. Likewise, pure vanilla extract is much more expensive than imitation vanilla extract, but worth it. I buy big bottles at Costco, but if you don't bake that often, a small bottle will take you through many batches. Conversely, certain luxury ingredients aren't worth the money. Inexpensive baking chocolate is indistinguishable from expensive imported chocolate when baked in brownies. But for frostings, I prefer the high-end stuff.

Follow directions. With any recipe, the keys to success are reading carefully and following directions exactly. If the directions say refrigerate the dough before baking, don't skip that step. If you are instructed to line a baking pan with parchment paper or aluminum foil, just do it! Pay special attention to any hints for success in the recipe headnotes. If I put a warning about a possible mistake in there, chances are good to excellent that I made the mistake the first time I baked the cookies.

Measure carefully. You may be able to eyeball it when you're making tomato sauce or bean dip, but don't try it with cookies. Like all successful chemistry experiments, successful cookie baking depends on the exact measuring of ingredients so that they will react to each other in the expected way.

When making substitutions, use common sense. In general, limit substitutions to ingredients that are add-ons to cookies: nuts, chocolate chips, dried fruit. If you prefer walnuts to almonds, go for it. The same is true for dried cranberries and raisins. These items add texture and flavor to cookies but don't affect the chemistry of the dough. Other substitutions can ruin a recipe. Avoid substituting one kind of sugar for another (brown sugar contains more moisture than white sugar, and will make the finished cookies dense and wet). Don't substitute baking soda for baking powder or your cookies won't rise properly (baking soda doesn't have acid, but baking powder does; that's why baking soda is used only in doughs with acidic ingredients).

When in doubt, pull them out. During college, I had a bad reputation—for baking the world's hardest chocolate chip cookies. What was wrong with my recipe, I wondered, every time someone made fun of my just-baked, rock-hard specimens. When I moved into my first apartment, I figured it out. Here I was able to make perfectly soft, chewy cookies from the same recipe. The oven in my college dorm must have run hot, so when I baked my cookies for the recommended time, they overcooked. Use an oven thermometer to check that your oven is running at the temperature it is set for. Even after you determine that your oven is at the correct temperature, keep a close eye on your cookies. They are much smaller than cakes and muffins, and a minute or two can mean the difference between a perfectly baked and an overbaked batch. If you have any doubt that they need more time in the oven, pull them out. It's okay if the cookies still feel soft or even look a little underdone. They will continue to cook as they cool.

The Cookie Baker's Pantry

How will you respond when your child waits until bedtime to tell you that it's your turn to bring the snack for the Girl Scout meeting the next day? That will depend on how well stocked your pantry is. If you are out of flour, brown sugar, and eggs, then it'll be a quick stop at the 7-Eleven on the way to school for a bag of Oreos. When well supplied with baking essentials, you can easily put together Pantry Blondies (page 95) as the kids fall asleep. Here is a list of ingredients that will allow you to bake on the spur of the moment. Having a stocked pantry will also make shopping for ingredients for a particular recipe much easier and less expensive when you get to the cash register.

Butter: There are a couple of recipes in this book that use vegetable oil or shortening, but the vast majority are made with unsalted butter. Butter lends baked goods a delicious flavor that's missing with those other fats. I prefer unsalted butter because it has a purer, fresher flavor than salted butter, which is sometimes too salty for desserts.

Candy: I have a beautiful antique bread box in my kitchen that I originally bought to keep bread, of course. But since my children began attending birthday parties and bringing home goody bags stuffed with loose candy, it's become the candy box. If you have a similar candy stash, save some for cookie decorating. I enjoy using candy in cookies so much that I've written a whole chapter on cookies incorporating candy. For these recipes, you might have to make an extra trip to the store.

Chocolate: Inexpensive baking squares work very well in recipes where the chocolate must be melted. Unsweetened cocoa powder is a great pantry staple. I keep both natural (nonalkalized) cocoa powder and Dutch-processed cocoa powder on hand for different recipes. Pay attention to the type called for in a recipe, because they react differently when mixed into dough.

Chocolate Chips: This is a major food group in my house. I prefer Ghirardelli Double Chocolate Chips, but my kids like Nestlé's better and call me on it every time I try to sneak the richer-tasting chips into cookies. I buy big bags of chips at the warehouse club when I can, because I go through them rather quickly. I buy less frequently used chips—butterscotch, white chocolate, milk chocolate, peanut butter, toffee bits—when I need them.

Coconut: I use both sweetened flaked and unsweetened dried coconut. If you can't find unsweetened coconut in the supermarket, look in the natural foods store.

Dried Fruit: Choose plump, moist dried fruit. If your raisins are old and dry, they will absorb moisture from the cookie dough, affecting the texture of your cookies.

Eggs: All the recipes in the book call for large eggs. It makes no difference whether they are white or brown.

Flour: I use unbleached all-purpose flour, either King Arthur or Hecker's, in my cookies.

Food Coloring: A small set from the supermarket will take you through any cookie project, but if you are mail-ordering other items from King Arthur Flour The Baker's Catalogue (see Resources, page 257) anyway, splurge and buy a larger set of 8 or 12, just for fun.

Jams and Jellies: Seeds or no seeds, it's a matter of taste. Likewise, substitute different flavors of jams and jellies in recipes depending on what your kids like.

Meringue Powder: This powder is the secret ingredient to good royal icing. Buy or mail-order (see Resources, page 257) one container and it will see you through 10 years of gingerbread houses.

Nonstick Cooking Spray: This is a good substitute for parchment paper, to ensure that your cookies won't stick to the baking sheets.

Nuts: Nuts are expensive, so I like to buy them in economy-size bags. I keep even small quantities of nuts in the freezer, because they go rancid quickly if stored at room temperature.

Peanut Butter: Over the years I've gone back and forth about what kind of peanut butter is best in cookies. Right now, I'm in a Jif/Skippy phase. Although I love Smucker's All-Natural Peanut Butter (which is made by Jif) on sandwiches because it's less sweet, I think that peanut butter without any additives produces a slightly greasier cookie. At any rate, don't use freshly ground peanut butter from the natural foods store in cookies. It is too coarse and grainy to produce good results.

Rolled Oats: I use Quaker old-fashioned rolled oats in my oatmeal cookies. You can substitute Quaker quick-cooking oats, which are really just rolled oats that have been chopped up a little bit. But don't use instant oats, because they've been precooked and dehydrated and will turn to mush in baked goods.

Spices: Small jars of cinnamon, nutmeg, allspice, and ground cloves will allow you to make the spicier cookies in this book.

Sprinkles: I keep a large container of multicolored sprinkles in the cabinet, to use on cookies as well as the occasional ice cream cone. I mail-order individual colors (see Resources, page 257) because everyone in my house has a favorite, and it's fun to sprinkle cookies with custom colors for different holidays.

Sugar: I keep granulated, light brown, dark brown, and confectioners' sugar in my pantry at all times. Stored in zipper-lock plastic bags or airtight containers, sugar will keep indefinitely, so there's no reason not to buy economy-size bags. I also have a box of turbinado sugar (sugar in the raw), which I like to sprinkle on some cookies. In addition, I have a rainbow of colored sanding sugars for decorating (see Resources, page 257).

Vanilla Extract: Pure vanilla extract gives many cookies their intoxicating aroma and pure flavor. To my taste buds, cookies baked with artificial vanilla taste weird and fake in comparison.

Essential Equipment for Easy Cookie Baking

None of the cookies in this book require special equipment. If you've baked before, you probably already own most of the stuff below. A small investment in a few unusual but extremely helpful items (a small cookie scoop, a roll of parchment paper) will pay off in convenience— I guarantee it.

Baking Pans: You'll need an 8-inch square baking pan for brownies and bars, a 9-inch springform pan for the Cookie Pizza (page 202), and a 10-inch round cake pan for the Giant Chocolate Chip Cookie (page 203).

Baking Sheets: If you are in the market for new baking sheets, look for good-quality, heavy sheets that won't warp in the oven. Cookies baked on flimsy, light-weight sheets tend to scorch before they are cooked through. It's handy to have both rimmed and rimless baking sheets. Cookies baked on parchment paper–covered rimless sheets are easy to slide right onto racks for cooling. Rimmed sheets are good for catching errant sprinkles and sanding sugar that would other-wise cover the floor or the bottom of your oven.

Cookie Cutters: I have inexpensive sets of small metal cookie cutters for Halloween, Christmas, Valentine's Day, and Easter. You can find them in cookware shops and online. I also have some special, more expensive large cutters to make impressive cookies (a large copper star, a large copper maple leaf). And of course, I have a selection that's just for fun: a dog bone, an airplane, a set of circus animals, the letters of the alphabet. I prefer metal cutters to plastic, which don't cut through cookie dough as well. Hand wash and then quickly dry metal cookie cutters to prevent rusting.

Craft Sticks: These make great icing spreaders when you are decorating cookies with kids. Unlike metal spreaders, they're cheap and disposable, so you can replace them every time one of the kids sticks one in the wrong color icing or in his mouth!

Double Boiler: The gentle heat of a double boiler melts chocolate without turning it grainy. If you don't own one (I don't), you can improvise by placing a stainless steel bowl over a saucepan of gently simmering water.

Electric Mixer: A stand mixer like my heavy-duty KitchenAid is great, and it is worth the investment if you bake cakes and breads as well as cookies. A hand-held mixer will work just fine for mixing most cookie doughs.

Food Processor: Although I love them for making pizza pie dough, I think that food processors overmix cookie doughs, making a gummy mess. I use mine for chopping nuts and pureeing fruit fillings for cookies, but a chef's knife and a blender will do those jobs just as well.

Ice Cream Scoop: A small ice cream or cookie scoop (specifically, #40, which holds 1 table-spoon) will help you produce a batch of uniform, beautifully round drop cookies. Buy one and you'll never go back to the rounded tablespoon method again.

Measuring Cups and Spoons: All successful baking requires precise measuring, and cookie

baking is no exception. Use clear liquid measuring cups for liquid ingredients, plastic or metal measuring cups for large quantities of dry ingredients, and measuring spoons for small quantities. Fill cups and spoons completely and level off ingredients with a knife.

Mixing Bowls: Mixing bowls are essential for mixing cookie dough, of course, but they are also extremely handy for organizing ingredients before getting started (chefs call this *mise en place*). Measuring out all your ingredients in bowls before you get started is a good way to ensure that you don't get halfway through a recipe before realizing that you're out of brown sugar. It is also a great way to prepare the kitchen for cooking with kids. If all ingredients are premeasured, then it's easy for even small children to participate by adding them to the big mixing bowl. Look for nesting bowls made of heatproof glass, plastic, and stainless steel for easy storage.

Parchment Paper: Along with my ice cream scoop, this is one item I simply must have before baking cookies. No matter how sticky the cookies, they simply peel away from the paper after cooling. And there's no cleanup afterward. You simply toss the paper away. Parchment is sold in rolls next to the aluminum foil and plastic wrap at the supermarket, but if you bake a lot of cookies you might consider mail-ordering a larger quantity in precut sheets (see Resources, page 257).

Pastry Bag and Tips: I use disposable plastic pastry bags because I find it difficult to completely clean the canvas ones. I have a deluxe set of decorating tips, but I use only the plain ones for decorating cookies. Pastry bags and tips are available in cookware shops and by mail (see Resources, page 257).

Rolling Pin: I use a wooden rolling pin that I inherited from my mom when I went to college. It's untapered, with wooden handles. But any kind of pin you already own or that you are comfortable with will work to roll out cookie dough.

Spatulas: I use several kinds of spatulas for baking cookies. Rubber spatulas are essential for scraping down the sides of a mixing bowl. A wide flexible metal spatula or turner is good for lifting cookies from cookie sheets. A small offset spatula works great for spreading frostings over cookies and brownies.

Wire Racks: These are important for cooling cookies properly, because they allow air to circulate underneath as well as above. Buy two or three so you'll have enough for big batches.

Wire Whisk: A small whisk is useful for blending dry ingredients together before adding them to wet ingredients. A whisk also comes in handy for stirring melting chocolate and breaking up eggs.

Storing Your Homemade Cookies

I don't need to tell you that most cookies taste best when they are fresh from the oven. Do let them cool to warm room temperature before eating them, however. Hot cookies may fall apart or burn your tongue.

Leftover cookies should be stored at room temperature in airtight containers unless the recipe says otherwise. Before packing them away, make sure they are completely cooled, or they will get soggy from condensation. If cookies are filled or frosted, it's best to separate layers with waxed or parchment paper to preserve their looks.

If you think you won't eat them within a day or two, you can freeze baked cookies to preserve their freshness. Pack them as described above in airtight containers for up to 1 month. Uncut brownies and blondies keep well this way. (Don't frost them if you plan on freezing them.) Let the cookies, brownies, or blondies come to room temperature on the counter. Brownies and blondies can be eaten as soon as they are defrosted. Other cookies may benefit from a crisping up in a 300°F oven for 5 minutes or so.

Personally, I prefer freezing cookie dough to freezing baked cookies. It's just so convenient to bake as many or as few as you want, whenever you want. I do this with logs of slice-and-bake dough, of course, but also with portioned-out balls of drop cookie dough. Recipes will note when this is an option. This way, there's no temptation to eat an entire batch of cookies before they go stale. I just bake as many cookies as I think I'll need for a given day and freeze the rest of the dough in zipper-lock plastic bags. When my kids want a couple of cookies after school, I take their orders and bake the cookies in a matter of minutes. And when surprise guests drop in, I like to work some freezer-to-oven magic, producing fresh, warm cookies as if I had planned on baking all along.

THE BIG THREE:
chocolate chip, oatmeal, and peanut butter cookies

CLOCKWISE FROM TOP: Oatmeal Cookies with Cranberries and Butterscotch Chips, Chocolate Chip Marble Cookies, Classic Peanut Butter Cookies, Mom's Chocolate Chip Cookies

Many moms never venture much beyond the three
most popular kinds of American cookies, except for maybe a brief excursion into brownie territory. It's no wonder why. There's nothing more reassuring to kids than a plate of their favorite chocolate chip, oatmeal, or peanut butter cookies. And when you and your family get a little bit bored with the basics, there are countless variations to explore.

If you are one of those bakers who has been following the recipes on the back of the chocolate chip bag, oatmeal canister, or peanut butter jar but who has been yearning to stretch a little, this chapter is for you. The 30 recipes here (and some more recipes scattered throughout the book—see opposite) will allow you to experiment while never leaving the comfort zone of your favorite ingredients.

When it comes to the basics, I've tried to distill the standard chocolate chip, oatmeal, and peanut butter cookie recipes to their essence. If I'm going to make one of these, I want it to be the best chocolate chip, oatmeal, or peanut butter cookie it can be. When I create a variation, it's not just for the sake of variety. Any addition or substitution in the recipe has to make sense. Cinnamon and chocolate have an affinity for each other, so Mexican Chocolate Chip Cookies (page 30) are a natural. Rice Krispies stirred into chocolate chip cookie dough to create Crispy Chocolate Chip Cookies (page 29) add crunch when nuts are not an option.

Here are a few of my opinions on ingredients and techniques for making the Big Three.

Chocolate Chip Cookies

A debate rages on about chewy versus crispy chocolate chip cookies and how to bake the best of either type. For me, it's as simple as this: Chewy cookies are baked 1 to 2 minutes less than crispy ones. If you like yours chewy (as I do), pull your cookies out of the oven on the early side of the recommended baking time, so that they are still soft on top. If you like them crispy, let them bake until they are dry on top and browned around the edges.

Whipping too much air into softened butter will cause your cookies to fall flat when they cool. I prefer to melt the butter before I combine it with the sugar. The result is a shapelier cookie, with no waiting around for the butter to soften. This is true for most oatmeal and peanut butter cookie doughs, as well, and for drop cookies in general.

The pastry chef in me prefers the more intense chocolate flavor of Ghirardelli, Callebaut, and Guittard chocolate chips (see Resources, page 257). But my kids and their friends have a decided preference for the sweeter Nestlé and Hershey brands. When I want to satisfy myself, I buy an upscale brand. When baking to please them, I'll go with the kids' choice.

More Big Three Cookie Recipes

Chocolate chips, oatmeal, and peanut butter are such elemental cookie ingredients that they can be found in cookie recipes throughout this book. Check out the following recipes for more ideas:

* Slice-and-Bake Chocolate Chippers (page 63)
* Oatmeal-Date Icebox Cookies (page 73)
* Reese's Pieces Autumn Oatmeal Cookies (page 133)
* Slice-and-Bake Peanuts (page 74)
* Flourless Peanut Butter Cookies (page 81)
* Instant Chocolate Chip–Peanut Butter Cookies (page 84)
* Peanut Butter Kisses (page 131)

Oatmeal Cookies

Old-fashioned rolled oats are the best way to go. They have more texture than instant oats, which dissolve into mush when stirred into cookie dough. And they are more tender than steel-cut or Irish oats, which are great for breakfast but too tough for cookies. You may substitute quick-cooking oats with good results.

Oatmeal is the perfect medium for fruit and nut combinations. Orange and pecan, apricot and pistachio, banana and walnut are all terrific. Feel free to use the basic recipe as a base for your own favorite match.

As a kid I never liked oatmeal cookies, and it wasn't until recently that I figured out why. My mom always used a lot of spices—cinnamon, nutmeg, cloves, mace—and the flavors were just too much for me back then. Now I'm a total spice junkie, but my own kids like their cookies mild. Most of my recipes call for small to moderate amounts of these powerful flavorings. If you know your kids are fussy about spices, cut them from the recipe and use ½ teaspoon additional vanilla extract to compensate. No kid has ever objected to vanilla in a cookie!

Peanut Butter Cookies

Will it sound fickle of me to say that I go back and forth between all-natural Smuckers or Arrowhead Mills peanut butter and commercial brands like Jif and Skippy, which contain corn syrup? Right now, I prefer commercial brands. The peanut butter cookie recipes here will work with both types. There will be a slight difference between cookies baked with one or the other—the cookies made with commercial peanut butter will be a little bit sweeter and a little less sandy in texture. But don't go out and buy a new jar if you already have enough all-natural.

Use salted, rather than unsalted, chopped peanuts in the dough. The extra salt really brings out the flavor of the peanuts and peanut butter.

mom's chocolate chip cookies

Makes about
48 cookies

This recipe, from my book *Mom's Big Book of Baking* (The Harvard Common Press, 2001), uses melted butter instead of softened butter as in the traditional Toll House recipe. Not only does this allow for spontaneous cookie baking (waiting for butter to soften is such a drag), but it results in cookies with superb texture—soft, chewy, and thick. Make sure to refrigerate the dough for at least 10 minutes before portioning it out. This will firm up the dough and prevent too much spreading in the oven.

2¼ cups unbleached all-purpose flour
1 teaspoon baking soda
1 teaspoon salt
1 cup (2 sticks) unsalted butter, melted
   and cooled slightly
1 cup firmly packed light brown sugar
½ cup granulated sugar
2 large eggs
1 teaspoon pure vanilla extract
2 cups semisweet chocolate chips
1½ cups chopped walnuts (optional)

1. Preheat the oven to 375°F.

2. Combine the flour, baking soda, and salt in a medium-size mixing bowl.

3. Cream the cooled melted butter and sugars together in a large mixing bowl with a wooden spoon until smooth. Add the eggs and vanilla extract and beat until smooth. Stir in the flour mixture until just incorporated. Stir in the chocolate chips and the nuts, if you are using them. Place the bowl in the refrigerator for 10 minutes (or up to 6 hours) to let the dough firm up.

4. Drop the dough by heaping tablespoonfuls onto ungreased baking sheets, leaving about 3 inches between each cookie. (Balls of dough may be placed next to each other on parchment paper–lined baking sheets, frozen, transferred to zipper-lock plastic freezer bags, and stored in the freezer for up to 1 month. Frozen cookies may be placed in the oven directly from the freezer and baked as directed.)

5. Bake the cookies until golden around the edges but still soft on top, 9 to 11 minutes (a minute or two longer for frozen dough). Let the cookies stand on the baking sheet for 5 minutes, then remove them with a metal spatula to a wire rack to cool completely. Mom's Chocolate Chip Cookies will keep at room temperature in an airtight container for 2 to 3 days.

obsessive mom's chocolate chip cookies

Makes about 44 cookies

For everyday baking, I wouldn't bother replacing vanilla extract with real vanilla bean seeds or substituting hazelnut butter (available at natural foods stores) for some of the butter in my basic recipe. But every once in a while I like to distinguish myself by using these ingredients to produce superior cookies. If you want to outdo everyone at the bake sale, this is the recipe for you.

2¼ cups unbleached all-purpose flour
1 teaspoon baking soda
1 teaspoon salt
½ cup (1 stick) unsalted butter, melted
    and cooled slightly
¼ cup hazelnut butter
¾ cup firmly packed light brown sugar
¾ cup granulated sugar
2 large eggs
1 vanilla bean, split lengthwise
2 cups semisweet or bittersweet
    chocolate chips
¾ cup finely chopped skinned hazelnuts
    (optional)

1. Preheat the oven to 375°F.

2. Combine the flour, baking soda, and salt in a medium-size mixing bowl.

3. Cream the cooled melted butter, hazelnut butter, and sugars together in a large mixing bowl with a wooden spoon until smooth. Add the eggs and beat until smooth. Scrape the seeds of the vanilla bean into the bowl and stir until well distributed. Stir in the flour mixture until just incorporated. Stir in the chocolate chips and the nuts, if you are using them. Place the bowl in the refrigerator for 10 minutes (or up to 6 hours) to let the dough firm up.

4. Drop the dough by heaping tablespoonfuls onto ungreased baking sheets, leaving about 3 inches between each cookie. (Balls of dough may be placed next to each other on parchment paper–lined baking sheets, frozen, transferred to zipper-lock plastic freezer bags, and stored in the freezer for up to 1 month. Frozen cookies may be placed in the oven directly from the freezer and baked as directed.)

5. Bake the cookies until golden around the edges but still soft on top, 9 to 11 minutes (a minute or two longer for frozen dough). Let the cookies stand on the baking sheet for 5 minutes, then remove them with a metal spatula to a wire rack to cool completely. Obsessive Mom's Chocolate Chip Cookies will keep at room temperature in an airtight container for 2 to 3 days.

white house chocolate chip cookies

Makes 48 large cookies

If it's good enough for the White House, it's good enough for my house. This recipe is adapted from legendary White House Pastry Chef Roland Mesnier's famous chocolate chip cookies, which he served to five U.S. presidents and their families and guests. Chef Mesnier's secret ingredient is molasses, which gives his cookies a more intense brown sugar flavor than Toll House–type cookies have. I like them with milk chocolate chips, but semisweet may be substituted.

3 cups unbleached all-purpose flour
1 teaspoon baking soda
¼ teaspoon salt
1 cup (2 sticks) unsalted butter, melted and cooled slightly
1 cup granulated sugar
½ cup firmly packed light brown sugar
¼ cup molasses
2 large eggs
1 teaspoon pure vanilla extract
2 cups milk chocolate chips
1½ cups chopped walnuts or pecans (optional)

1. Preheat the oven to 375°F.

2. Combine the flour, baking soda, and salt in a medium-size mixing bowl.

3. Cream the cooled melted butter and sugars together in a large mixing bowl with a wooden spoon until smooth. Add the molasses, eggs, and vanilla extract and beat until smooth. Stir in the flour mixture until just incorporated. Stir in the chocolate chips and the nuts, if you are using them. Place the bowl in the refrigerator for 10 minutes (or up to 6 hours) to let the dough firm up.

4. Drop the dough by heaping tablespoonfuls onto ungreased baking sheets, leaving about 3 inches between each cookie. (Balls of dough may be placed next to each other on parchment paper–lined baking sheets, frozen, transferred to zipper-lock plastic freezer bags, and stored in the freezer for up to 1 month. Frozen cookies may be placed in the oven directly from the freezer and baked as directed.)

5. Bake the cookies until golden around the edges but still soft on top, 8 to 10 minutes (a minute or two longer for frozen dough). Let the cookies stand on the baking sheet for 5 minutes, then remove them with a metal spatula to a wire rack to cool completely. White House Chocolate Chip Cookies will keep at room temperature in an airtight container for 2 to 3 days.

A Good Excuse to Make White House Chocolate Chip Cookies

When your child runs for class president, celebrate with these superb cookies. They won't guarantee victory if passed around on the campaign trail, but they certainly can't hurt....

chocolate chip cookies with sea salt

Makes about 48 cookies

Although sprinkling chocolate chip cookie dough with salt may sound weird, I had some good reasons for trying it. When I was a kid at sleep-away camp, I used to hang around in the kitchen with the camp director's wife, who was also the cook. After frosting my birthday cake, she'd spread some of the leftover chocolate frosting on saltines and let me eat them. My own children are absolute salt fiends, and Maldon Sea Salt, a brand from England that comes in papery flakes, is my daughters' favorite condiment of all time. Any other high-quality, medium-grain (not coarse) sea salt, such as *fleur de sel*, may be substituted.

2¼ cups unbleached all-purpose flour
1 teaspoon baking soda
¼ teaspoon kosher salt
1 cup (2 sticks) unsalted butter, melted and cooled slightly
1 cup firmly packed light brown sugar
½ cup granulated sugar
2 large eggs
1 teaspoon pure vanilla extract
2 cups semisweet chocolate chips
2 tablespoons Maldon Sea Salt or other best-quality sea salt

1. Preheat the oven to 375°F.

2. Combine the flour, baking soda, and salt in a medium-size mixing bowl.

3. Cream the cooled melted butter and sugars together in a large mixing bowl with a wooden spoon until smooth. Add the eggs and vanilla extract and beat until smooth. Stir in the flour mixture until just incorporated. Stir in the chocolate chips. Place the bowl in the refrigerator for 10 minutes (or up to 6 hours) to let the dough firm up.

4. Drop the dough by heaping tablespoonfuls onto ungreased baking sheets, leaving about 3 inches between each cookie. (Balls of dough may be placed next to each other on parchment paper–lined baking sheets, frozen, transferred to zipper-lock plastic freezer bags, and stored in the freezer for up to 1 month. Frozen cookies may be placed in the oven directly from the freezer and baked as directed.) Sprinkle each cookie with ⅛ teaspoon sea salt.

5. Bake the cookies until golden around the edges but still soft on top, 9 to 11 minutes (a minute or two longer for frozen dough). Let the cookies stand on the baking sheet for 5 minutes, then remove them with a metal spatula to a wire rack to cool completely. Chocolate Chip Cookies with Sea Salt will keep at room temperature in an airtight container for 2 to 3 days.

A Good Excuse to Make Chocolate Chip Cookies with Sea Salt

Pack these cookies in the cooler for a beach day, to enjoy their sea saltiness right at the ocean.

GOOD (Ice cream this flavor is better than cookies!)

coffee heath bar crunch–chip cookies

Makes about
48 cookies

I remember vividly the day my older daughter had her first Coffee Heath Bar Crunch ice cream cone. After that, it was a long time before she ordered plain vanilla again! Espresso might sound like a grown-up flavor, but when chocolate chip cookie dough is infused with rich coffee flavor and sprinkled with Heath Bar baking bits, it has definite kid appeal. The Heath Bar bits contribute to the crispness of this chocolate chip cookie. So if you are a crispy-cookie fan, this one's for you.

2¼ cups unbleached all-purpose flour
1 teaspoon baking soda
1 teaspoon salt
1 cup (2 sticks) unsalted butter, melted and cooled slightly
1 cup firmly packed light brown sugar
½ cup granulated sugar
2 large eggs
1 teaspoon pure vanilla extract
1½ tablespoons instant espresso powder
1 cup semisweet chocolate chips
1 cup Heath Bar Milk Chocolate Toffee Bits *—or crushed Heath Bars (Add pecans) - better w/nuts*

1. Preheat the oven to 375°F.

2. Combine the flour, baking soda, and salt in a medium-size mixing bowl.

3. Cream the cooled melted butter and sugars together in a large mixing bowl with a wooden spoon until smooth. Add the eggs, vanilla extract, and espresso powder and beat until smooth. Stir in the flour mixture until just incorporated. Stir in the chocolate chips and Heath Bar bits. Place the bowl in the refrigerator for 10 minutes (or up to 6 hours) to let the dough firm up.

4. Drop the dough by heaping table-spoonfuls onto ungreased baking sheets, leaving about 3 inches between each cookie. (Balls of dough may be placed next to each other on parchment paper–lined baking sheets, frozen, transferred to zipper-lock plastic freezer bags, and stored in the freezer for up to 1 month. Frozen cookies may be placed in the oven directly from the freezer and baked as directed.)

5. Bake the cookies until golden around the edges but still soft on top, about 10 minutes (a minute or two longer for frozen dough). Let the cookies stand on the baking sheet for 5 minutes, then remove them with a metal spatula to a wire rack to cool completely. Coffee Heath Bar Crunch–Chip Cookies will keep at room temperature in an airtight container for 2 to 3 days.

crispy chocolate chip cookies

Makes about 32 cookies

Puffed rice cereal gives these cookies kid-friendly crunch. They are great when you want a chocolate chip cookie with some texture, but don't want to use nuts.

1¼ cups unbleached all-purpose flour
½ teaspoon baking soda
½ teaspoon salt
½ cup (1 stick) unsalted butter, melted and cooled slightly
½ cup firmly packed light brown sugar
½ cup granulated sugar
1 large egg
1 teaspoon pure vanilla extract
1 cup semisweet chocolate chips
2 cups Rice Krispies cereal

1. Preheat the oven to 350°F.

2. Combine the flour, baking soda, and salt in a medium-size mixing bowl.

3. Cream the cooled melted butter and sugars together in a large mixing bowl with a wooden spoon until smooth. Add the egg and vanilla extract and beat until smooth. Stir in the flour mixture until just incorporated. Stir in the chocolate chips and Rice Krispies. Place the bowl in the refrigerator for 10 minutes (or up to 6 hours) to let the dough firm up.

4. Drop the dough by heaping tablespoonfuls onto ungreased baking sheets, leaving about 3 inches between each cookie. (Balls of dough may be placed next to each other on parchment paper–lined baking sheets, frozen, transferred to zipper-lock plastic freezer bags, and stored in the freezer for up to 1 month. Frozen cookies may be placed in the oven directly from the freezer and baked as directed.)

5. Bake the cookies until golden around the edges but still soft on top, 10 to 12 minutes (a minute or two longer for frozen dough). Let the cookies stand on the baking sheet for 5 minutes, then remove them with a metal spatula to a wire rack to cool completely. Crispy Chocolate Chip Cookies will keep at room temperature in an airtight container for 2 to 3 days.

mexican chocolate chip cookies

Makes about 48 cookies

Unsweetened natural cocoa powder and ground cinnamon give these cookies the flavor of Mexican hot chocolate. The pepitas (pumpkin seeds—look for them at natural foods stores and many supermarkets) are appropriate here, but any nuts may be substituted.

2¼ cups unbleached all-purpose flour
1 teaspoon baking soda
1 teaspoon salt
6 tablespoons unsweetened Dutch-processed cocoa powder
1 teaspoon ground cinnamon
1 cup (2 sticks) unsalted butter, melted and cooled slightly
1 cup firmly packed light brown sugar
½ cup granulated sugar
2 large eggs
1 teaspoon pure vanilla extract
2 cups semisweet chocolate chips
1 cup unsalted pepitas (optional)

1. Preheat the oven to 375°F.

2. Combine the flour, baking soda, salt, cocoa powder, and cinnamon in a medium-size mixing bowl.

3. Cream the cooled melted butter and sugars together in a large mixing bowl with a wooden spoon until smooth. Add the eggs and vanilla extract and beat until smooth. Stir in the flour mixture until just incorporated. Stir in the chocolate chips and the pepitas, if you are using them. Place the bowl in the refrigerator for 10 minutes (or up to 6 hours) to let the dough firm up.

4. Drop the dough by heaping table-spoonfuls onto ungreased baking sheets, leaving about 3 inches between each cookie. (Balls of dough may be placed next to each other on parchment paper–lined baking sheets, frozen, transferred to zipper-lock plastic freezer bags, and stored in the freezer for up to 1 month. Frozen cookies may be placed in the oven directly from the freezer and baked as directed.)

5. Bake the cookies until golden around the edges but still soft on top, 9 to 11 minutes (a minute or two longer for frozen dough). Let the cookies stand on the baking sheet for 5 minutes, then remove them with a metal spatula to a wire rack to cool completely. Mexican Chocolate Chip Cookies will keep at room temperature in an airtight container for 2 to 3 days.

A Good Excuse to Make Mexican Chocolate Chip Cookies

Back when I was a kid, spaghetti and meatballs was a kid's favorite dinner. Today, it's just as likely to be tacos, fajitas, or quesadillas. Serve these cookies after a simple Tex-Mex dinner if your kids appreciate theme meals.

favorite jumble chocolate chip cookies

Makes about 54 cookies

There are many ways to jazz up a chocolate chip cookie, but this particular combination of apricots, coconut, and macadamia nuts is my favorite. The nuts and apricots, especially, take me back to my own childhood, when my grandfather would bring me apricot fruit leather and small jars of precious macadamia nuts as treats when he visited.

2¼ cups unbleached all-purpose flour
1 teaspoon baking soda
¼ teaspoon salt
1 cup (2 sticks) unsalted butter, melted and cooled slightly
1 cup firmly packed light brown sugar
½ cup granulated sugar
2 large eggs
1 teaspoon pure vanilla extract
1 cup white chocolate chips
1 cup semisweet chocolate chips
1½ cups apricots, chopped to about the size of chocolate chips
1 cup sweetened flaked coconut
1½ cups chopped macadamia nuts

1. Preheat the oven to 350°F.

2. Combine the flour, baking soda, and salt in a medium-size mixing bowl.

3. Cream the cooled melted butter and sugars together in a large mixing bowl with a wooden spoon until smooth. Add the eggs and vanilla and beat until smooth. Stir in the flour mixture until just incorporated. Stir in the chocolate chips, apricots, coconut, and nuts. Place the bowl in the refrigerator for 10 minutes (or up to 6 hours) to let the dough firm up.

4. Drop the dough by heaping tablespoonfuls onto ungreased baking sheets, leaving about 3 inches between each cookie. (Balls of dough may be placed next to each other on parchment paper–lined baking sheets, frozen, transferred to zipper-lock plastic freezer bags, and stored in the freezer for up to 1 month. Frozen cookies may be placed in the oven directly from the freezer and baked as directed.)

5. Bake the cookies until golden around the edges but still soft on top, 9 to 11 minutes (a minute or two longer for frozen dough). Let the cookies stand on the baking sheet for 5 minutes, then remove them with a metal spatula to a wire rack to cool completely. Favorite Jumble Chocolate Chip Cookies will keep at room temperature in an airtight container for 2 to 3 days.

Kids Can Help

My younger daughter sometimes gets bored with the nuts and bolts of cookie making, so it's become a ritual to call her to the mixer when it's time for the "fun" part—adding in the chips, fruit, coconut, and nuts. We do this when making these jumbles, but also with any cookie that's got lots of good stuff going in at the end.

giant triple chocolate chippers

Makes about 34 cookies

I like to make these extra large, the better to showcase the three kinds of chocolate featured in the dough.

3¼ cups plus 2 tablespoons unbleached all-purpose flour
1½ teaspoons baking soda
1½ teaspoons salt
1½ cups (3 sticks) unsalted butter, melted and cooled slightly
1½ cups firmly packed light brown sugar
¾ cup granulated sugar
3 large eggs
2 teaspoons pure vanilla extract
1 cup semisweet chocolate chips
1 cup milk chocolate chips
1 cup white chocolate chips
1½ cups chopped walnuts (optional)

1. Preheat the oven to 375°F.

2. Combine the flour, baking soda, and salt in a medium-size mixing bowl.

3. Cream the cooled melted butter and sugars together in a large mixing bowl with a wooden spoon until smooth. Add the eggs and vanilla extract and beat until smooth. Stir in the flour mixture until just incorporated. Stir in the chocolate chips and the nuts, if you are using them. Place the bowl in the refrigerator for 10 minutes (or up to 6 hours) to let the dough firm up.

4. Drop the dough in ¼-cup mounds on ungreased baking sheets, leaving about 3 inches between each cookie. (Balls of dough may be placed next to each other on parchment paper–lined baking sheets, frozen, transferred to zipper-lock plastic freezer bags, and stored in the freezer for up to 1 month. Frozen cookies may be placed in the oven directly from the freezer and baked as directed.)

5. Bake the cookies until golden around the edges but still soft on top, 11 to 13 minutes (a minute or two longer for frozen dough). Let the cookies stand on the baking sheet for 5 minutes, then remove them with a metal spatula to a wire rack to cool completely. Giant Triple Chocolate Chippers will keep at room temperature in an airtight container for 2 to 3 days.

chocolate chip marble cookies

Makes about
40 cookies

It's easy to achieve this fun marbled effect with chocolate chip cookie dough. Just divide the dough in half before you stir the chips in, and add cocoa powder to one half. Then roll a small ball of each kind of dough together into one cookie.

2¼ cups unbleached all-purpose flour
1 teaspoon baking soda
1 teaspoon salt
1 cup (2 sticks) unsalted butter, melted and cooled slightly
1 cup firmly packed light brown sugar
½ cup granulated sugar
2 large eggs
1 teaspoon pure vanilla extract
¼ cup unsweetened Dutch-processed cocoa powder, sifted
1 cup white chocolate chips
1½ cups chopped walnuts (optional)
1 cup semisweet chocolate chips

1. Preheat the oven to 375°F.

2. Combine the flour, baking soda, and salt in a medium-size mixing bowl.

3. Cream the cooled melted butter and sugars together in a large mixing bowl with a wooden spoon until smooth. Add the eggs and vanilla and beat until smooth. Stir in the flour mixture until just incorporated.

4. Spoon half of the dough into another mixing bowl. Stir the sifted cocoa powder into the bowl. Stir the white chocolate chips and ¾ cup of the nuts, if you are using them, into the cocoa powder dough. Stir the semisweet chocolate chips and the remaining ¾ cup nuts, if you are using them, into the other bowl of dough. Place both bowls in the refrigerator for 10 minutes (or up to 6 hours) to let the dough firm up.

5. To shape the cookies, take a rounded teaspoonful of one dough and a rounded teaspoonful of the other dough and roll them together between your palms to form a single ball. Place on ungreased baking sheets, leaving about 3 inches between each cookie. (Balls of dough may be placed next to each other on parchment paper–lined baking sheets, frozen, transferred to zipper-lock plastic freezer bags, and stored in the freezer for up to 1 month. Frozen cookies may be placed in the oven directly from the freezer and baked as directed.)

6. Bake the cookies until golden around the edges but still soft on top, about 10 minutes (a minute or two longer for frozen dough). Let the cookies stand on the baking sheet for 5 minutes, then remove them with a metal spatula to a wire rack to cool completely. Chocolate Chip Marble Cookies will keep at room temperature in an airtight container for 2 to 3 days.

Kids Can Help

Kids enjoy rolling together the two types of dough in this recipe, so when you're finished mixing, let them take over.

reverse chocolate chunk cookies

Makes about
48 cookies

These brownie-like cookies are a chocolate lover's fantasy. They look great, too—shiny dark chocolate dotted with the white chips.

4 ounces (4 squares) unsweetened chocolate, finely chopped

1½ cups semisweet chocolate chips, or 9 ounces semisweet chocolate, finely chopped

½ cup (1 stick) unsalted butter, cut into 8 pieces

¾ cup unbleached all-purpose flour

½ teaspoon baking powder

½ teaspoon salt

4 large eggs

1½ cups sugar

2 teaspoons pure vanilla extract

1½ cups white chocolate chips

1. Preheat the oven to 350°F. Line baking sheets with parchment paper.

2. Put 1 inch of water in the bottom of a double boiler or medium-size saucepan and bring to a bare simmer. Combine the unsweetened chocolate, the semisweet chocolate, and the butter in the top of the double boiler or in a stainless-steel bowl set on top of the simmering water, making sure that the water doesn't touch the bottom of the bowl. Heat, whisking occasionally, until the chocolate and butter are completely melted. Set aside to cool slightly.

3. Combine the flour, baking powder, and salt in a small bowl.

4. Combine the eggs and sugar in a large mixing bowl and, with an electric mixer, beat on high speed until they are thick and pale, about 5 minutes. Stir in the chocolate mixture and vanilla extract on low speed until smooth. Stir in the flour mixture on low speed until just combined. Stir in the white chocolate chips. Place the bowl in the refrigerator for 30 minutes (or up to 6 hours) to let the dough firm up.

5. Drop the dough by heaping tablespoonfuls onto the lined baking sheets, leaving about 3 inches between each cookie. (Balls of dough may be placed next to each other on parchment paper–lined baking sheets, frozen, transferred to zipper-lock plastic freezer bags, and stored in the freezer for up to 1 month. Frozen cookies may be placed in the oven directly from the freezer and baked as directed.)

6. Bake the cookies until the tops are cracked and shiny, 10 to 12 minutes (a minute or two longer for frozen dough). Carefully slide the entire parchment sheet with the cookies from the pan to a wire rack and let the cookies cool completely. Reverse Chocolate Chunk Cookies will keep at room temperature in an airtight container for 2 to 3 days.

black forest chocolate chip cookies

When I was a kid, I loved chocolate-covered cherries, and this cookie reminds me of that favorite confection.

4 ounces (4 squares) unsweetened
chocolate, finely chopped
1½ cups semisweet chocolate chips, or
9 ounces semisweet chocolate, finely
chopped
½ cup (1 stick) unsalted butter, cut into
8 pieces
¾ cup unbleached all-purpose flour
½ teaspoon baking powder
½ teaspoon salt
4 large eggs
1½ cups sugar
2 teaspoons pure vanilla extract
1 cup semisweet chocolate chips
1⅓ cups dried cherries

1. Preheat the oven to 350°F. Line baking sheets with parchment paper.

2. Put 1 inch of water in the bottom of a double boiler or medium-size saucepan and bring to a bare simmer. Combine the unsweetened chocolate, the semisweet chocolate, and the butter in the top of the double boiler or in a stainless-steel bowl set on top of the simmering water, making sure that the water doesn't touch the bottom of the bowl. Heat, whisking occasionally, until the chocolate and butter are completely melted. Set aside to cool slightly.

3. Combine the flour, baking powder, and salt in a small bowl.

4. Combine the eggs and sugar in a large mixing bowl and, with an electric mixer, beat on high speed until they are thick and pale, about 5 minutes. Stir in the chocolate mixture and vanilla extract on low speed until smooth. Stir in the flour mixture on low speed until just combined. Stir in the chocolate chips and cherries. Place the bowl in the refrigerator for 30 minutes (or up to 6 hours) to let the dough firm up.

5. Drop the dough by heaping tablespoonfuls onto the lined baking sheets, leaving about 3 inches between each cookie. Balls of dough may be placed next to each other on parchment paper–lined baking sheets, frozen, transferred to zipper-lock plastic freezer bags, and stored in the freezer for up to 1 month. Frozen cookies may be placed in the oven directly from the freezer and baked as directed.)

6. Bake the cookies until the tops are cracked and shiny, 10 to 12 minutes (a minute or two longer for frozen dough). Carefully slide the entire parchment sheet with the cookies from the pan to a wire rack and let the cookies cool completely. Black Forest Chocolate Chip Cookies will keep at room temperature in an airtight container for 2 to 3 days.

sour cream chocolate mint chip cookies

**Makes about
48 cookies**

Mint and chocolate is a favorite combination of mine. But just stirring mint-flavored morsels (I use the Andes brand, but Nestlé and Hershey make them, too) into chocolate chip cookie dough seemed weird. I kept coming across recipes for chocolate cookies made with sour cream and that sounded more like the right base for these chips. So here it is.

2 cups unbleached all-purpose flour
**⅔ cup unsweetened Dutch-processed
   cocoa powder, sifted**
1 teaspoon baking powder
½ teaspoon baking soda
¼ teaspoon salt
2 large eggs
2 teaspoons pure vanilla extract
⅔ cup full-fat or low-fat sour cream
**¾ cup (1½ sticks) unsalted butter,
   softened**
1⅓ cups sugar
**2 cups Andes Crème de Menthe Baking
   Chips or other mint chocolate chips**

1. Preheat the oven to 350°F. Line baking sheets with parchment paper.

2. Combine the flour, cocoa powder, baking powder, baking soda, and salt in a small bowl. Whisk together the eggs, vanilla extract, and sour cream in a medium-size bowl.

3. Combine the butter and sugar in a large mixing bowl and, with an electric mixer, beat on medium speed until well combined. Add half of the egg mixture and beat until just combined. Add half of the flour mixture and beat until just combined. Repeat with the remaining egg mixture and remaining flour mixture, scraping down the sides of the bowl once or twice as necessary. Stir in the Andes chips. Place the bowl in the refrigerator for 30 minutes (or up to 6 hours) to let the dough firm up.

4. Drop the dough by heaping tablespoonfuls onto the lined baking sheets, leaving about 3 inches between each cookie. (Balls of dough may be placed next to each other on parchment paper–lined baking sheets, frozen, transferred to zipper-lock plastic freezer bags, and stored in the freezer for up to 1 month. Frozen cookies may be placed in the oven directly from the freezer and baked as directed.)

5. Bake the cookies until the tops are cracked and shiny, 10 to 12 minutes (a minute or two longer for frozen dough). Carefully slide the entire parchment sheet with the cookies from the pan to a wire rack and let the cookies cool completely. Sour Cream Chocolate Mint Chip Cookies will keep at room temperature in an airtight container for 2 to 3 days.

sour cream chocolate chip cookies

**Makes about
40 cookies**

Sour cream and regular granulated (instead of brown) sugar give these cookies a mild flavor and cake-like texture.

2¼ cups unbleached all-purpose flour
1 teaspoon baking soda
1 teaspoon salt
½ cup full-fat or low-fat sour cream
**½ cup (1 stick) unsalted butter, melted
  and cooled slightly**
1½ cups sugar
2 large eggs
2 teaspoons pure vanilla extract
2 cups milk chocolate chips
1½ cups chopped walnuts (optional)

1. Preheat the oven to 375°F.

2. Combine the flour, baking soda, and salt in a medium-size mixing bowl.

3. Cream the sour cream, cooled melted butter, and sugar together in a large mixing bowl with a wooden spoon until smooth. Add the eggs and vanilla extract and beat until smooth. Stir in the flour mixture until just incorporated. Stir in the chocolate chips and the nuts, if you are using them. Place the bowl in the refrigerator for 10 minutes (or up to 6 hours) to let the dough firm up.

4. Drop the dough by heaping table-spoonfuls onto ungreased baking sheets, leaving about 3 inches between each cookie. (Balls of dough may be placed next to each other on parchment paper–lined baking sheets, frozen, transferred to zipper-lock plastic freezer bags, and stored in the freezer for up to 1 month. Frozen cookies may be placed in the oven directly from the freezer and baked as directed.)

5. Bake the cookies until golden around the edges but still soft on top, 9 to 11 minutes (a minute or two longer for frozen dough). Let the cookies stand on the baking sheet for 5 minutes, then remove them with a metal spatula to a wire rack to cool completely. Sour Cream Chocolate Chip Cookies will keep at room temperature in an airtight container for 2 to 3 days.

mom's oatmeal cookies

**Makes about
48 cookies**

Here's my gold-standard oatmeal cookie. The raisins are optional, since some
kids love them and some don't.

1½ cups unbleached all-purpose flour
1 teaspoon baking soda
½ teaspoon salt
¼ teaspoon ground nutmeg
1 cup (2 sticks) unsalted butter, melted
and cooled slightly
1 cup firmly packed light brown sugar
½ cup granulated sugar
2 large eggs
1 teaspoon pure vanilla extract
3 cups old-fashioned rolled oats (not
instant)
1 cup raisins (optional)
1 cup chopped walnuts (optional)

1. Preheat the oven to 350°F.

2. Combine the flour, baking soda, salt,
and nutmeg in a medium-size mixing
bowl.

3. Combine the butter and sugars in a
large mixing bowl and, with an electric
mixer, beat on medium speed until well
combined. Add the eggs and vanilla
extract and beat until smooth. Stir in the
flour mixture until just combined. Stir in
the oats and the raisins and walnuts, if you
are using them. Place the bowl in the
refrigerator for 10 minutes (or up to 6
hours) to let the dough firm up.

4. Drop the dough by heaping tablespoonfuls onto ungreased baking sheets,
leaving about 3 inches between each
cookie. (Balls of dough may be placed
next to each other on parchment paper–
lined baking sheets, frozen, transferred to
zipper-lock plastic freezer bags, and stored
in the freezer for up to 1 month. Frozen
cookies may be placed in the oven directly
from the freezer and baked as directed.)

5. Bake the cookies until they are golden
around the edges but still soft on top, 15
to 17 minutes (a minute or two longer for
frozen dough). Let them stand on the
baking sheet for 5 minutes, then remove
them with a metal spatula to a wire rack
to cool completely. Mom's Oatmeal
Cookies will keep at room temperature in
an airtight container for 2 to 3 days.

oatmeal cookies with peanut butter and chocolate chips

Makes about 48 cookies

When I saw a bag of Nestlé Milk Chocolate & Peanut Butter Morsels at the supermarket, I got so excited. (This product is a mixture of milk chocolate chips and peanut butter–flavored chips—if you can't find it, you can buy the two kinds of chips separately.) I stir them into oatmeal cookie dough to satisfy everyone in the room—whether they love chocolate chip, oatmeal, or peanut butter cookies best.

1½ cups unbleached all-purpose flour
1 teaspoon baking soda
½ teaspoon salt
1 cup (2 sticks) unsalted butter, melted and cooled slightly
1 cup firmly packed light brown sugar
½ cup granulated sugar
2 large eggs
1 teaspoon pure vanilla extract
3 cups old-fashioned rolled oats (not instant)
One 12-ounce bag Nestlé Milk Chocolate & Peanut Butter Morsels
½ cup coarsely chopped salted peanuts

1. Preheat the oven to 350°F.

2. Combine the flour, baking soda, and salt in a medium-size mixing bowl.

3. Combine the butter and sugars in a large mixing bowl and, with an electric mixer, beat on medium speed until well combined. Add the eggs and vanilla extract and beat until smooth. Beat in the flour mixture until just combined. Stir in the oats, chocolate morsels and peanut butter, and peanuts. Place the bowl in the refrigerator for 10 minutes (or up to 6 hours) to let the dough firm up.

4. Drop the dough by heaping tablespoonfuls onto ungreased baking sheets, leaving about 3 inches between each cookie. (Balls of dough may be placed next to each other on parchment paper–lined baking sheets, frozen, transferred to zipper-lock plastic freezer bags, and stored in the freezer for up to 1 month. Frozen cookies may be placed in the oven directly from the freezer and baked as directed.)

5. Bake the cookies until they are golden around the edges but still soft on top, 13 to 15 minutes (a minute or two longer for frozen dough). Let them stand on the baking sheet for 5 minutes, then remove them with a metal spatula to a wire rack to cool completely. Oatmeal Cookies with Peanut Butter and Chocolate Chips will keep at room temperature in an airtight container for 2 to 3 days.

oatmeal cookies with cranberries and butterscotch chips

Makes about
48 cookies

Tart cranberries are the perfect companion for very sweet butterscotch chips, especially when both are stirred into chewy oatmeal cookies.

1½ cups unbleached all-purpose flour
1 teaspoon baking soda
½ teaspoon salt
½ teaspoon ground cinnamon
1 cup (2 sticks) unsalted butter, melted and cooled slightly
1 cup firmly packed light brown sugar
½ cup granulated sugar
2 large eggs
1 teaspoon pure vanilla extract
3 cups old-fashioned rolled oats (not instant)
2 cups butterscotch chips
1 cup dried cranberries

1. Preheat the oven to 350°F.

2. Combine the flour, baking soda, salt, and cinnamon in a medium-size mixing bowl.

3. Combine the butter and sugars in a large mixing bowl and, with an electric mixer, beat on medium speed until well combined. Add the eggs and vanilla extract and beat until smooth. Stir in the flour mixture until just combined. Stir in the oats, butterscotch chips, and cranberries. Place the bowl in the refrigerator for 10 minutes (or up to 6 hours) to let the dough firm up.

4. Drop the dough by heaping tablespoonfuls onto ungreased baking sheets, leaving about 3 inches between each cookie. (Balls of dough may be placed next to each other on parchment paper–lined baking sheets, frozen, transferred to zipper-lock plastic freezer bags, and stored in the freezer for up to 1 month. Frozen cookies may be placed in the oven directly from the freezer and baked as directed.)

5. Bake the cookies until they are golden around the edges but still soft on top, 13 to 15 minutes (a minute or two longer for frozen dough). Let them stand on the baking sheet for 5 minutes, then remove them with a metal spatula to a wire rack to cool completely. Oatmeal Cookies with Cranberries and Butterscotch Chips will keep at room temperature in an airtight container for 2 to 3 days.

oatmeal cookies with apricots and pistachios

Just a couple of simple substitutions from the previous recipe yield a very different, but equally delicious, cookie.

1½ cups unbleached all-purpose flour
1 teaspoon baking soda
½ teaspoon salt
½ teaspoon ground cinnamon
⅛ teaspoon ground cloves
1 cup (2 sticks) unsalted butter, melted and cooled slightly
1 cup firmly packed light brown sugar
½ cup granulated sugar
2 large eggs
1 teaspoon pure vanilla extract
3 cups old-fashioned rolled oats (not instant)
1 cup apricots, cut into raisin-size pieces
1 cup unsalted pistachio nuts, chopped

1. Preheat the oven to 350°F.

2. Combine the flour, baking soda, salt, cinnamon, and cloves in a medium-size mixing bowl.

3. Combine the butter and sugars in a large mixing bowl and, with an electric mixer, beat on medium speed until well combined. Add the eggs and vanilla extract and beat until smooth. Beat in the flour mixture until just combined. Stir in the oats, apricots, and pistachios. Place the bowl in the refrigerator for 10 minutes (or up to 6 hours) to let the dough firm up.

4. Drop the dough by heaping tablespoonfuls onto ungreased baking sheets, leaving about 3 inches between each cookie. (Balls of dough may be placed next to each other on parchment paper–lined baking sheets, frozen, transferred to zipper-lock plastic freezer bags, and stored in the freezer for up to 1 month. Frozen cookies may be placed in the oven directly from the freezer and baked as directed.)

5. Bake the cookies until they are golden around the edges but still soft on top, 15 to 17 minutes (a minute or two longer for frozen dough). Let them stand on the baking sheet for 5 minutes, then remove them with a metal spatula to a wire rack to cool completely. Oatmeal Cookies with Apricots and Pistachios will keep at room temperature in an airtight container for 2 to 3 days.

orange-pecan oatmeal cookies

Orange zest makes these cookies so fragrant, and pecans give them richness and flavor. I like to use tiny currants here, but golden raisins are also great.

1½ cups unbleached all-purpose flour
1 teaspoon baking soda
½ teaspoon salt
1 cup (2 sticks) unsalted butter, melted and cooled slightly
1 cup firmly packed light brown sugar
½ cup granulated sugar
2 large eggs
1 teaspoon pure vanilla extract
2 teaspoons grated orange zest
3 cups old-fashioned rolled oats (not instant)
1 cup currants
1 cup chopped pecans

1. Preheat the oven to 350°F.

2. Combine the flour, baking soda, and salt in a medium-size mixing bowl.

3. Combine the butter and sugars in a large mixing bowl and, with an electric mixer, beat on medium speed until well combined. Add the eggs, vanilla extract, and orange zest and beat until smooth. Beat in the flour mixture until just combined. Stir in the oats, currants, and pecans. Place the bowl in the refrigerator for 10 minutes (or up to 6 hours) to let the dough firm up.

4. Drop the dough by heaping table-spoonfuls onto ungreased baking sheets, leaving about 3 inches between each cookie. (Balls of dough may be placed next to each other on parchment paper–lined baking sheets, frozen, transferred to zipper-lock plastic freezer bags, and stored in the freezer for up to 1 month. Frozen cookies may be placed in the oven directly from the freezer and baked as directed.)

5. Bake the cookies until they are golden around the edges but still soft on top, 15 to 17 minutes (a minute or two longer for frozen dough). Let them stand on the baking sheet for 5 minutes, then remove them with a metal spatula to a wire rack to cool completely. Orange-Pecan Oatmeal Cookies will keep at room temperature in an airtight container for 2 to 3 days.

oatmeal cookies with coconut and mango

Makes about 48 cookies

Unsweetened coconut, available in natural foods stores and many supermarkets, is essential here. Sweetened flaked coconut will make these cookies spread and burn. Dried mango can also be found in natural foods stores. Macadamia nuts are optional, but I like them for their tropical flavor.

1½ cups unbleached all-purpose flour
1 teaspoon baking soda
½ teaspoon salt
1 teaspoon ground ginger
1 cup (2 sticks) unsalted butter, melted and cooled slightly
1 cup firmly packed light brown sugar
½ cup granulated sugar
2 large eggs
1 teaspoon pure vanilla extract
3 cups old-fashioned rolled oats (not instant)
1 cup chopped dried mango
¾ cup unsweetened dried coconut
⅔ cup chopped unsalted macadamia nuts (optional)

1. Preheat the oven to 350°F.

2. Combine the flour, baking soda, salt, and ginger in a medium-size mixing bowl.

3. Combine the butter and sugars in a large mixing bowl and, with an electric mixer, beat on medium speed until well combined. Add the eggs and vanilla extract and beat until smooth. Beat in the flour mixture until just combined. Stir in the oats, mango, and coconut. Stir in the nuts, if you are using them. Place the bowl in the refrigerator for 10 minutes (or up to 6 hours) to let the dough firm up.

4. Drop the dough by heaping table-spoonfuls onto ungreased baking sheets, leaving about 3 inches between each cookie. (Balls of dough may be placed next to each other on parchment paper–lined baking sheets, frozen, transferred to zipper-lock plastic freezer bags, and stored in the freezer for up to 1 month. Frozen cookies may be placed in the oven directly from the freezer and baked as directed.)

5. Bake the cookies until they are golden around the edges but still soft on top, 15 to 17 minutes (a minute or two longer for frozen dough). Let them stand on the baking sheet for 5 minutes, then remove them with a metal spatula to a wire rack to cool completely. Oatmeal Cookies with Coconut and Mango will keep at room temperature in an airtight container for 2 to 3 days.

A Good Excuse to Make Oatmeal Cookies with Coconut and Mango

Make a trip to the natural foods store to buy bulk quantities of nuts and dried fruit. While you're there, pick up some coconut and mango to make these cookies.

banana-walnut oatmeal cookies

Makes about 40 cookies

If you like banana bread, these oatmeal cookies are for you. Use very ripe (that means brown!) bananas for the best flavor.

1½ cups unbleached all-purpose flour
1 teaspoon baking soda
½ teaspoon salt
¼ teaspoon ground nutmeg
¾ cup (1½ sticks) unsalted butter, melted and cooled slightly
1 cup firmly packed light brown sugar
1 cup mashed ripe bananas (about 2 medium-size bananas)
1 large egg
1 teaspoon pure vanilla extract
2½ cups old-fashioned rolled oats (not instant)
1 cup chopped walnuts

1. Preheat the oven to 350°F.

2. Combine the flour, baking soda, salt, and nutmeg in a medium-size mixing bowl.

3. Combine the butter and sugar in a large mixing bowl and, with an electric mixer, beat on medium speed until well combined. Add the bananas, egg, and vanilla extract and beat until smooth. Stir in the flour mixture until just combined. Stir in the oats and walnuts. Place the bowl in the refrigerator for 10 minutes (or up to 6 hours) to let the dough firm up.

4. Drop the dough by heaping table-spoonfuls onto ungreased baking sheets, leaving about 3 inches between each cookie. (Balls of dough may be placed next to each other on parchment paper–lined baking sheets, frozen, transferred to zipper-lock plastic freezer bags, and stored in the freezer for up to 1 month. Frozen cookies may be placed in the oven directly from the freezer and baked as directed.)

5. Bake the cookies until they are golden around the edges but still soft on top, 15 to 17 minutes (a minute or two longer for frozen dough). Let them stand on the baking sheet for 5 minutes, then remove them with a metal spatula to a wire rack to cool completely. Banana-Walnut Oatmeal Cookies will keep at room temperature in an airtight container for 2 to 3 days.

A Good Excuse to Make Banana-Walnut Oatmeal Cookies

What more of an excuse do you need than those brown bananas sitting on your counter that no one wants to eat?

applesauce oatmeal cookies

**Makes about
48 cookies**

These have an aroma and flavor reminiscent of apple pie. Any kind of apple-sauce will work in these cookies, but I like unsweetened Mott's for its pure flavor.

1½ cups unbleached all-purpose flour
1 teaspoon baking soda
½ teaspoon salt
1 teaspoon ground cinnamon
¼ teaspoon ground allspice
¾ cup (1½ sticks) unsalted butter, melted and cooled slightly
1 cup firmly packed light brown sugar
½ cup granulated sugar
¾ cup applesauce
1 large egg
1 large egg white
1 teaspoon pure vanilla extract
3 cups old-fashioned rolled oats (not instant)
1 cup currants or raisins
1 cup chopped walnuts

1. Preheat the oven to 350°F.

2. Combine the flour, baking soda, salt, cinnamon, and allspice in a medium-size mixing bowl.

3. Combine the butter and sugars in a large mixing bowl and, with an electric mixer, beat on medium speed until well combined. Add the applesauce, eggs, and vanilla extract and beat until smooth. Stir in the flour mixture until just combined. Stir in the oats, dried fruit, and walnuts. Place the bowl in the refrigerator for 10 minutes (or up to 6 hours) to let the dough firm up.

4. Drop the dough by heaping table-spoonfuls onto ungreased baking sheets, leaving about 3 inches between each cookie. (Balls of dough may be placed next to each other on parchment paper–lined baking sheets, frozen, transferred to zipper-lock plastic freezer bags, and stored in the freezer for up to 1 month. Frozen cookies may be placed in the oven directly from the freezer and baked as directed.)

5. Bake the cookies until they are golden around the edges but still soft on top, 15 to 17 minutes (a minute or two longer for frozen dough). Let them stand on the baking sheet for 5 minutes, then remove them with a metal spatula to a wire rack to cool completely. Applesauce Oatmeal Cookies will keep at room temperature in an airtight container for 2 to 3 days.

chocolate oatmeal cookies

Makes about 24 cookies

This is a rich shortbread-type cookie, but it also has a lot of great texture because of the oats.

1¼ cups unbleached all-purpose flour
½ cup unsweetened Dutch-processed cocoa powder, sifted
1 teaspoon baking soda
½ teaspoon salt
1 cup (2 sticks) unsalted butter, softened
1 cup firmly packed light brown sugar
1 teaspoon pure vanilla extract
½ cup old-fashioned rolled oats (not instant)

1. Preheat the oven to 350°F.

2. Combine the flour, cocoa powder, baking soda, and salt in a medium-size mixing bowl.

3. Combine the butter and sugar in a large mixing bowl and, with an electric mixer, beat on medium speed until well combined. Add the vanilla extract. Stir in the flour mixture until just combined. Stir in the oats.

4. Drop the dough by heaping tablespoonfuls onto ungreased baking sheets, leaving about 3 inches between each cookie. Flatten each ball slightly with the palm of your hand. (Balls of dough may be placed next to each other on parchment paper–lined baking sheets, frozen, transferred to zipper-lock plastic freezer bags, and stored in the freezer for up to 1 month. Frozen cookies may be placed in the oven directly from the freezer and baked as directed.)

5. Bake the cookies until they are set around the edges and cracked on top, 12 to 15 minutes (a minute or two longer for frozen dough). Let them stand on the baking sheet for 5 minutes, then remove them with a metal spatula to a wire rack to cool completely. Chocolate Oatmeal Cookies will keep at room temperature in an airtight container for 2 to 3 days.

Kids Can "Help"

I feel like a real Scrooge when I say no, but for safety's sake I usually don't let my kids sample raw cookie dough. Doughs made without eggs, however, don't present the risk of salmonella, so when I make Chocolate Oatmeal Cookies I happily let them help "clean" the bowl.

oatmeal toffee lace cookies

Makes about
24 cookies

A sprinkling of toffee bits in the batter makes these delicate but child-pleasing treats more like candy than cookies. Miniature chocolate chips may be substituted for the toffee bits if you prefer a more chocolatey oatmeal cookie.

1½ cups old-fashioned rolled oats (not instant)

¾ cup sugar

2 tablespoons unbleached all-purpose flour

½ teaspoon salt

1 teaspoon pure vanilla extract

¾ cup (1½ sticks) unsalted butter, melted and cooled slightly

1 large egg, lightly beaten

½ cup Heath Bar Milk Chocolate Toffee Bits

1. Preheat the oven to 325°F. Line baking sheets with parchment paper.

2. Combine the oats, sugar, flour, and salt in a large mixing bowl. With a wooden spoon, stir in the vanilla extract and cooled melted butter until combined. Stir in the egg until combined. Stir in the toffee bits.

3. Drop the dough by scant tablespoonfuls onto the lined baking sheets, leaving about 3 inches between each cookie. Bake the cookies until they are golden around the edges, 12 to 13 minutes. Carefully slide the entire parchment sheet with the cookies from the pan to a wire rack and let them cool completely. Oatmeal Toffee Lace Cookies will keep at room temperature in an airtight container for 2 to 3 days.

classic peanut butter cookies

The roasted salted peanuts called for here are essential to achieve the most intense peanut flavor.

1 cup roasted salted peanuts
2 cups unbleached all-purpose flour
½ teaspoon baking soda
½ teaspoon baking powder
½ teaspoon salt
1 cup (2 sticks) unsalted butter, melted
  and cooled slightly
1 cup firmly packed light brown sugar
1 cup granulated sugar
2 large eggs
1 teaspoon pure vanilla extract
1 cup smooth peanut butter

1. Preheat the oven to 350°F. Line baking sheets with parchment paper.

2. Place the peanuts in a food processor and finely chop. Combine the flour, baking soda, baking powder, and salt in a medium-size bowl. Combine the butter and sugars in a large mixing bowl and, with an electric mixer, beat on medium speed until well combined. Add the eggs, vanilla extract, and peanut butter and beat until smooth. Stir in the flour mixture until just combined. Stir in the chopped peanuts. Place the bowl in the refrigerator for 10 minutes (or up to 6 hours) to let the dough firm up.

3. Scoop a heaping tablespoonful of dough and roll it between your palms to form a ball. Place the balls on the lined baking sheets, leaving about 3 inches between each cookie. Press each cookie with the back of a fork twice, in opposite directions, to make a crisscross pattern. (Balls of dough may be placed next to each other on parchment paper–lined baking sheets, frozen, transferred to zipper-lock plastic freezer bags, and stored in the freezer for up to 1 month. Frozen cookies may be placed in the oven directly from the freezer and baked as directed.)

4. Bake the cookies until they are lightly colored, about 15 minutes (a minute or two longer for frozen dough). Let them stand on the baking sheet for 5 minutes, then carefully slide the entire parchment sheet with the cookies from the pan to a wire rack and let them cool completely. Classic Peanut Butter Cookies will keep at room temperature in an airtight container for 2 to 3 days.

peanut butter and honey cookies

Makes about
48 cookies

Honey in place of brown sugar gives these cookies a special sweetness all their own. Use honey-roasted peanuts instead of roasted salted peanuts if you like.

1 cup roasted salted peanuts
2 cups unbleached all-purpose flour
½ teaspoon baking soda
½ teaspoon baking powder
½ teaspoon salt
½ cup (1 stick) unsalted butter, melted and cooled slightly
1 cup honey
1 cup sugar
2 large eggs
1 teaspoon pure vanilla extract
1 cup smooth peanut butter

1. Preheat the oven to 350°F. Line baking sheets with parchment paper.

2. Place the peanuts in a food processor and finely chop. Combine the flour, baking soda, baking powder, and salt in a medium-size bowl. Combine the butter, honey, and sugar in a large mixing bowl and, with an electric mixer, beat on medium speed until well combined. Add the eggs, vanilla, and peanut butter and beat until smooth. Stir in the flour mixture until just combined. Stir in the chopped peanuts. Place the bowl in the refrigerator for 10 minutes (or up to 6 hours) to let the dough firm up.

3. Scoop a heaping tablespoonful of dough and roll it between your palms to form a ball. Place the balls on the lined baking sheets, leaving about 3 inches between each cookie. Press each cookie with the back of a fork twice, in opposite directions, to make a crisscross pattern.

(Balls of dough may be placed next to each other on parchment paper–lined baking sheets, frozen, transferred to zipper-lock plastic freezer bags, and stored in the freezer for up to 1 month. Frozen cookies may be placed in the oven directly from the freezer and baked as directed.)

4. Bake the cookies until they are lightly colored, about 15 minutes (a minute or two longer for frozen dough). Let them stand on the baking sheet for 5 minutes, then carefully slide the entire parchment sheet with the cookies from the pan to a wire rack and let them cool completely. Peanut Butter and Honey Cookies will keep at room temperature in an airtight container for 2 to 3 days.

Peanut Butter Thumbprints

The dough for Classic Peanut Butter Cookies or Peanut Butter and Honey Cookies can be used to make peanut butter thumbprint cookies with jelly filling. Instead of making the crosshatch decoration with the fork, make an impression in the center of each ball of dough with a small measuring spoon. Bake as directed, cool completely, and then fill with your favorite jam or jelly. I am partial to apricot, but my kids prefer grape. So I make some of both and everybody is very, very happy.

chocolate peanut butter cookies

Makes about
40 cookies

Cocoa powder and chocolate and peanut butter chips transform peanut butter cookie dough into a chocolate lover's peanut butter cookie.

1½ cups unbleached all-purpose flour
¾ cup unsweetened Dutch-processed cocoa powder, sifted
½ teaspoon baking soda
½ teaspoon baking powder
½ teaspoon salt
1 cup (2 sticks) unsalted butter, melted and cooled slightly
½ cup firmly packed light brown sugar
1 cup granulated sugar
2 large eggs
1 teaspoon pure vanilla extract
1 cup smooth peanut butter
1 cup peanut butter chips
1 cup milk chocolate chips

1. Preheat the oven to 350°F.

2. Combine the flour, cocoa powder, baking soda, baking powder, and salt in a medium-size bowl. Combine the butter and sugars in a large mixing bowl and, with an electric mixer, beat on medium speed until well combined. Add the eggs, vanilla extract, and peanut butter and beat until smooth. Stir in the flour mixture until just combined. Stir in the peanut butter and milk chocolate chips. Place the bowl in the refrigerator for 10 minutes (or up to 6 hours) to let the dough firm up.

3. Drop the dough by heaping tablespoonfuls onto ungreased baking sheets, leaving about 3 inches between each cookie. (Balls of dough may be placed next to each other on parchment paper–lined baking sheets, frozen, transferred to zipper-lock plastic freezer bags, and stored in the freezer for up to 1 month. Frozen cookies may be placed in the oven directly from the freezer and baked as directed.)

4. Bake the cookies until they are firm around the edges but still a little soft in the center, 10 to 12 minutes (a minute or two longer for frozen dough). Let them stand on the baking sheet for 5 minutes, then carefully slide the entire parchment sheet with the cookies from the pan to a wire rack and let them cool completely. Chocolate Peanut Butter Cookies will keep at room temperature in an airtight container for 2 to 3 days.

salted peanut and brown sugar cookies

Makes about 40 cookies

This simple cookie doesn't contain peanut butter, but it does have an abundance of salted peanuts in a brown sugar–sweetened dough. It's another great sweet-salty combination. Other salted nuts may be substituted if you prefer. I love cashews, which should be coarsely chopped before being added.

2¼ cups unbleached all-purpose flour
1 teaspoon baking soda
½ teaspoon salt
1 cup (2 sticks) unsalted butter, melted and cooled slightly
1½ cups firmly packed light brown sugar
2 large eggs
1 teaspoon pure vanilla extract
2 cups salted peanuts

1. Preheat the oven to 375°F.

2. Combine the flour, baking soda, and salt in a medium-size mixing bowl.

3. Cream the cooled melted butter and brown sugar together in a large mixing bowl with a wooden spoon until smooth. Add the eggs and vanilla extract and beat until smooth. Stir in the flour mixture until just incorporated. Stir in the peanuts. Place the bowl in the refrigerator for 10 minutes (or up to 6 hours) to let the dough firm up.

4. Drop the dough by heaping table-spoonfuls onto ungreased baking sheets, leaving about 3 inches between each cookie. (Balls of dough may be placed next to each other on parchment paper–lined baking sheets, frozen, transferred to zipper-lock plastic freezer bags, and stored in the freezer for up to 1 month. Frozen cookies may be placed in the oven directly from the freezer and baked as directed.)

5. Bake the cookies until golden around the edges but still soft on top, 9 to 11 minutes (a minute or two longer for frozen dough). Let the cookies stand on the baking sheet for 5 minutes, then remove them with a metal spatula to a wire rack to cool completely. Salted Peanut and Brown Sugar Cookies will keep at room temperature in an airtight container for 2 to 3 days.

trail mix cookies

Makes about
50 cookies

The best way to get my kids out on a hike is to pack these energy-boosting cookies containing raisins, peanuts, chocolate chips, sunflower seeds, and lots of oats.

1½ cups unbleached all-purpose flour
1 teaspoon baking soda
½ teaspoon salt
½ cup (1 stick) unsalted butter, melted and cooled slightly
1 cup firmly packed light brown sugar
½ cup honey
2 large eggs
1 cup smooth peanut butter
1½ teaspoons pure vanilla extract
3 cups old-fashioned rolled oats (not instant)
1 cup raisins
1 cup salted peanuts, coarsely chopped
1 cup semisweet chocolate chips
1 cup sunflower seeds

1. Preheat the oven to 350°F.

2. Combine the flour, baking soda, and salt in a medium-size mixing bowl.

3. Combine the butter, sugar, and honey in a large mixing bowl and, with an electric mixer, beat on medium speed until well combined. Add the eggs, peanut butter, and vanilla extract and beat until smooth. Stir in the flour mixture until just combined. Stir in the oats, raisins, peanuts, chocolate chips, and sunflower seeds. Place the bowl in the refrigerator for 10 minutes (or up to 6 hours) to let the dough firm up.

4. Drop the dough by heaping table-spoonfuls onto ungreased baking sheets, leaving about 3 inches between each cookie. (Balls of dough may be placed next to each other on parchment paper–lined baking sheets, frozen, transferred to zipper-lock plastic freezer bags, and stored in the freezer for up to 1 month. Frozen cookies may be placed in the oven directly from the freezer and baked as directed.)

5. Bake the cookies until they are golden around the edges but still soft on top, 12 to 15 minutes (a minute or two longer for frozen dough). Let them stand on the baking sheet for 5 minutes, then remove them with a metal spatula to a wire rack to cool completely. Trail Mix Cookies will keep at room temperature in an airtight container for 2 to 3 days.

A Good Excuse to Make Trail Mix Cookies

Sometimes our hikes get rained out, and I'll make these cookies to cheer everyone up. So I also recommend them as an accompaniment to rainy day DVD and board game marathons.

peanut butter shortbread

Makes 16 wedges
or squares

I like to sprinkle this peanut butter dough with cinnamon sugar, but if you like you can drizzle the cooled cookies with melted chocolate instead. To pack down the dough tightly in the pan, try using the bottom of a juice glass or glass measuring cup.

1 tablespoon granulated sugar
1 teaspoon ground cinnamon
1 cup unsalted dry-roasted peanuts
1 cup firmly packed light brown sugar
¾ cup (1½ sticks) unsalted butter, softened
¼ cup smooth peanut butter
1 teaspoon pure vanilla extract
2 cups unbleached all-purpose flour

1. Preheat the oven to 325°F. Spray a 9-inch fluted tart pan with removable bottom or an 8-inch square baking pan with nonstick cooking spray.

2. Combine the granulated sugar and cinnamon in a small bowl and set aside.

3. Combine the peanuts and ¼ cup of the brown sugar in the work bowl of a food processor and process until the mixture resembles coarse meal.

4. Cream the butter, peanut butter, vanilla extract, and the remaining ¾ cup brown sugar together in a large mixing bowl with an electric mixer on medium speed until fluffy, 3 to 4 minutes. Stir in the flour until the dough just comes together. Stir in the peanut–brown sugar mixture. Do not overmix.

5. Turn the dough into the prepared pan and press the dough to the edges with your fingertips, packing it down tightly. It will come up to the top of the pan. Sprinkle with the cinnamon sugar. Bake until the shortbread is firm at the edges but still soft in the center, about 55 minutes.

6. Let cool completely on a wire rack, then cut the shortbread into wedges or squares. Peanut Butter Shortbread will keep at room temperature in an airtight container for 3 days.

FRESH FROM THE FREEZER:
slice-and-bake cookies for instant gratification

LEFT TO RIGHT: Slice-and-Bake Sugar Cookies, Chocolate-Cherry-Pistachio Swirls, Fig-Filled Slice-and-Bakes

I have long been a passionate advocate of freezing
cookie dough. With frozen dough, I can have homemade cookies, warm
from the oven, anytime I want them, without having to pull out the mixer,
hunt for ingredients, or wash the dishes afterward. Freezing unbaked dough
also allows me to control portions. I'd rather bake just as many cookies as
I need or want rather than bake too many. Extra cookies get stale, or, more
often, lead to overeating and then a lot of moaning and groaning about
indigestion and tight jeans. To avoid either of these tragic outcomes, I usually
bake some of my cookie dough on the day that I make it and reserve the
rest for a cookie emergency.

Many types of cookie dough can be frozen (when freezing is an option,
I note this in the recipes throughout the book), but the simplest way to
ensure that you always have cookie dough on hand is to make a batch of
the slice-and-bake variety. In these recipes, cookie dough is shaped into
logs that are wrapped in plastic and refrigerated or frozen, and then sliced
into cookie shapes just before baking. The cookies themselves don't have
to be shaped ahead of time, and the logs store compactly in the freezer, a
benefit if yours is stuffed to overflowing, as mine is.

Slice-and-bake cookies can be as plain and simple as the vanilla sugar
cookies that kick off this chapter (page 58), but there are also plenty of
opportunities to have fun and get creative with the form. To make Brown
Sugar Buttons (page 71) beautiful as well as tasty, I brush the dough logs
with egg white and then roll them in turbinado sugar to create a sparkly
border for the finished cookies. Chocolate cookie dough can be rolled out
into a flat square, spread with a mixture of chopped pistachio nuts and
cherry preserves, and then rolled into a tight cylinder so that when the
dough is sliced, the filling swirls through each cookie (page 65). Vanilla
and chocolate doughs can be rolled up together to create a two-toned look
(page 62). These fancier icebox cookies are all the more impressive because
they can appear to be conjured instantly and at will.

Here are a few tips for successfully making, freezing, and baking icebox
cookies:

To form evenly shaped logs, pinch and press the dough into a rough log of the specified length. Then turn it onto a piece of waxed or parchment paper and roll it inside the paper to smooth it and round it.

To prevent drying out and freezer burn, tightly wrap the dough logs in plastic before refrigerating or freezing. When well wrapped, dough will stay fresh in the freezer for a month or longer.

There's a reason that these are also called icebox cookies. Slice-and-bake cookie dough doesn't have to be frozen, but it does need to be well chilled before it is sliced. Dough that is too soft will be difficult to cut into rounds, because it will get squashed as the knife cuts through it.

When you're ready to bake, use a sharp chef's knife to cut away as much dough from the frozen log as you need. This can be done while the dough is still frozen solid. Re-wrap what you don't need with fresh plastic wrap. Let the dough you are using stand on the counter for 15 minutes to defrost slightly before slicing into cookies. Rock-hard dough may crumble when cut with a knife.

Any of the dough logs can be embellished with chopped nuts, sanding sugar, or sprinkles. Spread the coating of your choice in an even layer on a rimmed baking sheet. Brush the dough logs with egg white, then roll the logs in the coating to completely cover. Slice and bake as directed.

Rotate the logs often as you slice, so that one side doesn't become flattened by the repeated pressure of the knife.

Planning Ahead for a Spur-of-the-Moment Cookie Party

When I have some extra time on my hands, I like to make a few different kinds of icebox cookie doughs that go well with each other. I wrap them in plastic, put them together in a large zipper-lock freezer bag, and label them so that I don't forget what they are. Then, when the class mother calls or the Brownie troop descends, I'm covered. Here are a few combinations that I like:

* Classic collection: Slice-and-Bake Chocolate Chippers (page 63), Oatmeal-Date Icebox Cookies (page 73), Slice-and-Bake Peanuts (page 74)
* For chocolate fiends: Thin Mints (page 60), Spiral Cookies (page 62), Chocolate-Walnut Slice-and-Bakes (page 64)
* Tea party favorites: Lime-Coconut Cookies (page 77), Slice-and-Bake Sugar Cookies (page 58), Pecan Sandies (page 67)
* Instant holiday party: Chocolate-Cherry-Pistachio Swirls (page 65), Molasses Spice Slices (page 72), Cornmeal Cranberry Squares (page 76)

slice-and-bake sugar cookies

Makes about 60 cookies

If you like, this basic cookie dough can be dressed up with sprinkles or colored sugar for colorful cookies in a flash. You may either sprinkle them on the tops of the cookies after slicing or brush unsliced logs with egg white and roll in sugar before slicing for a border effect.

2 cups unbleached all-purpose flour
½ teaspoon baking powder
½ teaspoon salt
1 cup (2 sticks) unsalted butter, softened
¾ cup sugar
1 large egg
2 teaspoons pure vanilla extract

1. Combine the flour, baking powder, and salt in a medium-size mixing bowl.

2. Combine the butter and sugar in a large mixing bowl and, with an electric mixer, beat on medium-high speed until fluffy, 2 to 3 minutes. Add the egg and vanilla extract and beat until smooth. Stir in the flour mixture until just incorporated.

3. Divide the dough into 2 equal portions. Turn 1 portion onto a piece of waxed paper and shape it, rolling it inside the paper, into a log about 10 inches long and 1½ inches in diameter. Wrap the dough in plastic wrap and refrigerate it for at least 2 hours or up to 24 hours. Repeat with the remaining dough. (Dough logs may be wrapped tightly in plastic and frozen for up to 1 month. Slice and bake directly from the freezer.)

4. Preheat the oven to 350°F.

5. Slice the dough into ⅓-inch-thick rounds, rotating the dough often so it doesn't become flattened as you cut.

6. Place the cookies on ungreased baking sheets at least 2 inches apart. Bake until they are pale golden around the edges but still soft on top, 13 to 15 minutes (a minute or two longer for frozen dough). Let them stand on the baking sheet for 5 minutes, then remove them with a metal spatula to a wire rack to cool completely. Slice-and-Bake Sugar Cookies will keep at room temperature in an airtight container for 2 to 3 days.

A Good Excuse to Make Slice-and-Bake Sugar Cookies

I don't know about you, but when I see those quart-size containers of rainbow sprinkles at Costco, I can't resist the urge to take one home. Whenever I buy a new container of sprinkles, I make a double batch of Slice-and-Bake Sugar Cookie dough to go with them, so I know that the sprinkles won't sit unused in my pantry for very long.

slice-and-bake chocolate cookies

Makes about 60 cookies

This is the chocolate cookie version of the previous recipe. Try rolling these in chocolate sprinkles for a total chocolate effect.

1½ cups unbleached all-purpose flour
½ cup unsweetened Dutch-processed cocoa powder
½ teaspoon baking powder
½ teaspoon salt
1 cup (2 sticks) unsalted butter, softened
½ cup firmly packed light brown sugar
¼ cup granulated sugar
1 large egg
2 teaspoons pure vanilla extract

1. Sift together the flour, cocoa powder, baking powder, and salt in a medium-size mixing bowl.

2. Combine the butter, brown sugar, and granulated sugar in a large mixing bowl and, with an electric mixer, beat on medium-high speed until fluffy, 2 to 3 minutes. Add the egg and vanilla extract and beat until smooth. Beat in the flour mixture until just incorporated.

3. Divide the dough into 2 equal portions. Turn 1 portion onto a piece of waxed paper and shape it, rolling it inside the paper, into a log about 10 inches long and 1½ inches in diameter. Wrap the dough in plastic wrap and refrigerate it for at least 2 hours or up to 24 hours. Repeat with the remaining dough. (Dough logs may be wrapped tightly in plastic and frozen for up to 1 month. Slice and bake directly from the freezer.)

4. Preheat the oven to 350°F.

5. Slice the dough into ⅓-inch-thick rounds, rotating the dough often so it doesn't become flattened as you cut.

6. Place the cookies on ungreased baking sheets at least 2 inches apart. Bake until they are firm around the edges but still soft on top, 13 to 15 minutes (a minute or two longer for frozen dough). Let them stand on the baking sheet for 5 minutes, then remove them with a metal spatula to a wire rack to cool completely. Slice-and-Bake Chocolate Cookies will keep at room temperature in an airtight container for 2 to 3 days.

thin mints

Makes about 60 cookies

Here's a home-style version of the Girl Scout cookie-sale favorite. I'd never knock the Girl Scouts (I'd be in big trouble with my six-year-old daughter), but their cookies will never have the luscious, buttery richness of these. Using best-quality chocolate in the glaze elevates the cookies even higher. Make sure that you use peppermint extract, not spearmint, or else your cookies will taste like chewing gum.

1½ cups unbleached all-purpose flour
½ cup unsweetened Dutch-processed cocoa powder
1 teaspoon baking powder
½ teaspoon salt
1 cup (2 sticks) unsalted butter, softened
¾ cup sugar
1 large egg
2 teaspoons pure vanilla extract
½ teaspoon peppermint extract
7 ounces bittersweet chocolate, finely chopped
1 teaspoon vegetable oil

1. Sift together the flour, cocoa powder, baking powder, and salt in a medium-size mixing bowl.

2. Combine the butter and sugar in a large mixing bowl and, with an electric mixer, beat on medium-high speed until fluffy, 2 to 3 minutes. Add the egg and the extracts and beat until smooth. Stir in the flour mixture until just incorporated.

3. Divide the dough into 2 equal portions. Turn 1 portion onto a piece of waxed paper and shape it, rolling it inside the paper, into a log about 10 inches long and 1½ inches in diameter. Wrap the dough in plastic wrap and refrigerate it for at least 2 hours or up to 24 hours. Repeat with the remaining dough. (Dough logs may be wrapped tightly in plastic and frozen for up to 1 month. Slice and bake directly from the freezer.)

4. Preheat the oven to 350°F.

5. Slice the dough into ⅓-inch-thick rounds, rotating the dough often so it doesn't become flattened as you cut. Place the cookies on ungreased baking sheets at least 2 inches apart. Bake until they are firm around the edges but still soft on top, 13 to 15 minutes (a minute or two longer for frozen dough). Let them stand on the baking sheet for 5 minutes, then remove them with a metal spatula to a wire rack to cool completely.

6. Put 1 inch of water in the bottom of a double boiler or a large saucepan and bring to a bare simmer. Place the chocolate and vegetable oil in the top of the double boiler or in a stainless-steel bowl big enough to rest on top of the saucepan, making sure that the water doesn't touch the bottom of the bowl. Heat, whisking occasionally, until the chocolate is completely melted. Remove from the heat and whisk until completely smooth.

7. Line 2 baking sheets with parchment paper or aluminum foil. Use a small offset spatula to spread a thin layer of the chocolate glaze over the top of each cookie. Place the cookies, chocolate side up, on the baking sheets and refrigerate until the glaze is firm, about 15 minutes. Thin Mints will keep at room temperature in an airtight container for 4 to 5 days.

A Good Excuse to Make Thin Mints

Just because you gave birth only to boys doesn't mean you have to live without Girl Scout cookies. When your Boy Scouts return from a hike or camping trip, treat them to homemade Thin Mints.

spiral cookies

Makes about
24 large cookies

I can't tell you how impressed I was with myself when I sliced and baked these for the first time. They look great and their flavor is fantastic. Rolling the two doughs together takes just a few minutes more than rolling them into separate logs. So if you are making either one, consider throwing together a batch of the other and trying this fun cookie.

**½ batch freshly made Slice-and-Bake
Sugar Cookie dough (page 58)**
**½ batch freshly made Slice-and-Bake
Chocolate Cookie dough (page 59)**
2 teaspoons cold water

1. Spread a large piece of plastic wrap on a work surface and sprinkle lightly with flour. Use a rolling pin to roll the sugar cookie dough into a rough 8½-inch square. Trim the edges of the dough so that it is a neat 8-inch square. Repeat with the chocolate cookie dough.

2. Brush the sugar cookie dough with the water. Carefully invert the chocolate cookie dough onto the sugar cookie dough so that the two doughs are lined up, one on top of the other. Use the plastic wrap to push and roll the doughs into a neat, tight log. Tightly wrap the dough in plastic wrap and freeze until firm, at least 2 hours and up to 1 month.

3. Preheat the oven to 350°F.

4. Slice the dough into ⅓-inch-thick rounds, rotating the dough often so it doesn't become flattened as you cut. Place the cookies on ungreased baking sheets at least 2 inches apart. Bake until they are pale golden around the edges but still soft on top, 13 to 15 minutes. Let them stand on the baking sheet for 5 minutes, then remove them with a metal spatula to a wire rack to cool completely. Spiral Cookies will keep at room temperature in an airtight container for 2 to 3 days.

slice-and-bake chocolate chippers

Makes about 48 cookies

These have a sandier, more refined texture than drop cookies. Large chocolate chips are difficult to slice, so use mini chips when making slice-and-bake cookies.

2 cups unbleached all-purpose flour
½ teaspoon baking powder
¼ teaspoon salt
10 tablespoons (1 stick plus 2 tablespoons) unsalted butter, softened
½ cup firmly packed light brown sugar
¼ cup granulated sugar
2 large eggs
1 teaspoon pure vanilla extract
1 cup mini semisweet chocolate chips

1. Combine the flour, baking powder, and salt in a medium-size mixing bowl.

2. Combine the butter and sugars in a large mixing bowl and, with an electric mixer, beat on medium-high speed until fluffy, 2 to 3 minutes. Add the eggs and vanilla extract and beat until smooth. Stir in the flour mixture until just incorporated. Stir in the chocolate chips.

3. Divide the dough into 2 equal portions. Turn 1 portion onto a piece of waxed paper and shape it, rolling it inside the paper, into a log about 8 inches long and 2 inches in diameter. Wrap the dough in plastic wrap and refrigerate it for at least 2 hours or up to 24 hours. Repeat with the remaining dough. (Dough logs may be wrapped tightly in plastic and frozen for up to 1 month. Slice and bake directly from the freezer.)

4. Preheat the oven to 350°F.

5. Slice the dough into ⅓-inch-thick rounds, rotating the dough often so it doesn't become flattened as you cut. Place the cookies on ungreased baking sheets at least 2 inches apart. Bake until they are pale golden around the edges but still soft on top, 13 to 15 minutes (a minute or two longer for frozen dough). Let them stand on the baking sheet for 5 minutes, then remove them with a metal spatula to a wire rack to cool completely. Slice-and-Bake Chocolate Chippers will keep at room temperature in an airtight container for 2 to 3 days.

chocolate-walnut slice-and-bakes

While the chocolate is primary here, small amounts of cinnamon and ground cloves give these cookies a mysteriously delicious flavor. Almonds or pecans may be substituted for the walnuts if you like.

1½ cups unbleached all-purpose flour
½ cup unsweetened Dutch-processed
    cocoa powder
1 teaspoon baking powder
½ teaspoon salt
½ teaspoon ground cinnamon
Pinch of ground cloves
1 cup (2 sticks) unsalted butter,
    softened
¾ cup firmly packed light brown sugar
1 large egg
1 teaspoon pure vanilla extract
1 cup walnuts, finely chopped

1. Sift together the flour, cocoa powder, baking powder, salt, cinnamon, and cloves in a medium-size mixing bowl.

2. Combine the butter and brown sugar in a large mixing bowl and, with an electric mixer, beat on medium-high speed until fluffy, 2 to 3 minutes. Add the egg and vanilla extract and beat until smooth. Beat in the flour mixture until just incorporated. Stir in the walnuts.

3. Divide the dough into 2 equal portions. Turn 1 portion onto a piece of waxed paper and shape it, rolling it inside the paper, into a log about 10 inches long and 1½ inches in diameter. Wrap the dough in plastic wrap and refrigerate it for at least 2 hours or up to 24 hours. Repeat with the remaining dough. (Dough logs may be wrapped tightly in plastic and frozen for up to 1 month. Slice and bake directly from the freezer.)

4. Preheat the oven to 350°F.

5. Slice the dough into ⅓-inch-thick rounds, rotating the dough often so it doesn't become flattened as you cut. Place the cookies on ungreased baking sheets at least 2 inches apart. Bake until they are pale golden around the edges but still soft on top, 13 to 15 minutes (a minute or two longer for frozen dough). Let them stand on the baking sheet for 5 minutes, then remove them with a metal spatula to a wire rack to cool completely. Chocolate-Walnut Slice-and-Bakes will keep at room temperature in an airtight container for 2 to 3 days.

chocolate-cherry-pistachio swirls

Makes about 60 cookies

I love classic pairings like pistachio and cherry, and I also love the look of the green-and-red swirl in this chocolate cookie. This is a good choice at holiday time, both for the colors and for the rich, festive combination of fruit, chocolate, and nuts.

½ cup cherry preserves
2 cups unbleached all-purpose flour
½ teaspoon baking powder
½ teaspoon salt
1 cup (2 sticks) unsalted butter, softened
¾ cup sugar
1 large egg
1 teaspoon pure vanilla extract
2 ounces (2 squares) unsweetened chocolate, melted and cooled
⅔ cup unsalted pistachio nuts, finely chopped

1. Place the cherry preserves in a blender or the work bowl of a food processor and blend until smooth. Combine the flour, baking powder, and salt in a medium-size mixing bowl.

2. Combine the butter and sugar in a large mixing bowl and, with an electric mixer, beat on medium-high speed until fluffy, 2 to 3 minutes. Add the egg and vanilla extract and beat until smooth. Stir in the chocolate. Beat in the flour mixture until just incorporated.

3. Divide the dough into 2 equal portions. Spread a large piece of plastic wrap on a work surface and sprinkle lightly with flour. Use a rolling pin to roll 1 portion of the dough into a rough 10-inch square. Trim the edges of the dough so that it is a neat 9-inch square. Spread half of the preserves in a thin layer over the dough.

Sprinkle with half of the pistachio nuts. Press lightly on the nuts with your fingertips so that they adhere. Use the plastic wrap to push and roll the dough into a neat, tight log. Tightly wrap the dough in plastic wrap and freeze until firm, at least 2 hours and up to 2 weeks. Repeat the process with the remaining dough, preserves, and nuts. (Dough logs may be wrapped tightly in plastic and frozen for up to 1 month. Slice and bake directly from the freezer.)

4. Preheat the oven to 350°F.

5. Slice the dough into ⅓-inch-thick rounds, rotating the dough often so it doesn't become flattened as you cut. Place the cookies on ungreased baking sheets at least 2 inches apart. Bake until they are firm around the edges but still soft on top, 13 to 15 minutes. Let them stand on the baking sheet for 5 minutes, then remove them with a metal spatula to a wire rack to cool completely. Chocolate-Cherry-Pistachio Swirls will keep at room temperature in an airtight container for 2 to 3 days.

Kids Can Help

Spreading the preserves, sprinkling the nuts, and rolling up the dough into logs are fun tasks for kids.

fig-filled slice-and-bakes

Makes about 40 cookies

These are tiny pillows of rich pastry, filled with a delicious fig-and-nut mixture spiced with cinnamon.

2 cups unbleached all-purpose flour
½ teaspoon baking powder
¼ teaspoon salt
½ cup (1 stick) unsalted butter, softened
½ cup granulated sugar
2 large eggs
1 teaspoon pure vanilla extract
1 cup (about 6 ounces) dried figs, stems removed and finely chopped
¼ cup firmly packed light brown sugar
¼ cup water
⅛ teaspoon ground cinnamon
½ cup finely chopped walnuts

1. Combine the flour, baking powder, and salt in a medium-size mixing bowl.

2. Combine the butter and sugar in a large mixing bowl and, with an electric mixer, beat on medium-high speed until fluffy, 2 to 3 minutes. Add the eggs and vanilla extract and beat until smooth. Beat in the flour mixture until just incorporated.

3. Divide the dough into 2 equal portions. Turn 1 portion onto a piece of waxed paper and shape it, rolling it inside the paper, into a log about 10 inches long and 1½ inches in diameter. Wrap the dough in plastic wrap and refrigerate it for at least 2 hours or up to 24 hours. Repeat with the remaining dough. (Dough logs may be wrapped tightly in plastic and frozen for up to 1 month. Slice and bake directly from the freezer.)

4. Combine the figs, brown sugar, water, and cinnamon in a small saucepan and bring to a boil. Reduce the heat to low and simmer until the figs have absorbed most of the liquid, about 5 minutes. Place in a food processor and process until smooth. Transfer to a small bowl, stir in the walnuts, and let cool completely.

5. Preheat the oven to 375°F.

6. Slice the dough into ⅛-inch-thick rounds, rotating the dough often so it doesn't become flattened as you cut. Place half of the cookies on ungreased baking sheets about 1½ inches apart. Place ½ teaspoon of the filling in the center of each cookie. Top with another cookie and gently press the edges of the cookies together. Bake until they are pale golden around the edges but still soft on top, 10 to 12 minutes (a minute or two longer for frozen dough). Let them stand on the baking sheet for 5 minutes, then remove them with a metal spatula to a wire rack to cool completely. Fig-Filled Slice-and-Bakes will keep at room temperature in an airtight container for 2 to 3 days.

A Good Excuse to Make Fig-Filled Slice-and-Bakes

Bake these Fig Newton–like cookies, along with Chocolate Sandwich Cookies (page 159) and homemade graham crackers (see Abraham Lincoln Stovepipe Hats, page 223), to approximate (and put to shame) the cookie selection at the supermarket.

pecan sandies

Makes about
60 cookies

This classic slice-and-bake cookie belongs in every mom's repertoire. Its sweet-salty flavor is irresistible, it's simple to make, and it's very pretty with its pecan garnish.

1½ cups pecans, plus about 60 pecan halves for garnish
¾ cup (1½ sticks) unsalted butter, softened
¼ cup confectioners' sugar
½ cup firmly packed light brown sugar
1 large egg yolk
1½ cups unbleached all-purpose flour
¼ teaspoon salt

1. Finely chop the 1½ cups pecans in a food processor fitted with a metal blade.

2. Combine the butter and sugars in a large mixing bowl and, with an electric mixer, beat on medium-high speed until fluffy, 2 to 3 minutes. Add the egg and beat until smooth. Stir in the flour and salt until just incorporated. Stir in the chopped nuts.

3. Divide the dough into 2 equal portions. Turn 1 portion onto a piece of waxed paper and shape it, rolling it inside the paper, into a log about 10 inches long and 1½ inches in diameter. Wrap the dough in plastic wrap and refrigerate it for at least 2 hours or up to 24 hours. Repeat with the remaining dough. (Dough logs may be wrapped tightly in plastic and frozen for up to 1 month. Slice and bake directly from the freezer.)

4. Preheat the oven to 350°F.

5. Slice the dough into ⅓-inch-thick rounds, rotating the dough often so it doesn't become flattened as you cut. Place the cookies on ungreased baking sheets at least 2 inches apart. Place a pecan half in the center of each cookie. Bake until they are pale golden around the edges but still soft on top, 15 to 17 minutes (a minute or two longer for frozen dough). Let them stand on the baking sheet for 5 minutes, then remove them with a metal spatula to a wire rack to cool completely. Pecan Sandies will keep at room temperature in an airtight container for 2 to 3 days.

Kids Can Help

Give the littlest ones the important job of choosing 60 nice-looking pecan halves and then placing them on the cookies.

macadamia nut sandies
with white chocolate frosting

**Makes about
60 cookies**

Macadamia nuts and white chocolate have an affinity for each other, so it's only natural to dress up these sandies with a simple white chocolate glaze.

1½ cups salted macadamia nuts, plus about 60 whole macadamia nuts for garnish
¾ cup (1½ sticks) unsalted butter, softened
¼ cup confectioners' sugar
½ cup firmly packed light brown sugar
1 large egg yolk
½ teaspoon pure vanilla extract
1½ cups unbleached all-purpose flour
Pinch of salt
4 ounces white chocolate, finely chopped
½ teaspoon vegetable oil

1. Finely chop the 1½ cups macadamia nuts in a food processor fitted with a metal blade.

2. Combine the butter and sugars in a large mixing bowl and, with an electric mixer, beat on medium-high speed until fluffy, 2 to 3 minutes. Add the egg yolk and vanilla extract and beat until smooth. Beat in the flour and salt until just incorporated. Stir in the chopped nuts.

3. Divide the dough into 2 equal portions. Turn 1 portion onto a piece of waxed paper and shape it, rolling it inside the paper, into a log about 10 inches long and 1½ inches in diameter. Wrap the dough in plastic wrap and refrigerate it for at least 2 hours or up to 24 hours. Repeat with the remaining dough. (Dough logs may be wrapped tightly in plastic and frozen for up to 1 month. Slice and bake directly from the freezer.)

4. Preheat the oven to 350°F.

5. Slice the dough into ⅓-inch-thick rounds, rotating the dough often so it doesn't become flattened as you cut. Place the cookies on ungreased baking sheets at least 2 inches apart. Bake until they are pale golden around the edges but still soft on top, 15 to 17 minutes (a minute or two longer for frozen dough). Let them stand on the baking sheet for 5 minutes, then remove them with a metal spatula to a wire rack to cool completely.

6. Put 1 inch of water in the bottom of a double boiler or a large saucepan and bring to a bare simmer. Place the chocolate and vegetable oil in the top of the double boiler or in a stainless-steel bowl big enough to rest on top of the saucepan, making sure that the water doesn't touch the bottom of the bowl. Heat, whisking occasionally, until the chocolate is completely melted. Remove from the heat and whisk until completely smooth.

7. Line 2 baking sheets with parchment paper or aluminum foil. Use a small offset spatula to spread a thin layer of the chocolate glaze over the top of each cookie. Place a whole macadamia nut on top of each cookie. Place the cookies, chocolate side up, on the baking sheets and refrigerate until the glaze is firm, about 15 minutes. Macadamia Nut Sandies with White Chocolate Frosting will keep at room temperature in an airtight container for 4 to 5 days.

hazelnut biscuits

Makes 36 cookies

These crunchy nut cookies keep well and are sturdy enough that they won't crumble easily, making them ideal for filling cookie jars and packing into lunch boxes and picnic baskets.

1 cup hazelnuts
1½ cups unbleached all-purpose flour
½ teaspoon baking powder
¼ teaspoon salt
1⅓ cups sugar
3 large eggs
1 teaspoon pure vanilla extract

1. Preheat the oven to 350°F. Line baking sheets with parchment paper.

2. Place the nuts on a baking sheet and bake until fragrant, about 10 minutes. Remove the pan from the oven, wrap the nuts in a clean kitchen towel, and allow to cool for 10 to 15 minutes. Rub the nuts with the towel to remove the skins (it's okay if bits of skin stick to some of the nuts). Let cool completely and finely chop.

3. Combine the flour, baking powder, and salt in a medium-size mixing bowl.

4. Combine the sugar, 2 of the eggs, and the vanilla extract in a large mixing bowl and beat until smooth. Stir in the flour mixture until just incorporated. Stir in the hazelnuts.

5. Turn the dough out onto a lightly floured sheet of plastic wrap and pat into a 9 x 3-inch rectangle. Wrap in the plastic and freeze until firm, at least 1 hour or up to 2 days.

6. Preheat the oven to 350°F.

7. Cut the dough into ¼-inch-thick slices. Place the cookies on the lined baking sheets at least 2 inches apart. Lightly beat the remaining egg and brush the tops of the cookies with the egg. Bake until the cookies begin to brown, 13 to 15 minutes. Let them stand on the baking sheet for 5 minutes, then remove them with a metal spatula to a wire rack to cool completely. Hazelnut Biscuits will keep at room temperature in an airtight container for 1 week.

A Good Excuse to Make Hazelnut Biscuits

A day at the beach, a hike, a vacation that involves a long car or plane ride—I make these cookies any time that I know my family will need a treat that packs and travels well.

raspberry-almond icebox thumbprints

Makes about
60 cookies

Blanched almonds and almond extract give these cookies a wonderful flavor and fragrance. I like raspberry jam, but any flavor may be substituted.

1½ cups blanched whole almonds
2 cups unbleached all-purpose flour
½ teaspoon baking powder
½ teaspoon salt
1 cup (2 sticks) unsalted butter, softened
½ cup firmly packed light brown sugar
6 tablespoons granulated sugar
1 large egg
1 teaspoon pure almond extract
½ cup best-quality raspberry jam

1. Place the nuts in a food processor and finely chop. Don't overprocess; the nuts should look dry, not oily. Combine the flour, baking powder, and salt in a medium-size bowl.

2. Combine the butter and sugars in a large mixing bowl and, with an electric mixer, beat on medium-high speed until fluffy, 2 to 3 minutes. Add the egg and the almond extract and beat until smooth. Stir in the flour mixture until just incorporated.

3. Divide the dough into 2 equal portions. Turn 1 portion onto a piece of waxed paper and shape it, rolling it inside the paper, into a log about 10 inches long and 1½ inches in diameter. Wrap the dough in plastic wrap and refrigerate it for at least 2 hours or up to 24 hours. Repeat with the remaining dough. (Dough logs may be wrapped tightly in plastic and frozen for up to 1 month. Slice and bake directly from the freezer.)

4. Preheat the oven to 325°F.

5. Slice the dough into ⅓-inch-thick rounds, rotating the dough often so it doesn't become flattened as you cut. Place the cookies on ungreased baking sheets at least 2 inches apart. Bake for 15 minutes (a minute or two longer for frozen dough), remove the baking sheets from the oven, and make an indentation in each cookie with the back of a small measuring spoon. Return the baking sheets to the oven and bake until the edges of the cookies are pale golden, 5 to 7 minutes longer. Let them stand on the baking sheet for 5 minutes, then remove them with a metal spatula to a wire rack to cool completely.

6. Carefully fill each cookie indentation with about 1 teaspoon of jam. Raspberry-Almond Icebox Thumbprints will keep at room temperature in an airtight container for 2 to 3 days.

brown sugar buttons

This is a very easy dough to work with. I like to roll it into long logs and make a lot of tiny, delicate cookies. Turbinado sugar, otherwise known as sugar in the raw, makes a nice coating for these cookies because it has a hint of molasses flavor. It is available in the supermarket, right next to the granulated sugar. If you'd prefer, use granulated or coarse sanding sugar instead.

1¾ cups unbleached all-purpose flour
½ teaspoon baking powder
¼ teaspoon salt
10 tablespoons (1 stick plus 2 tablespoons) unsalted butter, softened
¾ cup firmly packed dark brown sugar
1 large egg, separated
1 teaspoon pure vanilla extract
⅔ cup turbinado sugar (often called sugar in the raw)

1. Combine the flour, baking powder, and salt in a medium-size mixing bowl.

2. Combine the butter and brown sugar in a large mixing bowl and, with an electric mixer, beat on medium-high speed until fluffy, 2 to 3 minutes. Add the egg yolk and the vanilla extract and beat until smooth. Stir in the flour mixture until just incorporated.

3. Divide the dough into 2 equal portions. Turn 1 portion onto a piece of waxed paper and shape it, rolling it inside the paper, into a log about 12 inches long and 1 inch in diameter. Wrap the dough in plastic wrap and refrigerate it for at least 2 hours or up to 24 hours. Repeat with the remaining dough. (Dough logs may be wrapped tightly in plastic and frozen for up to 1 month. Slice and bake directly from the freezer.)

4. Preheat the oven to 350°F.

5. Spread the turbinado sugar in an even layer on a rimmed baking sheet. Brush the dough logs with the egg white. Roll the logs in the sugar to coat them. Slice the dough into ⅓-inch-thick rounds, rotating the dough often so it doesn't become flattened as you cut.

6. Place the cookies on ungreased baking sheets at least 2 inches apart. Bake until they are pale golden around the edges but still soft on top, 10 to 12 minutes (a minute or two longer for frozen dough). Let them stand on the baking sheet for 5 minutes, then remove them with a metal spatula to a wire rack to cool completely. Brown Sugar Buttons will keep at room temperature in an airtight container for 2 to 3 days.

molasses spice slices

Makes about
60 cookies Slice and bake some of these mildly spicy cookies in the fall and serve them with warm apple cider.

2¼ cups unbleached all-purpose flour
½ teaspoon baking soda
½ teaspoon salt
1 teaspoon ground ginger
1 teaspoon ground cinnamon
½ teaspoon ground cloves
1 cup (2 sticks) unsalted butter, softened
½ cup sugar
1 large egg
¼ cup dark (not light or blackstrap) molasses

1. Combine the flour, baking soda, salt, ginger, cinnamon, and cloves in a medium-size mixing bowl.

2. Combine the butter and sugar in a large mixing bowl and, with an electric mixer, beat on medium-high speed until fluffy, 2 to 3 minutes. Add the egg and molasses and beat until smooth. Stir in the flour mixture until just incorporated.

3. Divide the dough into 2 equal portions. Turn 1 portion onto a piece of waxed paper and shape it, rolling it inside the paper, into a log about 10 inches long and 1½ inches in diameter. Wrap the dough in plastic wrap and refrigerate it for at least 2 hours or up to 24 hours. Repeat with the remaining dough. (Dough logs may be wrapped tightly in plastic and frozen for up to 1 month. Slice and bake directly from the freezer.)

4. Preheat the oven to 375°F.

5. Slice the dough into ⅓-inch-thick rounds, rotating the dough often so it doesn't become flattened as you cut. Place the cookies on ungreased baking sheets at least 2 inches apart. Bake until they are just firm on top, 13 to 15 minutes (a minute or two longer for frozen dough). Let them stand on the baking sheet for 5 minutes, then remove them with a metal spatula to a wire rack to cool completely. Molasses Spice Slices will keep at room temperature in an airtight container for 2 to 3 days.

oatmeal-date icebox cookies

Makes about 48 cookies

Here's a slice-and-bake version of the classic oatmeal-date cookie. The dough is soft, so it's easier to shape into squared-off logs than rounded ones.

1½ cups unbleached all-purpose flour
1 teaspoon baking powder
½ teaspoon salt
¼ teaspoon ground cinnamon
⅛ teaspoon ground nutmeg
1 cup (2 sticks) unsalted butter, softened
1 cup firmly packed light brown sugar
½ cup granulated sugar
2 large eggs
1 teaspoon pure vanilla extract
3 cups old-fashioned rolled oats (not instant)
1 cup finely chopped dates

1. Combine the flour, baking powder, salt, cinnamon, and nutmeg in a medium-size mixing bowl.

2. Combine the butter and sugars in a large mixing bowl and, with an electric mixer, beat on medium-high speed until fluffy, 2 to 3 minutes. Add the eggs and vanilla extract and beat until smooth. Stir in the flour mixture until just incorporated. Stir in the oats and dates.

3. Divide the dough into 2 equal portions. Turn 1 portion onto a piece of waxed paper and shape it, rolling it inside the paper and pressing it flat on four sides, into a squared-off log about 8 inches long and 2 inches in diameter. Wrap the dough in plastic wrap and refrigerate it for at least 2 hours or up to 24 hours. Repeat with the remaining dough. (Dough logs may be wrapped tightly in plastic and frozen for up to 1 month. Slice and bake directly from the freezer.)

4. Preheat the oven to 350°F.

5. Slice the dough into ⅓-inch-thick rounds, rotating the dough often so it doesn't become flattened as you cut. Place the cookies on ungreased baking sheets at least 2 inches apart. Bake until they are pale golden around the edges but still soft on top, 13 to 15 minutes (a minute or two longer for frozen dough). Let them stand on the baking sheet for 5 minutes, then remove them with a metal spatula to a wire rack to cool completely. Oatmeal-Date Icebox Cookies will keep at room temperature in an airtight container for 2 to 3 days.

slice-and-bake peanuts

Pinching the slices slightly at their centers creates a peanut shape for these simple peanut butter cookies. If you want to bake the cookies straight from the freezer, just let the slices thaw for a few extra minutes on the cookie sheet before pinching. This makes a big batch of dough, so I'll often just bake from one log and keep the rest in the freezer for a later date.

1 cup roasted salted peanuts
2 cups unbleached all-purpose flour
½ teaspoon baking powder
¼ teaspoon salt
¾ cup (1½ sticks) unsalted butter, softened
1½ cups firmly packed light brown sugar
½ cup granulated sugar
2 large eggs
1 teaspoon pure vanilla extract
1 cup creamy peanut butter
1 cup finely chopped dry-roasted peanuts

1. Place the roasted salted peanuts in a food processor and finely chop. Combine the flour, baking powder, and salt in a medium-size mixing bowl.

2. Combine the butter and sugars in a large mixing bowl and, with an electric mixer, beat on medium-high speed until fluffy, 2 to 3 minutes. Add the eggs and vanilla extract and beat until smooth. Add the peanut butter and beat until smooth. Stir in the flour mixture until just incorporated. Stir in the chopped dry-roasted peanuts.

3. Divide the dough into 2 equal portions. Turn 1 portion onto a piece of waxed paper and shape it, rolling it inside the paper, into a log about 12 inches long and 2 inches in diameter. Wrap the dough in plastic wrap and refrigerate it for at least 2 hours or up to 24 hours. Repeat with the remaining dough. (Dough logs may be wrapped tightly in plastic and frozen for up to 1 month. Slice and bake directly from the freezer.)

4. Preheat the oven to 350°F.

5. Slice the dough into ⅓-inch-thick rounds, rotating the dough often so it doesn't become flattened as you cut. Place the cookies on ungreased baking sheets at least 2 inches apart. Gently pinch the opposite sides of each slice together at the middle of the cookie to create a peanut shape. Bake until they are lightly colored, 13 to 15 minutes (a minute or two longer for frozen dough). Let them stand on the baking sheet for 5 minutes, then remove them with a metal spatula to a wire rack to cool completely. Slice-and-Bake Peanuts will keep at room temperature in an airtight container for 2 to 3 days.

Kids Can Help

Younger children will be happy to pinch rounds of cookie dough into peanut shapes.

lemon–cream cheese meltaways

Makes about 60 cookies

A little cream cheese in the dough gives these tender cookies a pleasantly tangy flavor. Sift some confectioners' sugar over the cookies just before serving for a pretty finish.

¾ cup (1½ sticks) unsalted butter, softened
4 ounces cream cheese, softened
1 cup confectioners' sugar, plus more for dusting if desired
1 large egg
1 teaspoon pure vanilla extract
2 teaspoons finely grated lemon zest
2¼ cups unbleached all-purpose flour
¼ teaspoon salt

1. Combine the butter, cream cheese, and confectioners' sugar in a large mixing bowl and, with an electric mixer, beat on medium-high speed until fluffy, 2 to 3 minutes. Add the egg, vanilla extract, and lemon zest, and beat until smooth. Stir in the flour and salt until just incorporated.

2. Divide the dough into 2 equal portions. Turn 1 portion onto a piece of waxed paper and shape it, rolling it inside the paper, into a log about 10 inches long and 1½ inches in diameter. Wrap the dough in plastic wrap and refrigerate it for at least 2 hours or up to 24 hours. Repeat with the remaining dough. (Dough logs may be wrapped tightly in plastic and frozen for up to 1 month. Slice and bake directly from the freezer.)

3. Preheat the oven to 350°F.

4. Slice the dough into ⅓-inch-thick rounds, rotating the dough often so it doesn't become flattened as you cut. Place the cookies on ungreased baking sheets at least 2 inches apart. Bake until they are pale golden around the edges but still soft on top, 15 to 17 minutes (a minute or two longer for frozen dough). Let them stand on the baking sheet for 5 minutes, then remove them with a metal spatula to a wire rack to cool completely. Sift some confectioners' sugar over the cookies before serving, if desired. Lemon–Cream Cheese Meltaways will keep at room temperature in an airtight container for 2 to 3 days.

cornmeal cranberry squares

Makes about
60 cookies

I love the combination of cornmeal and dried cranberries. The colors are beautiful, and the flavors and textures contrast wonderfully. This dough is quite soft, so it's easier to square off the sides of the log than attempt to roll it into a cylinder shape. Freeze rather than refrigerate it for easy slicing.

1 cup unbleached all-purpose flour
1 cup yellow cornmeal
½ teaspoon baking powder
¼ teaspoon salt
10 tablespoons (1 stick plus 2 tablespoons) unsalted butter, softened
½ cup firmly packed light brown sugar
¼ cup granulated sugar
2 large eggs
½ teaspoon pure vanilla extract
1 cup dried cranberries, coarsely chopped

1. Combine the flour, cornmeal, baking powder, and salt in a medium-size mixing bowl.

2. Combine the butter and sugars in a large mixing bowl and, with an electric mixer, beat on medium-high speed until fluffy, 2 to 3 minutes. Add the eggs and vanilla extract and beat until smooth. Stir in the flour mixture until just incorporated. Stir in the cranberries.

3. Divide the dough into 2 equal portions. Turn 1 portion onto a piece of waxed paper and shape it, rolling it inside the paper and pressing it flat on four sides, into a squared-off log about 10 inches long and 1½ inches in diameter. Wrap the dough in plastic wrap and freeze for at least 2 hours. Repeat with the remaining dough. (Dough logs may be wrapped tightly in plastic and frozen for up to 1 month. Slice and bake directly from the freezer.)

4. Preheat the oven to 350°F.

5. Slice the dough into ⅓-inch-thick rounds, rotating the dough often so it doesn't become flattened as you cut. Place the cookies on ungreased baking sheets at least 2 inches apart. Bake until they are pale golden around the edges but still soft on top, 13 to 15 minutes. Let them stand on the baking sheet for 5 minutes, then remove them with a metal spatula to a wire rack to cool completely. Cornmeal Cranberry Squares will keep at room temperature in an airtight container for 2 to 3 days.

lime-coconut cookies

Makes about 60 cookies

Sweetened flaked coconut and lime zest added to sugar cookie dough make for a wonderful slice-and-bake variation. If your kids love lemon-flavored cookies, as mine do, let them try these. They will be familiar, yet fun and new.

2 cups unbleached all-purpose flour
½ teaspoon baking powder
½ teaspoon salt
1 cup (2 sticks) unsalted butter, softened
¾ cup sugar
1 large egg
1½ teaspoons grated lime zest
1 teaspoon pure vanilla extract
½ cup sweetened flaked coconut

1. Combine the flour, baking powder, and salt in a medium-size mixing bowl.

2. Combine the butter and the sugar in a large mixing bowl and, with an electric mixer, beat on medium-high speed until fluffy, 2 to 3 minutes. Add the egg, lime zest, and vanilla extract and beat until smooth. Stir in the flour mixture until just incorporated. Stir in the coconut.

3. Divide the dough into 2 equal portions. Turn 1 portion onto a piece of waxed paper and shape it, rolling it inside the paper, into a log about 10 inches long and 1½ inches in diameter. Wrap the dough in plastic wrap and refrigerate it for at least 2 hours or up to 24 hours. Repeat with the remaining dough. (Dough logs may be wrapped tightly in plastic and frozen for up to 1 month. Slice and bake directly from the freezer.)

4. Preheat the oven to 350°F.

5. Slice the dough into ⅓-inch-thick rounds, rotating the dough often so it doesn't become flattened as you cut. Place the cookies on ungreased baking sheets at least 2 inches apart. Bake until they are pale golden around the edges but still soft on top, 13 to 15 minutes (a minute or two longer for frozen dough). Let them stand on the baking sheet for 5 minutes, then remove them with a metal spatula to a wire rack to cool completely. Lime-Coconut Cookies will keep at room temperature in an airtight container for up to 2 days.

A Good Excuse to Make Lime-Coconut Cookies

If you have some of this dough in the freezer, you'll be able to have these cookies baked and ready to sell when your kids want to open up their sidewalk lemonade stand.

DESPERATION COOKIES: what to bake when you have no ingredients in the house

LEFT TO RIGHT: Baby Elephant Ears, Homemade Milk Chocolate Crunch, Cornmeal Muffin Bites

Anyone who bakes cookies for and with their

children on a regular basis has lived the following scenario at one point:

Mom: "Who wants homemade cookies today?"

Kids: "We do! We do!"

Mom: "Then let's bake." (*walks to the pantry*) "Oh, no! We're out of flour!"

Kids: (*desperate wailing and crying, thrashing around on the floor, tearing of hair, rending of garments, etc.*)

Over the years, I've devised a strategy to avoid this frightening moment. No, it does not involve getting organized or checking the pantry before I speak. Instead, I've collected a bunch of recipes that give me the ability to conjure cookies from whatever random ingredients I happen to have on hand.

I do make every effort to keep my pantry, refrigerator, and freezer stocked with items I need if I want to bake at a moment's notice (see pages 16–17 on tips for stocking up). But inevitably, just when I've suggested cookies, I'll notice that I'm out of a key ingredient. With these "desperation" recipes and a flexible attitude, I can usually deliver on my promise. No flour? No problem. Let's make Flourless Peanut Butter Cookies (opposite) or Cocoa Meringue Cookies (page 91). No eggs? Shortbread cookies to the rescue (pages 88–90). No chocolate for brownies? Bar cookies like Pantry Blondies (page 95) or Apricot-Almond Squares (page 94) will do in a pinch.

The following recipes may be cobbled together with such random items as graham cracker crumbs, sweetened condensed milk, jelly, and Rice Krispies, but each one has met my high standards for great taste. In fact, I often find myself turning to these recipes just because I like them, even if the cupboard isn't bare. Orange–Cream Cheese Spiral Cookies (page 86) and Baby Elephant Ears (page 93) are so beloved in my house that they have made it onto my list of special-occasion cookies.

flourless peanut butter cookies

Makes about 24 cookies

When I began to notice recipes for flourless peanut butter cookies in different cookbooks and magazines, I knew I had to include a version in this chapter. This one calls for just 4 ingredients, and the proportions are so simple—1 egg, 1 cup sugar, 1 teaspoon vanilla, 1 cup peanut butter—that you can commit them to memory as you are making the dough.

1 large egg
1 cup sugar
1 teaspoon pure vanilla extract
1 cup creamy peanut butter

1. Preheat the oven to 350°F. Line baking sheets with parchment paper.

2. Combine the egg, sugar, and vanilla extract in a large mixing bowl and, with an electric mixer, beat on medium speed until smooth. Stir in the peanut butter and beat until smooth. Place the bowl in the refrigerator for 10 minutes (or up to 6 hours) to let the dough firm up.

3. Scoop a heaping tablespoonful of dough and roll it between your palms to form a ball. Place the balls on the lined baking sheets, leaving about 3 inches between each cookie. Press each cookie with the back of a fork twice, in opposite directions, to make a crisscross pattern.

4. Bake the cookies until they are lightly colored, 12 to 15 minutes. Let them stand on the baking sheet for 5 minutes, then carefully slide the entire parchment sheet with the cookies from the pan to a wire rack and let them cool completely. Flourless Peanut Butter Cookies will keep at room temperature in an airtight container for 2 to 3 days.

Kids Can Help

If you are looking for recipes to make with your children, these are all good choices. Each one requires only a handful of ingredients and is super easy to make, perfect for beginning cooks who like to measure and mix alongside Mom.

brown sugar cookies

I always wondered what would happen if you made chocolate chip cookie dough but left out the chocolate chips—because I often have those desperate days when I have all of the ingredients except that bag of morsels. Here is the resulting cookie, and it's actually very good. I've added a little extra flour to the dough to help the cookies keep their shape and a little extra vanilla to boost their flavor. Dark brown sugar gives these cookies a deep color and molasses flavor, but light brown sugar also works fine.

2½ cups unbleached all-purpose flour
1 teaspoon baking soda
1 teaspoon salt
1 cup (2 sticks) unsalted butter, melted
  and cooled slightly
1½ cups firmly packed dark or light
  brown sugar
2 large eggs
2 teaspoons pure vanilla extract

1. Preheat the oven to 375°F.

2. Combine the flour, baking soda, and salt in a medium-size mixing bowl.

3. Cream the cooled melted butter and sugar together in a large mixing bowl with a wooden spoon until smooth. Add the eggs and vanilla extract and beat until smooth. Stir in the flour mixture until just incorporated. Place the bowl in the refrigerator for 10 minutes (or up to 6 hours) to let the dough firm up.

4. Drop the dough by heaping tablespoonfuls onto ungreased baking sheets, leaving about 3 inches between each cookie. (Balls of dough may be placed next to each other on parchment paper–lined baking sheets, frozen, transferred to zipper-lock plastic freezer bags, and stored in the freezer for up to 1 month. Frozen cookies may be placed in the oven directly from the freezer and baked as directed.)

5. Bake the cookies until golden around the edges but still soft on top, 9 to 11 minutes (a minute or two longer for frozen dough). Let the cookies stand on the baking sheet for 5 minutes, then remove them with a metal spatula to a wire rack to cool completely. Brown Sugar Cookies will keep at room temperature in an airtight container for 2 to 3 days.

cornmeal muffin bites

Makes about
60 muffin bites
or 30 larger cookies

I absolutely love the flavor, color, and crunch of yellow cornmeal, and I almost always have some cornmeal in my pantry, since I use it constantly to make muffins and polenta and to dust my pizza stone before baking bread. So when I'm desperate for cookies and don't have much to work with, I grab the cornmeal and make these. You can bake the dough in mini-muffin tins so that the cookies look like little muffin bites, but they are equally tasty (and probably simpler) just dropped onto cookie sheets and baked. To vary the recipe, substitute 1 teaspoon grated lemon zest for the vanilla, and/or add ¾ cup dried blueberries or dried cranberries to the dough.

1¼ cups unbleached all-purpose flour
1 cup yellow cornmeal
1 teaspoon baking powder
½ teaspoon salt
1 cup (2 sticks) unsalted butter, melted and cooled slightly
¾ cup sugar
1 large egg
1 teaspoon pure vanilla extract

1. Preheat the oven to 350°F. Line mini-muffin tins with liners or baking sheets with parchment paper.

2. Combine the flour, cornmeal, baking powder, and salt in a medium-size mixing bowl.

3. Cream the cooled melted butter and sugar together in a large mixing bowl with a wooden spoon until smooth. Add the egg and vanilla extract and beat until smooth. Stir in the flour mixture until just incorporated. Place the bowl in the refrigerator for 10 minutes (or up to 6 hours) to let the dough firm up.

4. Scoop rounded teaspoonfuls of dough into the mini-muffin tins, or drop tablespoonfuls onto the lined baking sheets, leaving about 2 inches between each cookie.

5. Bake until the cookies are dry on top and just golden around the edges, 7 to 10 minutes for muffin bites, 10 to 12 minutes for cookies. Let them stand in the muffin tins or on the baking sheet for 5 minutes, then carefully remove them from the tins or slide the entire parchment sheet with the cookies from the pan to a wire rack and let them cool completely. Cornmeal Muffin Bites will keep at room temperature in an airtight container for 2 to 3 days.

instant chocolate chip peanut butter cookies

Makes about
28 cookies

This amazing recipe mimics real cookie dough, but does not require flour, baking powder, salt, or sugar. What are the secret ingredients? Sweetened condensed milk and graham cracker crumbs. This is a great recipe for kids who like to bake, because the ingredient list is so simple and easy to handle.

**One 15-ounce can sweetened
  condensed milk**
½ cup smooth peanut butter
1 teaspoon vanilla extract
2 cups graham cracker crumbs
½ cup chopped salted peanuts
½ cup semisweet chocolate chips

1. Preheat the oven to 350°F.

2. Combine the sweetened condensed milk, peanut butter, and vanilla extract in a large mixing bowl and, with an electric mixer, beat on medium speed until smooth. Stir in the graham cracker crumbs, peanuts, and chocolate chips.

3. Drop the batter by heaping tablespoonfuls onto ungreased baking sheets, leaving about 3 inches between each cookie. Bake until set, 12 to 15 minutes. Let the cookies stand on the baking sheet for 5 minutes, then remove them with a metal spatula to a wire rack to cool completely. Instant Chocolate Chip Peanut Butter Cookies will keep at room temperature in an airtight container for 2 to 3 days.

almond joy cookies

Makes about
24 cookies

You could probably mix this cookie dough in less time than it would take you to run to the store to buy the candy bar for which it is named.

**2 ounces (2 squares) unsweetened
  chocolate, finely chopped**
**One 15-ounce can sweetened
  condensed milk**
**One 7-ounce bag sweetened flaked
  coconut**
**½ cup finely chopped almonds, plus
  about 24 whole almonds**

1. Preheat the oven to 350°F. Line baking sheets with parchment paper.

2. Melt the chocolate in the microwave or on top of a double boiler.

3. Combine the chocolate, sweetened condensed milk, coconut, and chopped almonds in a large bowl and stir. Drop the batter by heaping tablespoonfuls onto the lined baking sheets, leaving about 3 inches between each cookie. Place a whole almond on top of each mound.

4. Bake until set, 12 to 15 minutes. Let the cookies stand on the baking sheet for 5 minutes, then remove them with a metal spatula to a wire rack to cool completely. Almond Joy Cookies will keep at room temperature in an airtight container for 4 to 5 days.

buttery raisin cookies

These simple butter cookies are great in a pinch, since most moms will have all of the ingredients on hand. They are an easy way to get your kids to eat those raisins that they may have begun to reject at snack time!

½ cup (1 stick) unsalted butter, softened
½ cup sugar
2 large eggs
1½ teaspoons pure vanilla extract
½ cup unbleached all-purpose flour
¼ teaspoon salt
1 cup raisins

1. Preheat the oven to 350°F. Line baking sheets with parchment paper.

2. Cream the butter and sugar together in a large mixing bowl with a wooden spoon until smooth. Add the eggs and vanilla extract and beat until smooth. Stir in the flour and salt until just incorporated. Stir in the raisins.

3. Drop rounded teaspoonfuls of the dough onto the lined baking sheets, leaving about 2 inches between each cookie. The cookies will spread quite a lot during baking.

4. Bake until the cookies are dry on top and just golden around the edges, 10 to 12 minutes. Let them stand on the baking sheet for 5 minutes, then carefully slide the entire parchment sheet with the cookies from the pan to a wire rack and let them cool completely. Buttery Raisin Cookies will keep at room temperature in an airtight container for 2 to 3 days.

orange–cream cheese spiral cookies

Makes about
30 cookies

This cookie came about when I looked in the refrigerator and saw half a package of cream cheese, half a jar of orange marmalade, and not much else. They are surprisingly fancy looking, considering their humble beginnings. It's important to whirl the marmalade in the food processor or blender so that it's easy to spread. Definitely bake these on parchment, because they get very sticky.

1 cup unbleached all-purpose flour
5 tablespoons sugar
¼ teaspoon salt
4 ounces (½ package) chilled cream
    cheese, cut into 8 pieces
½ cup (1 stick) unsalted butter, chilled,
    cut into 16 pieces
⅓ cup orange marmalade
¼ teaspoon ground cinnamon

1. Combine the flour, 2 tablespoons of the sugar, and the salt in a food processor and pulse to combine. Add the cream cheese and butter and pulse until the mixture resembles coarse meal (do not overprocess).

2. Turn the mixture out onto a lightly floured work surface and shape the dough into a 6-inch square. Wrap in plastic wrap and refrigerate it for at least 2 hours or up to 2 days.

3. Place the marmalade in a blender or the work bowl of a food processor and blend until smooth.

4. Using a lightly floured rolling pin, roll out the dough into a 10-inch square on a lightly floured work surface. Spread the marmalade evenly over the dough. Roll the dough into a tight cylinder. Wrap the cylinder in plastic wrap and place in the freezer for 1 hour to firm up.

5. Preheat the oven to 375°F. Line a baking sheet with parchment paper.

6. Combine the remaining 3 tablespoons sugar and the cinnamon in a small bowl. Slice the dough into ⅓-inch-thick rounds, rotating the dough often so it doesn't become flattened as you cut. Arrange the cookies on the baking sheet about 1 inch apart and sprinkle liberally with the cinnamon sugar. Bake until golden brown, 12 to 15 minutes. Transfer the baking sheet to a wire rack and let the cookies cool completely on the sheet. Orange–Cream Cheese Spiral Cookies will keep at room temperature in an airtight container for 2 to 3 days.

homemade milk chocolate crunch

Makes about 32 one-inch pieces

Although not technically cookies, these crunchy bites of candy satisfy kids just the same. They are so simple to put together, and kids age nine and up can make them by themselves.

1 cup (one 6-ounce bag) milk chocolate chips, or 6 ounces milk chocolate, chopped
1 tablespoon unsalted butter
1 cup Rice Krispies or other toasted rice cereal

1. Line an 8-inch square baking pan with heavy-duty aluminum foil, making sure that the foil is tucked into all the corners and that there is at least 1 inch overhanging the top of the pan on all sides.

2. Put 1 inch of water in the bottom of a double boiler or a large saucepan and bring to a bare simmer. Place the chocolate chips and butter in the top of the double boiler or in a stainless-steel bowl big enough to rest on top of the saucepan, making sure that the water doesn't touch the bottom of the bowl. Heat, whisking occasionally, until the chocolate and butter are completely melted. Remove from the heat and whisk until completely smooth. Stir in the Rice Krispies.

3. Spread the chocolate mixture across the bottom of the foil-covered baking pan in an even layer with an offset spatula. Refrigerate until hardened, about 1 hour. Grasping the overhanging foil on either side of the pan, lift out the crunch and place it on a cutting board. Break into pieces. Homemade Milk Chocolate Crunch will keep, refrigerated, in an airtight container for up to 3 days.

Kids Can Help

Let kids younger than nine break the bark into pieces once it is chilled. They'll be happy to do it, and you won't have to get your hands dirty.

scottish shortbread

Makes 16
shortbread wedges

Many cookbook authors and bakers prize these cookies for their tender and crumbly texture and buttery flavor. I cherish them as the cookie I make when I don't have any eggs in the house. If I have some coarse-grained sanding sugar on hand, I'll sprinkle some on just before baking to add some sparkle. But the cookies are wonderful without any embellishment, and they are particularly pleasing to kids who like plain and simple food.

1 cup (2 sticks) unsalted butter, softened
½ cup sugar
2 cups unbleached all-purpose flour
Pinch of salt

1. Combine the butter and sugar together in a large mixing bowl and, with an electric mixer, beat on medium speed until fluffy, 3 to 4 minutes. Stir in the flour and salt on low speed until the dough just comes together. Do not overmix. Turn the dough into a 10-inch tart pan with a removable bottom and press it into an even layer with your fingertips. Use the dull edge of a knife to score the dough into 16 wedges. Wrap the pan in plastic wrap and refrigerate for at least 2 hours and for up to 24 hours. (Dough may be wrapped tightly in plastic and frozen for up to 1 month. Defrost the dough in the refrigerator overnight before proceeding with the recipe.)

2. Preheat the oven to 250°F.

3. Bake the shortbread until it is dry and firm but has not yet begun to color, about 1 hour. Let cool completely in the pan on a wire rack, then remove the bottom from the pan and cut the shortbread with a sharp knife along the scored lines into 16 wedges. Scottish Shortbread will keep at room temperature in an airtight container for 3 to 4 days.

any nut shortbread

Makes about
20 cookies

I can usually scrounge up butter, flour, and sugar at my house. Ditto for nuts—at any one time, I probably have a bag of almonds, walnuts, or pecans in the freezer. So when I want something a little more exciting than Scottish Shortbread (opposite), I turn to this recipe. You may use one type of nut or a combination of two or more.

1 cup almonds, walnut pieces, unsalted pistachio nuts, and/or pecan halves
¾ cup sugar
1 cup (2 sticks) unsalted butter, softened
1¾ cups unbleached all-purpose flour
¼ teaspoon salt

1. Preheat the oven to 350°F. Place the nuts on a rimmed baking sheet and toast until fragrant, 5 to 7 minutes. Remove from the oven and let cool completely.

2. Combine the cooled nuts and ¼ cup of the sugar in the work bowl of a food processor and process until the mixture resembles coarse meal.

3. Combine the butter and another ¼ cup of the sugar together in a large mixing bowl and, with an electric mixer, beat on medium speed until fluffy, 3 to 4 minutes. Stir in the flour and salt on low speed until the dough just comes together. Stir in the nut mixture. Do not overmix. Divide the dough in half and roll each piece into a 1-inch-thick log that's about 5 inches long. Wrap each log in plastic wrap and refrigerate until firm, at least 1 hour and up to 1 day.

4. Preheat the oven to 350°F. Line baking sheets with parchment paper.

5. Cut the logs into ½-inch-thick circles. Place the cookies on the lined baking sheets, leaving about 1 inch between each cookie. Generously sprinkle with the remaining ¼ cup sugar.

6. Bake the cookies until they are golden around the edges, 14 to 17 minutes. Let them stand on the baking sheet for 5 minutes, then carefully slide the entire parchment sheet with the cookies from the pan to a wire rack and let the cookies cool completely. Any Nut Shortbread will keep at room temperature in an airtight container for 2 to 3 days.

simple lemon shortbread squares
with simple lemon glaze

Makes 16 squares I love this recipe because the glaze is made from two ingredients that you've already got out for the cookie dough. My younger daughter likes to serve these at her summertime tea parties, along with sweetened raspberry iced tea.

½ cup (1 stick) unsalted butter, chilled,
   cut into 16 pieces
1½ cups confectioners' sugar
1 teaspoon grated lemon zest
1¼ cups unbleached all-purpose flour
¼ teaspoon salt
2 tablespoons fresh lemon juice

1. Combine the butter, ½ cup of the confectioners' sugar, and ½ teaspoon of the lemon zest together in a large mixing bowl and, with an electric mixer, beat on medium speed until fluffy, 3 to 4 minutes. Stir in the flour and salt on low speed until the mixture resembles fine crumbs. Do not overmix.

2. Transfer the crumbs to an ungreased 8 x 8-inch baking pan and press into a compact, even layer with your fingertips. Cover with plastic wrap and refrigerate until the dough is well chilled, at least 1 hour and up to 1 day.

3. Preheat the oven to 300°F. Bake the shortbread until it is dry and firm and just beginning to color around the edges, about 35 minutes. While the shortbread is still warm and in the pan, cut it into 16 squares with a sharp paring knife. Let cool completely in the pan.

4. Combine the remaining 1 cup confectioners' sugar, the remaining ½ teaspoon lemon zest, and the lemon juice in a small bowl and whisk until smooth. Remove the shortbread squares from the pan and set them on a wire rack placed over a rimmed baking sheet. Spread the glaze on the tops of the squares with a small offset spatula. Let stand until the glaze is hardened, about 30 minutes. Simple Lemon Shortbread Squares with Simple Lemon Glaze will keep at room temperature in an airtight container for 2 to 3 days.

cocoa meringue cookies

Cocoa powder is a staple in my pantry, as are sugar and vanilla. When I combine these with a few egg whites I can turn out remarkably fudgy cookies without any flour or butter.

3 large egg whites
1 cup sugar
**3 tablespoons unsweetened Dutch-
    processed cocoa powder**
1 teaspoon pure vanilla extract

1. Position one oven rack in the top third of the oven and the other rack on the bottom third of the oven. Preheat the oven to 275°F. Line baking sheets with parchment paper.

2. Place the egg whites in a large mixing bowl. With an electric mixer fitted with the whisk attachment, beat the egg whites on medium speed until they are frothy, about 30 seconds. Turn the speed to high and pour the sugar into the bowl in a slow, steady stream. Continue to beat until the egg whites are stiff and shiny.

3. Hold a small fine-mesh strainer over the bowl and sift the cocoa powder into the bowl. Add the vanilla, and fold together with the egg whites, being careful not to deflate the meringue.

4. Drop heaping tablespoonfuls of the meringue onto the prepared baking sheets, leaving about 1½ inches between each cookie. Bake the meringues, using both oven racks, until they are firm on the outside but still soft on the inside, about 30 minutes. Let them cool on wire racks for 5 minutes, then carefully peel them off the parchment paper. Cocoa Meringue Cookies will keep at room temperature in an airtight container for several days.

**A Good Excuse to Make
Cocoa Meringue Cookies**

These cookies, which don't contain any butter, are the perfect simple Passover dessert. Serve them alongside Passover Macaroons (page 226).

cinnamon toast meringues

Makes about
24 cookies

When it's breakfast time and I realize I'm out of milk, eggs, and cereal, I often turn to cinnamon toast in desperation. Why not do the same when the cupboard is bare but I want to make cookies? Nuts give these cookies their toasty crunch. Pecans, walnuts, or almonds may be used here, depending upon what you can scrounge together.

¾ **cup pecans, walnuts, or almonds**
1 cup sugar
½ **teaspoon ground cinnamon**
3 large egg whites
1 teaspoon pure vanilla extract

1. Position one oven rack in the top third of the oven and the other rack on the bottom third of the oven. Preheat the oven to 275°F. Line 2 baking sheets with parchment paper.

2. Combine the nuts, ¼ cup of the sugar, and the cinnamon in a food processor and grind until fine.

3. Place the egg whites in a large mixing bowl. With an electric mixer fitted with the whisk attachment, beat the egg whites on medium speed until they are frothy, about 30 seconds. Turn the speed to high and pour the remaining ¾ cup sugar into the bowl in a slow, steady stream. Continue to beat until the egg whites are stiff and shiny. Fold in the nut mixture and vanilla extract with a rubber spatula, being careful not to deflate the meringue.

4. Drop heaping tablespoonfuls of the meringue batter onto the lined baking sheets, leaving about 1½ inches between each cookie. Bake the meringues, using both oven racks, until they are completely dry, about 40 minutes. Let them cool completely on wire racks, then carefully peel them off the parchment paper. Cinnamon Toast Meringues will keep at room temperature in an airtight container for several days.

baby elephant ears

Makes about 36 cookies

When they hear "elephant ears," kids just start to smile. These mini ears are just the right size for snacking. You can create these bakery-style treats with practically no effort and just two other ingredients if you keep some store-bought puff pastry in your freezer. Or make up the rolls ahead of time and freeze them for up to 2 weeks, then just slice and bake at your convenience. I like the Dufour brand of puff pastry, which is made with butter and makes these cookies especially delicious.

½ cup sugar, plus more for sprinkling the counter

1 teaspoon ground cinnamon

1 sheet (about 8 ounces) frozen puff pastry dough, thawed but well chilled

1 large egg, lightly beaten

1. Line several baking sheets with parchment paper. Combine ½ cup of the sugar and the cinnamon in a small bowl. Dust the work surface with a tablespoon or two of sugar. Quickly roll out the puff pastry dough on the sugar into a 12 x 9-inch rectangle.

2. Brush the puff pastry dough with the beaten egg. Sprinkle the cinnamon and sugar mixture over the dough, patting it lightly with your fingers so that it adheres. With the tip of a paring knife, mark a line (but do not cut through) lengthwise down the center of the dough. Fold the long sides of the rectangle toward the center line, leaving ⅓ inch uncovered on either side of the line. Wrap the folded dough in plastic wrap and freeze until firm, at least 1 hour and up to 2 weeks.

3. Preheat the oven to 400°F. Cut the pastry roll into ¼-inch slices. Arrange the slices, cut sides down, 1 inch apart on the lined baking sheets. Bake until golden brown, 15 to 20 minutes. Cool on the baking sheets for 15 to 20 minutes and serve at room temperature. Baby Elephant Ears will keep at room temperature in an airtight container for up to 3 days.

A Good Excuse to Make Baby Elephant Ears

I made these cookies for the nursery school class when it was "E" week. You could also bring them to school when you read a *Babar* story or *Horton Hears a Who!*

apricot-almond squares

The simple combination of flour, sugar, and nuts is used as both a crust and a topping in this recipe. This trick gives the appearance of hard work, but requires only a tiny bit of effort. Another reason this recipe is great in a pinch: You can use whatever kind of nuts and jam you have on hand. If your jam is very cold and chunky, stir it up to loosen it before spreading it over the crust.

½ cup whole almonds
½ cup sugar
½ cup unbleached all-purpose flour
¼ teaspoon ground cinnamon
¼ cup (½ stick) unsalted butter, chilled and cut into 8 pieces
⅔ cup apricot jam

1. Preheat the oven to 375°F. Line an 8-inch square baking pan with heavy-duty aluminum foil, making sure that the foil is tucked into all the corners and that there is at least 1 inch overhanging the top of the pan on all sides.

2. Place the almonds and sugar in the work bowl of a food processor and process until the nuts are finely ground. Add the flour, cinnamon, and butter, and process until the mixture is crumbly. Do not overprocess.

3. Transfer half of the almond mixture to the prepared pan and press it into a compact, even layer with your fingertips. Spread the jam evenly over the dough. Press the remaining almond mixture into loose, large crumbles and scatter evenly over the jam. Bake until the jam is bubbling and the topping is golden, 25 to 30 minutes. Let cool completely on a wire rack.

4. Grasping the overhanging foil on either side of the pan, lift the cooled squares out of the pan and place on a cutting board. Cut them into 16 squares. Apricot-Almond Squares will keep at room temperature in an airtight container for up to 3 days.

pantry blondies

Makes 16 blondies

This was my very first desperation recipe, and it is still one of my favorites. My mom wasn't a big baker, so if I wanted to make brownies, I had to let her know before she went shopping so she could pick up some unsweetened chocolate. But she always had a box of brown sugar in the house, along with flour, butter, and eggs. Once I discovered a version of this recipe in her copy of *The Joy of Cooking*, I was set. Eventually I grew to prefer these blondies to homemade brownies, and I often make them even when I do have chocolate in my pantry.

1 cup unbleached all-purpose flour
1 teaspoon baking powder
¼ teaspoon salt
½ cup (1 stick) unsalted butter
1 cup firmly packed light brown sugar
1 large egg
1 teaspoon pure vanilla extract
¾ cup chopped walnuts

1. Preheat the oven to 350°F. Line an 8-inch square baking pan with heavy-duty aluminum foil, making sure that the foil is tucked into all the corners and that there is at least 1 inch overhanging the top of the pan on all sides.

2. Combine the flour, baking powder, and salt in a small mixing bowl.

3. Melt the butter in a medium-size saucepan over low heat. Remove it from the heat. With a wooden spoon, stir in the brown sugar until it dissolves. Quickly whisk in the egg and vanilla extract. Stir in the flour mixture until just incorporated. Stir in the walnuts. Pour the batter into the prepared baking pan. Bake the blondies until they are just set in the center, 25 to 30 minutes. Let cool completely on a wire rack.

4. Grasping the overhanging foil on either side of the pan, lift out the blondies and place them on a cutting board. Cut them into 16 squares. Pantry Blondies will keep at room temperature in an airtight container for up to 3 days.

brownies, blondies, and beyond:
BAR COOKIES
to make and eat with kids

CLOCKWISE FROM TOP LEFT: Black Forest Brownies, Congo Bars, Orange Squares, Turtle Bars

Bar cookies appeal to kids and moms for so many
reasons. Kids love that bars are bigger, thicker, and all-around more of a mouthful than cookies, even when cut into kid-size portions. Moms love the fact that they are easy to prepare. No dropping, slicing, or rolling cookie dough. You just spread the mixture in the pan and put your feet up (or start dinner) while they bake. Ironically, the sliced squares often look more precise and elegant than the drop cookies you spent 45 minutes spooning out before baking.

Chocolate lovers like my daughter Rose enjoy brownies dozens of ways. Here I've included versions made with dark chocolate, milk chocolate, and white chocolate. You'll also find brownies with nuts, dried fruit, peanut butter, and raspberries stirred in (not all in the same batch, of course!). For caramel enthusiasts like my daughter Eve, there are blondies. These can also be varied endlessly, with mix-ins like coconut, oatmeal, or toffee bits. For people who just don't want to choose sides (that would be me and my husband), marble brownies swirled with blondie batter come to the rescue.

Beyond brownies, blondies, gingerbread, and granola squares, there are bar cookies with tender pastry crusts and delectable fillings. But they're still bar cookies, and I've done my best to keep them simple. In the recipes for Oatmeal-Date Bars, Nutella Ribbon Bars, and Peanut Butter and Jelly Crumb Squares (pages 117, 118, 119), the crust and crumb topping are made from the same dough. Half of it is patted into the pan, and the other half is crumbled over the filling. Classic Lemon Squares, Almond and Honey Squares, and Turtle Bars (pages 122, 124, 125) use a shortbread crust that's patted, not rolled, for ease. When you are ready to bake a new kind of bar, these recipes are only baby steps away from brownies and blondies in difficulty.

For superior bars with minimum fuss, take my advice:

Line the pan with heavy-duty aluminum foil. Unless otherwise directed (as in After-Dinner Microwave Brownies, page 104), line your pan with foil for easy removal of the bars. Once the bars have cooled completely in the pan, lift the foil from the pan and transfer the whole uncut batch to a cutting board. Peel the foil from the sides of the bars and slice. Unless otherwise noted, there's no need to butter or grease the foil. Not only does lining the pan this way make for easy cleanup, it also solves the problem of having to dig out that first bar from the corner of the pan, destroying it in the process, before you are able to remove the rest of the bars.

When in doubt, underbake. Brownies and bars cook from the outer edges in, so if you wait until the center of your pan is completely baked to remove the pan from the oven, the edges will likely be hard and dry. Take your brownies and blondies out of the oven when a cake tester comes out with a few moist crumbs clinging to it. The center of the pan will firm up as the bars cool.

It's especially important to remove bars with custard or cream fillings (such as Raspberry–Cream Cheese Brownies and Classic Lemon Squares, pages 110 and 122) from the oven when the centers are still a little jiggly. The fillings may look underdone, but they will continue to cook and will set up completely as the bars cool. If you keep these bars in the oven until their centers are completely set, the crusts will become intolerably hard and the fillings may curdle.

Be patient and let your bar cookies cool. It's tempting to dig into the pan before your bars have cooled completely, but if you try to cut any kind of bar cookies before they've had time to set up, you'll more than likely wind up with a plateful of crumbs. To guarantee neat, even slices with a minimum of crumbs, put the cooled bars in the refrigerator for 5 or 10 minutes. Chilling them slightly will make them even easier to cut.

Make portions small, but not too small. Even if you are not baking for kids, it's best to cut bars into small squares. This way, one batch can be stretched out for several days of after-school snacking or dessert. In most of the recipes that follow, I recommend 2-inch squares, which are large enough to satisfy without making anyone sick from overindulgence. In my experience, cutting bars any smaller than this is risky, because smaller squares tend to crumble.

best basic brownies

Makes 16 brownies I've tinkered with my old basic recipe a bit since I wrote *Mom's Big Book of Baking* (The Harvard Common Press, 2001). This new recipe is still chocolatey and tender, but the brownies will hold their shape even when knocked around in a lunch box or care package.

½ cup (1 stick) unsalted butter
2 ounces (2 squares) unsweetened chocolate
¾ cup unbleached all-purpose flour
½ teaspoon baking powder
¼ teaspoon salt
1 cup sugar
2 large eggs
1 teaspoon pure vanilla extract
¾ cup chopped walnuts or pecans (optional)

1. Preheat the oven to 350°F. Line an 8-inch square baking pan with heavy-duty aluminum foil, making sure the foil is tucked into all the corners and there is at least 1 inch overhanging the top of the pan on all sides.

2. Put 1 inch of water in the bottom of a double boiler or medium-size saucepan and bring to a bare simmer. Combine the butter and chocolate in the top of the double boiler or in a stainless-steel bowl set on top of the simmering water, making sure that the water doesn't touch the bottom of the bowl. Heat, whisking occasionally, until the chocolate and butter are completely melted. Set aside to cool slightly.

3. Combine the flour, baking powder, and salt in a small mixing bowl.

4. Whisk together the sugar and eggs in a large mixing bowl. With a wooden spoon, stir in the chocolate mixture and vanilla extract. Stir in the flour mixture until just incorporated. Stir in the nuts, if you are using them.

5. Pour the batter into the prepared baking dish. Bake the brownies until they are just set in the center, 30 to 35 minutes. Let them cool completely on a wire rack.

6. Grasping the overhanging foil on either side of the pan, lift out the brownies and place them on a cutting board. Cut into 16 squares. Best Basic Brownies will keep at room temperature in an airtight container for up to 3 days.

cocoa powder brownies

Makes 16 brownies This recipe is for all those times when you crave brownies but only have cocoa powder in the house. I like Dutch-processed cocoa. It's got a mellow flavor, with none of the bitterness of natural cocoa.

¾ cup unsweetened Dutch-processed cocoa powder
⅓ cup unbleached all-purpose flour
½ teaspoon baking powder
¼ teaspoon salt
1 cup sugar
2 large eggs
1 teaspoon pure vanilla extract
10 tablespoons (1¼ sticks) unsalted butter, melted and slightly cooled
¾ cup chopped walnuts or pecans (optional)

1. Preheat the oven to 350°F. Line an 8-inch square baking pan with heavy-duty aluminum foil, making sure the foil is tucked into all the corners and there is at least 1 inch overhanging the top of the pan on all sides.

2. Sift together the cocoa powder, flour, baking powder, and salt in a medium-size bowl.

3. Whisk together the sugar, eggs, and vanilla extract in a large mixing bowl until pale yellow, about 30 seconds. Whisk in the butter until smooth, another 30 seconds. Stir in the cocoa mixture until just incorporated. Stir in the nuts, if you are using them.

4. Pour the batter into the prepared baking dish. Bake the brownies until they are just set in the center, 25 to 30 minutes. Let cool completely on a wire rack.

5. Grasping the overhanging foil on either side of the pan, lift out the brownies and place them on a cutting board. Cut into 16 squares. Cocoa Powder Brownies will keep at room temperature in an airtight container for up to 3 days.

milk chocolate brownies

Makes 16 brownies

Here is a mild and sweet brownie, great for kids who find semisweet and bitter-sweet chocolate too intense.

½ cup (1 stick) unsalted butter
4 ounces milk chocolate
⅔ cup unbleached all-purpose flour
2 tablespoons unsweetened Dutch-processed cocoa powder, sifted
½ teaspoon baking powder
¼ teaspoon salt
½ cup sugar
2 large eggs
1 teaspoon pure vanilla extract
1 cup milk chocolate chips
¾ cup chopped walnuts or pecans (optional)

1. Preheat the oven to 350°F. Line an 8-inch square baking pan with heavy-duty aluminum foil, making sure the foil is tucked into all the corners and there is at least 1 inch overhanging the top of the pan on all sides.

2. Put 1 inch of water in the bottom of a double boiler or medium-size saucepan and bring to a bare simmer. Combine the butter and chocolate in the top of the double boiler or in a stainless-steel bowl set on top of the simmering water, making sure that the water doesn't touch the bottom of the bowl. Heat, whisking occasionally, until the chocolate and butter are completely melted. Set aside to cool slightly.

3. Combine the flour, cocoa powder, baking powder, and salt in a small mixing bowl.

4. Whisk together the sugar and eggs in a large mixing bowl. With a wooden spoon, stir in the chocolate mixture and vanilla extract. Stir in the flour mixture until just incorporated. Stir in the chocolate chips and the nuts, if you are using them.

5. Pour the batter into the prepared baking dish. Bake the brownies until they are just set in the center, 30 to 35 minutes. Let cool completely on a wire rack.

6. Grasping the overhanging foil on either side of the pan, lift out the brownies and place them on a cutting board. Cut into 16 squares. Milk Chocolate Brownies will keep at room temperature in an airtight container for up to 3 days.

white chocolate brownies

Makes 16 brownies I can't believe I never thought to try white chocolate in brownies, since I absolutely love the stuff, until I saw Dede Wilson's recipe in her inspirational *A Baker's Field Guide to Chocolate Chip Cookies* (The Harvard Common Press, 2004). Here's my version, inspired by hers. The walnuts cut the sweetness of the chocolate, and the dark chocolate chips add chocolate flavor.

½ cup (1 stick) unsalted butter
4 ounces best-quality white chocolate,
   such as Lindt
¾ cup unbleached all-purpose flour
½ teaspoon baking powder
¼ teaspoon salt
½ cup sugar
2 large eggs
1 teaspoon pure vanilla extract
¾ cup semisweet chocolate chips
¾ cup chopped walnuts

1. Preheat the oven to 350°F. Line an 8-inch square baking pan with heavy-duty aluminum foil, making sure the foil is tucked into all the corners and there is at least 1 inch overhanging the top of the pan on all sides.

2. Put 1 inch of water in the bottom of a double boiler or medium-size saucepan and bring to a bare simmer. Combine the butter and white chocolate in the top of the double boiler or in a stainless-steel bowl set on top of the simmering water, making sure that the water doesn't touch the bottom of the bowl. Heat, whisking occasionally, until the chocolate and butter are completely melted. Set aside to cool slightly.

3. Combine the flour, baking powder, and salt in a small mixing bowl.

4. Whisk together the sugar and eggs in a large mixing bowl. With a wooden spoon, stir in the chocolate mixture and vanilla extract. Stir in the flour mixture until just incorporated. Stir in the chocolate chips and walnuts.

5. Pour the batter into the prepared baking dish. Bake the brownies until they are just set in the center, 30 to 35 minutes. Let cool completely on a wire rack.

6. Grasping the overhanging foil on either side of the pan, lift out the brownies and place them on a cutting board. Cut into 16 squares. White Chocolate Brownies will keep at room temperature in an airtight container for up to 3 days.

after-dinner microwave brownies

Makes 16 brownies

This is my family's go-to recipe when we realize after dinner that we just have to have something warm from the oven. They're quick and easy enough to make and eat in the brief time we have between washing up the dinner dishes and reading bedtime stories. I've been tinkering with the recipe for microwave brownies for years now, and I think this is my simplest, best version yet. Everything is melted, stirred, and baked in the same dish.

½ cup (1 stick) unsalted butter, cut into 8 pieces
¾ cup unsweetened Dutch-processed cocoa powder
1½ cups sugar
3 large eggs
1 teaspoon pure vanilla extract
¾ cup unbleached all-purpose flour
¾ cup chopped walnuts (optional)

1. Place the butter and cocoa powder in an 8-inch square microwave-safe baking dish. Microwave on high until the butter is melted, 30 seconds to 1½ minutes, depending on the power and size of your oven.

2. Add the sugar and stir to combine. Whisk in the eggs and vanilla extract. Stir in the flour. Stir in the nuts, if you are using them. Smooth the top of the batter with a spatula.

3. Microwave on high until the brownies are just set in the center, 4 to 7 minutes, depending on the power and size of your oven. Let the brownies cool on a wire rack for 10 minutes.

4. Cut the brownies into 16 squares and serve immediately.

peanut butter swirl brownies

Makes 16 brownies Although in most of the recipes in this book you can use either commercial or natural peanut butter, be sure to use a supermarket brand like Jif or Skippy here. All-natural peanut butter will separate and make the brownies greasy.

½ cup (1 stick) unsalted butter
2 ounces (2 squares) unsweetened chocolate
¾ cup unbleached all-purpose flour
½ teaspoon baking powder
¼ teaspoon salt
1 cup sugar
2 large eggs
1 teaspoon pure vanilla extract
⅓ cup peanut butter, at room temperature

1. Preheat the oven to 350°F. Line an 8-inch square baking pan with heavy-duty aluminum foil, making sure the foil is tucked into all the corners and there is at least 1 inch overhanging the top of the pan on all sides.

2. Put 1 inch of water in the bottom of a double boiler or medium-size saucepan and bring to a bare simmer. Combine the butter and chocolate in the top of the double boiler or in a stainless-steel bowl set on top of the simmering water, making sure that the water doesn't touch the bottom of the bowl. Heat, whisking occasionally, until the chocolate and butter are completely melted. Set aside to cool slightly.

3. Combine the flour, baking powder, and salt in a small mixing bowl.

4. Whisk together the sugar and eggs in a large mixing bowl. With a wooden spoon, stir in the chocolate mixture and vanilla extract. Stir in the flour mixture until just incorporated.

5. Pour the batter into the prepared baking dish. Drop the peanut butter in 10 dollops on top of the batter. Gently run a knife through the batter in several figure-eight patterns to marble it. Bake the brownies until they are just set in the center, 25 to 30 minutes. Let cool completely on a wire rack.

6. Grasping the overhanging foil on either side of the pan, lift out the brownies and place them on a cutting board. Cut into 16 squares. Peanut Butter Swirl Brownies will keep at room temperature in an airtight container for up to 3 days.

nutella brownies

If you've never tried it, Nutella is a tempting chocolate-hazelnut spread that has been popular in Europe for years and is now widely available in this country (look for it next to the peanut butter at the supermarket). It adds wonderful depth and richness to these nut-studded brownies.

1¼ cups hazelnuts
½ cup (1 stick) unsalted butter
2 ounces (2 squares) unsweetened chocolate, finely chopped
¼ cup Nutella
¾ cup unbleached all-purpose flour
½ teaspoon baking powder
¼ teaspoon salt
¾ cup sugar
2 large eggs
1 teaspoon pure vanilla extract

1. Preheat the oven to 350°F. Line an 8-inch square baking pan with heavy-duty aluminum foil, making sure the foil is tucked into all the corners and there is at least 1 inch overhanging the top of the pan on all sides.

2. Place the hazelnuts on a baking sheet and bake until they are fragrant, about 10 minutes. Remove the nuts from the oven and wrap them in a clean kitchen towel. Let cool for 10 to 15 minutes. Rub the nuts with the towel to remove the skins (it's okay if bits of skin stick to some of the nuts). Finely chop and set aside.

3. Put 1 inch of water in the bottom of a double boiler or medium-size saucepan and bring to a bare simmer. Combine the butter, chocolate, and Nutella in the top of the double boiler or in a stainless-steel bowl set on top of the simmering water, making sure that the water doesn't touch the bottom of the bowl. Heat, whisking occasionally, until the chocolate, Nutella, and butter are completely melted. Set aside to cool slightly.

4. Combine the flour, baking powder, and salt in a small mixing bowl.

5. Whisk together the sugar and eggs in a large mixing bowl. With a wooden spoon, stir in the chocolate mixture and vanilla extract. Stir in the flour mixture until just incorporated. Stir in the chopped hazelnuts.

6. Pour the batter into the prepared baking dish. Bake the brownies until they are just set in the center, 30 to 35 minutes. Let cool completely on a wire rack.

7. Grasping the overhanging foil on either side of the pan, lift out the brownies and place them on a cutting board. Cut into 16 squares. Nutella Brownies will keep at room temperature in an airtight container for up to 3 days.

black forest brownies

Makes 16 brownies

I have loved the combination of chocolate and cherries since I was a kid, so this recipe brings back memories for me. The jam makes these brownies extremely moist and delicious, and the cherries add welcome tartness to balance the dark chocolate of the brownies.

½ cup (1 stick) unsalted butter
2 ounces (2 squares) unsweetened
    chocolate
¾ cup unbleached all-purpose flour
½ teaspoon baking powder
¼ teaspoon salt
¾ cup sugar
2 large eggs
½ teaspoon pure vanilla extract
¾ cup dried tart cherries
⅓ cup semisweet chocolate chips
¼ cup cherry preserves

1. Preheat the oven to 350°F. Line an 8-inch square baking pan with heavy-duty aluminum foil, making sure the foil is tucked into all the corners and there is at least 1 inch overhanging the top of the pan on all sides.

2. Put 1 inch of water in the bottom of a double boiler or medium-size saucepan and bring to a bare simmer. Combine the butter and chocolate in the top of the double boiler or in a stainless-steel bowl set on top of the simmering water, making sure that the water doesn't touch the bottom of the bowl. Heat, whisking occasionally, until the chocolate and butter are completely melted. Set aside to cool slightly.

3. Combine the flour, baking powder, and salt in a small mixing bowl.

4. Whisk together the sugar and eggs in a large mixing bowl. With a wooden spoon, stir in the chocolate mixture and vanilla extract. Stir in the flour mixture until just incorporated. Stir in the dried cherries, chocolate chips, and cherry preserves.

5. Pour the batter into the prepared baking dish. Bake the brownies until they are just set in the center, 30 to 35 minutes. Let cool completely on a wire rack.

6. Grasping the overhanging foil on either side of the pan, lift out the brownies and place them on a cutting board. Cut into 16 squares. Black Forest Brownies will keep at room temperature in an airtight container for up to 3 days.

A Good Excuse to Make
Black Forest Brownies

Call them "George Washington brownies" when you make them over the long Presidents' Day weekend, in honor of the man who couldn't tell a lie about chopping down the cherry tree.

s'mores brownies

Makes 16 brownies

You can thank my husband (my children are very grateful) for this ingenious variation on Best Basic Brownies.

¾ cup (1½ sticks) unsalted butter
¾ cup graham cracker crumbs
1 cup plus 1 tablespoon sugar
3 ounces (3 squares) unsweetened chocolate
¾ cup unbleached all-purpose flour
½ teaspoon baking powder
¼ teaspoon salt
2 large eggs
1 teaspoon pure vanilla extract
¾ cup chopped walnuts or pecans
2 cups mini marshmallows

1. Preheat the oven to 350°F. Line an 8-inch square baking pan with heavy-duty aluminum foil, making sure the foil is tucked into all the corners and there is at least 1 inch overhanging the top of the pan on all sides.

2. Melt 4 tablespoons of the butter. Combine the graham cracker crumbs, melted butter, and 1 tablespoon of the sugar in a medium-size bowl and stir until all of the crumbs are moistened. Press the mixture evenly across the bottom of the pan, packing it tightly with your fingertips so it is even and compacted. Bake until the crust is crisp, 6 to 8 minutes. Remove from the oven to cool.

3. Put 1 inch of water in the bottom of a double boiler or medium-size saucepan and bring to a bare simmer. Combine the remaining ½ cup butter and the chocolate in the top of the double boiler or in a stainless-steel bowl set on top of the simmering water, making sure that the water doesn't touch the bottom of the bowl. Heat, whisking occasionally, until the chocolate and butter are completely melted. Set aside to cool slightly.

4. Combine the flour, baking powder, and salt in a small mixing bowl.

5. Whisk together the remaining 1 cup sugar and the eggs in a large mixing bowl. With a wooden spoon, stir in the chocolate mixture and vanilla extract. Stir in the flour mixture until just incorporated. Pour the batter on top of the graham cracker crust. Bake the brownies until they are just set in the center, 30 to 35 minutes.

6. Remove the pan from the oven and turn on the broiler. Scatter the marshmallows in an even layer over the brownies. Broil until the marshmallows are lightly browned, 1 to 3 minutes. Watch the pan carefully, because the marshmallows will

A Good Excuse to Make S'mores Brownies

Make these brownies to cheer everyone up when your barbecue or campout has been called off because of rain. Other good s'mores substitutes: Chocolate-Marshmallow Cookies (page 210) and Rocky Road Cookies (page 136).

begin to burn very quickly after they brown. Remove from the oven and let cool completely on a wire rack.

7. Grasping the overhanging foil on either side of the pan, lift out the brownies and place them on a cutting board. Spray your knife with cooking spray before cutting the brownies to prevent them from sticking. Cut into 16 squares. S'mores Brownies will keep at room temperature in an airtight container for up to 3 days.

Brownie and Blondie Frostings

Although brownies are rich and delicious when unadorned, some kids (most kids?) love them better when they're frosted. Here are a few simple frostings and glazes to mix and match as you like. Each should be spread on top of a completely cooled batch of brownies or blondies that are still in the pan. Allow 1 to 2 hours for the frosting to set before removing the brownies from the pan and cutting as directed.

* Bittersweet Chocolate Glaze: Melt 8 ounces finely chopped bittersweet chocolate, 2 tablespoons vegetable oil, and 1 tablespoon corn syrup in the top of a double boiler over simmering water or in a small bowl in the microwave, stirring occasionally, until completely melted.

* Milk Chocolate Ganache: Place 4 ounces finely chopped milk chocolate and 1 tablespoon unsweetened Dutch-processed cocoa powder in a medium-size heatproof bowl. Bring 6 tablespoons heavy cream to a boil in a small saucepan. Pour over the chocolate and let stand 5 minutes. Whisk until smooth.

* Caramel-Nut Glaze: Combine 6 tablespoons sugar, 2½ tablespoons light corn syrup, ¼ cup water, and a pinch of salt in a heavy saucepan and cook over medium heat, stirring, until the sugar has dissolved. Bring to a boil without stirring and cook until the mixture turns light amber. Remove from the heat and stir in 3 tablespoons heavy cream and 1 teaspoon vanilla extract. Be careful—the mixture will bubble up. Stir in ¾ cup coarsely chopped pecans or walnuts.

* Peanut Butter Frosting: Combine 1 cup creamy peanut butter (not natural or freshly ground), 3 tablespoons softened unsalted butter, ⅔ cup confectioners' sugar, and 1 teaspoon vanilla extract in the bowl of an electric mixer and beat until fluffy and smooth.

raspberry–cream cheese brownies

Makes 16 brownies These are deluxe, triple-layer brownies with a fudgy bottom, a cheesecake middle, and a raspberry top. They should be just a little bit wobbly in the center when you take them out of the oven. The cheesecake layer will set up as they cool.

For the
brownie batter

- ½ cup (1 stick) unsalted butter
- 4 ounces (4 squares) unsweetened chocolate
- ⅔ cup unbleached all-purpose flour
- ½ teaspoon baking powder
- ¼ teaspoon salt
- 1½ cups sugar
- 2 large eggs
- 1 teaspoon pure vanilla extract

For the cream
cheese layer

- One 8-ounce package cream cheese, softened
- ¼ cup plus 1 tablespoon sugar
- 1 large egg
- ½ teaspoon pure vanilla extract
- ¼ teaspoon salt
- 1 tablespoon unbleached all-purpose flour

- 1½ cups raspberries

1. Preheat the oven to 325°F. Adjust the oven rack to the bottom third of the oven. Line an 8-inch square baking pan with heavy-duty aluminum foil, making sure the foil is tucked into all the corners and there is at least 1 inch overhanging the top of the pan on all sides.

2. Make the brownies: Put 1 inch of water in the bottom of a double boiler or medium-size saucepan and bring to a bare simmer. Combine the butter and chocolate in the top of the double boiler or in a stainless-steel bowl set on top of the simmering water, making sure that the water doesn't touch the bottom of the bowl. Heat, whisking occasionally, until the chocolate and butter are completely melted. Set aside to cool slightly.

3. Combine the flour, baking powder, and salt in a small mixing bowl.

4. Whisk together the sugar and eggs in a large mixing bowl. With a wooden spoon, stir in the chocolate mixture and vanilla extract. Stir in the flour mixture until just incorporated. Spread in an even layer into the prepared pan.

5. Make the cheesecake: Combine the cream cheese and ¼ cup of the sugar in a medium-size mixing bowl. With an electric mixer on medium-high speed, beat the mixture until very smooth. Add the egg and vanilla extract and beat again until smooth. Stir in the salt and flour.

6. Drop the cream cheese mixture by heaping tablespoonfuls over the brownie batter and smooth with a spatula to create an even layer. Sprinkle the raspberries over the cream cheese. Sprinkle with the remaining 1 tablespoon sugar.

7. Bake the brownies in the bottom third of the oven until they are set around the edges but still a little wobbly in the center, 50 to 55 minutes. Let cool completely on a wire rack.

8. Refrigerate them until they are completely chilled, at least 6 hours. Grasping

the overhanging foil on either side of the pan, lift out the brownies and place them on a cutting board. Cut into 16 squares.

Raspberry–Cream Cheese Brownies will keep in the refrigerator in an airtight container for up to 5 days.

marble brownies

Makes 32 brownies

To make these pretty and chewy brownies, just stir some melted chocolate into a portion of butterscotch blondie batter, swirl the two together in the pan, and bake.

1½ ounces (1½ squares) unsweetened chocolate
1 cup unbleached all-purpose flour
1 teaspoon baking powder
¼ teaspoon salt
½ cup (1 stick) unsalted butter
1 cup firmly packed light brown sugar
1 large egg
1 teaspoon pure vanilla extract

1. Preheat the oven to 350°F. Line an 8-inch square baking pan with heavy-duty aluminum foil, making sure the foil is tucked into all the corners and there is at least 1 inch overhanging the top of the pan on all sides.

2. Melt the chocolate over simmering water or in the microwave. Set aside to cool slightly. Combine the flour, baking powder, and salt in a small mixing bowl.

3. Melt the butter in a medium-size saucepan over low heat. Remove from the heat and, with a wooden spoon, stir in the brown sugar until it is dissolved. Quickly whisk in the egg and vanilla extract. Stir in the flour mixture until just incorporated.

4. Pour two-thirds of the batter into the prepared baking pan. Smooth with a spatula. Stir the chocolate into the remaining batter until incorporated. Drop dollops of the chocolate mixture into the pan. Gently run a knife through the batter in several figure-eight patterns to marble it. Bake the brownies until they are just set in the center, 25 to 30 minutes. Let cool completely on a wire rack.

5. Grasping the overhanging foil on either side of the pan, lift out the brownies and place them on a cutting board. Cut into 16 squares. Marble Brownies will keep at room temperature in an airtight container for up to 3 days.

A Good Excuse to Make Marble Brownies

If your family is divided along the blondie-brownie line, make Marble Brownies to satisfy everyone.

congo bars

Makes 16 bars Unsweetened coconut is lighter and less sticky than sweetened flaked coconut, and won't weigh down these bars. A combination of white and dark chocolate chips is nice, but you can certainly use one or the other if you only have one type on hand.

¾ **cup unsweetened dried coconut**
1 **cup unbleached all-purpose flour**
1 **teaspoon baking powder**
¼ **teaspoon salt**
½ **cup (1 stick) unsalted butter**
1 **cup firmly packed light brown sugar**
1 **large egg**
1 **teaspoon pure vanilla extract**
½ **cup white chocolate chips**
½ **cup semisweet chocolate chips**
¾ **cup chopped walnuts or pecans**

1. Preheat the oven to 350°F. Line an 8-inch square baking pan with heavy-duty aluminum foil, making sure the foil is tucked into all the corners and there is at least 1 inch overhanging the top of the pan on all sides.

2. Place the coconut on a rimmed baking sheet and toast, stirring once or twice, until golden, about 5 minutes. Set aside to cool completely.

3. Combine the flour, baking powder, and salt in a small mixing bowl.

4. Melt the butter in a medium-size saucepan over low heat. Remove it from the heat and, with a wooden spoon, stir in the brown sugar until it is dissolved. Quickly whisk in the egg and vanilla extract. Stir in the flour mixture until just incorporated. Stir in the coconut, white and semisweet chocolate chips, and nuts.

5. Pour the batter into the prepared baking pan. Bake the bars until they are just set in the center, 25 to 30 minutes. Let cool completely on a wire rack.

6. Grasping the overhanging foil on either side of the pan, lift out the bars and place them on a cutting board. Cut into 16 squares. Congo Bars will keep at room temperature in an airtight container for up to 3 days.

coffee toffee blondies

Makes 16 blondies

I am always surprised at how many kids who pass through my house love coffee-flavored cookies, brownies, and ice cream, so I no longer reserve that flavor for the grownups. Toffee bits give these brownies a little crunch and make them extra kid friendly.

1 cup unbleached all-purpose flour
1 teaspoon baking powder
¼ teaspoon salt
½ cup (1 stick) unsalted butter
1 cup firmly packed dark brown sugar
2 teaspoons instant espresso powder
1 large egg
1 teaspoon pure vanilla extract
1 cup Heath Bar Milk Chocolate Toffee Bits

1. Preheat the oven to 350°F. Line an 8-inch square baking pan with heavy-duty aluminum foil, making sure the foil is tucked into all the corners and there is at least 1 inch overhanging the top of the pan on all sides.

2. Combine the flour, baking powder, and salt in a small mixing bowl.

3. Melt the butter in a medium-size saucepan over low heat. Remove it from the heat and, with a wooden spoon, stir in the brown sugar until it is dissolved. Stir in the espresso powder. Quickly whisk in the egg and vanilla extract. Stir in the flour mixture until just incorporated, then stir in the toffee bits.

4. Pour the batter into the prepared baking dish. Bake the blondies until they are just set in the center, 25 to 30 minutes. Immediately scatter the toffee bits over the blondies and press down lightly on them with the back of a spoon so they adhere. Let cool completely on a wire rack.

5. Grasping the overhanging foil on either side of the pan, lift out the blondies and place them on a cutting board. Cut into 16 squares. Coffee Toffee Blondies will keep at room temperature in an airtight container for up to 3 days.

oatmeal blondies

I love the combination of oatmeal and chocolate chips, but for a terrific variation you may substitute butterscotch chips for the chocolate and add ¾ cup dried cranberries and ½ teaspoon orange zest along with the chips.

1 cup unbleached all-purpose flour
1 teaspoon baking powder
¼ teaspoon salt
½ cup (1 stick) unsalted butter
1 cup firmly packed light brown sugar
½ cup milk
1 large egg
1 teaspoon pure vanilla extract
1¼ cups old-fashioned rolled oats (not instant)
¾ cup chopped walnuts (optional)
1 cup semisweet chocolate chips (optional)

1. Preheat the oven to 350°F. Line an 8-inch square baking pan with heavy-duty aluminum foil, making sure the foil is tucked into all the corners and there is at least 1 inch overhanging the top of the pan on all sides.

2. Combine the flour, baking powder, and salt in a small mixing bowl.

3. Melt the butter in a medium-size saucepan over low heat. Remove it from the heat and, with a wooden spoon, stir in the brown sugar until it is dissolved. Quickly whisk in the milk, egg, and vanilla extract. Stir in the flour mixture until just incorporated. Stir in the oats. Stir in the walnuts and chocolate chips, if you are using them.

4. Pour the batter into the prepared baking pan and smooth with a spatula. Bake the blondies until they are just set in the center, 25 to 30 minutes. Let cool completely on a wire rack. Grasping the overhanging foil on either side of the pan, lift out the blondies and place them on a cutting board. Cut into 16 squares. Oatmeal Blondies will keep at room temperature in an airtight container for up to 3 days.

chocolate chip gingerbread bars

Makes 16 bars These are cakey and not too sweet. To embellish, use either Bittersweet Chocolate Glaze (see page 109) or Milk Chocolate Ganache (see page 109).

¾ cup unbleached all-purpose flour

2 teaspoons unsweetened Dutch-processed cocoa powder

2 teaspoons ground ginger

1 teaspoon ground cinnamon

⅛ teaspoon ground cloves

⅛ teaspoon ground nutmeg

¼ teaspoon salt

¼ cup (½ stick) unsalted butter, softened

1 cup firmly packed dark brown sugar

¼ cup dark (not blackstrap) molasses

2 large eggs

½ teaspoon baking soda

1 teaspoon very hot tap water

1 cup semisweet or milk chocolate chips

1. Preheat the oven to 350°F. Spray an 8-inch square baking pan with nonstick cooking spray.

2. Combine the flour, cocoa powder, ginger, cinnamon, cloves, nutmeg, and salt in a small mixing bowl.

3. Cream together the butter and brown sugar in a large bowl using an electric mixer. Stir in the molasses. Beat in the eggs, scraping down the sides of the bowl once or twice as necessary, until smooth.

4. Dissolve the baking soda in the hot tap water. Stir half of the flour mixture into the egg mixture. Stir in the baking soda mixture. Stir in the remaining flour mixture. Stir in the chocolate chips.

5. Pour the batter into the prepared baking dish. Bake the gingerbread until it is just set in the center, 22 to 25 minutes. Let cool completely on a wire rack before cutting into 16 squares. Chocolate Chip Gingerbread Bars will keep at room temperature in an airtight container for up to 3 days.

gingery pumpkin bars with milk chocolate glaze

Makes 35 bars One can of pumpkin produces a batch of big, moist, gingery bars. A simple milk chocolate glaze is absolutely the best icing on the cake.

For the bars
- 2 cups unbleached all-purpose flour
- 1½ cups firmly packed light brown sugar
- ½ cup finely chopped crystallized ginger
- One 15-ounce can solid pack pumpkin
- 4 large eggs
- ¾ cup vegetable oil
- 1 cup finely chopped pecans

For the glaze
- 12 ounces milk chocolate, finely chopped
- 3 tablespoons vegetable oil
- 1½ tablespoons light corn syrup

1. Preheat the oven to 350°F. Spray a 15½ x 10½ x 1-inch rimmed baking sheet with nonstick cooking spray.

2. Make the bars: Combine the flour, brown sugar, and crystallized ginger in a large bowl. Stir to blend. Stir in the pumpkin, eggs, and oil and stir until well combined. Stir in the pecans.

3. Spread the batter in an even layer in the prepared pan, smoothing with a spatula. Bake until a cake tester or wooden skewer inserted in the middle comes out clean, about 25 minutes. Cool in the pan on a wire rack.

4. Make the glaze: Combine the chocolate, vegetable oil, and corn syrup in a micro-wavable bowl and heat on high until the chocolate is halfway melted. Whisk to melt the remaining chocolate. Spread the glaze over the cooled bars with an offset spatula.

5. Allow to set, about 2 hours, before cutting into 2-inch squares. Gingery Pumpkin Bars with Milk Chocolate Glaze will keep at room temperature in an airtight container for up to 3 days.

A Good Excuse to Make
Gingery Pumpkin Bars with Milk Chocolate Glaze

These are a nice alternative to cupcakes at a kids' Halloween party. Decorate each one with a plastic pumpkin, ghost, or bat toothpick.

oatmeal-date bars

Makes 16 bars These old-fashioned bars have all the goodness of classic oatmeal cookies, with a moist layer of date filling as a bonus.

1½ cups pitted dates, chopped
1½ cups water
½ cup unbleached all-purpose flour
½ teaspoon baking powder
½ teaspoon ground cinnamon
¼ teaspoon salt
⅔ cup firmly packed light brown sugar
½ cup (1 stick) unsalted butter, softened
1 large egg
1 teaspoon pure vanilla extract
1½ cups old-fashioned rolled oats (not instant)
¾ cup coarsely chopped walnuts

1. Preheat the oven to 375°F. Line an 8-inch square baking pan with heavy-duty aluminum foil, making sure the foil is tucked into all the corners and there is at least 1 inch overhanging the top of the pan on all sides.

2. Combine the dates and water in a small saucepan and bring to a boil. Turn the heat to low and simmer until the dates are very soft and almost all of the water has evaporated, about 15 minutes. Set aside to cool completely.

3. Combine the flour, baking powder, cinnamon, and salt in a small bowl.

4. Combine the brown sugar and butter together in a medium-size mixing bowl and cream together with an electric mixer until smooth. Stir in the egg. Stir in the vanilla extract. Stir in the flour mixture. Stir in the oats and nuts.

5. Sprinkle half of the mixture across the bottom of the prepared baking pan and press it with your fingertips into an even layer. Place the other half of the mixture in the freezer for 5 minutes.

6. Spread the dates in an even layer across the bottom of the pan. Scatter the remaining oatmeal mixture over the dates, squeezing it into grape-size crumbs as you do so. Bake until the top is golden, 25 to 30 minutes. Let the pan cool completely on a wire rack.

7. Grasping the overhanging foil on either side of the pan, lift out the bars and place them on a cutting board. Cut into 16 squares. Oatmeal-Date Bars will keep at room temperature in an airtight container for 2 days.

Kids Can Help

Squeezing crumb topping into grape- or pea-size pieces is a messy job, but someone's got to do it. So enlist your children to do the dirty work when making Oatmeal-Date Bars, Nutella Ribbon Bars (page 118), and Peanut Butter and Jelly Crumb Squares (page 119). These bars may become their favorites for this reason alone.

nutella ribbon bars

Makes 16 bars These chewy oatmeal bars have a ribbon of Nutella, the decadent chocolate-hazelnut spread, running through their centers. Walnuts may be substituted for the hazelnuts if it's more convenient or preferred.

¾ **cup skinned, chopped hazelnuts**
½ **cup unbleached all-purpose flour**
½ **teaspoon baking powder**
⅔ **cup firmly packed light brown sugar**
¼ **teaspoon salt**
½ **cup (1 stick) unsalted butter, melted**
1 **teaspoon pure vanilla extract**
1½ **cups old-fashioned rolled oats (not instant)**
¾ **cup Nutella**

1. Preheat the oven to 375°F. Line an 8-inch square baking pan with heavy-duty aluminum foil, making sure the foil is tucked into all the corners and there is at least 1 inch overhanging the top of the pan on all sides.

2. Grind the hazelnuts coarsely in a food processor. Add the flour, baking powder, sugar, and salt and pulse once or twice to combine. Add the melted butter and vanilla extract and pulse once or twice until all the ingredients are moistened. Add the oats and pulse once or twice to combine.

3. Sprinkle half the mixture across the bottom of the prepared baking pan and press it with your fingertips into an even layer. Place the other half of the mixture in the freezer for 5 minutes.

4. Spread the Nutella in an even layer on top of the crust. Scatter the remaining crumb mixture over the Nutella, squeezing it into pea-size crumbs as you do so. Bake until the top is golden, 25 to 30 minutes. Let the pan cool completely on a wire rack.

5. Grasping the overhanging foil on either side of the pan, lift out the bars and place them on a cutting board. Cut into 16 squares. Nutella Ribbon Bars will keep at room temperature in an airtight container for up to 2 days.

Top 10 Uses for Leftover Nutella

Aside from eating it straight from the jar, here are my favorite things to do with Nutella.

1. Spread Nutella on graham crackers as an after-school snack.
2. Spoon a dollop onto Belgian waffles or French toast for a special breakfast.
3. Make a sandwich on soft white bread with Nutella and sliced bananas.
4. Stir ⅓ cup of Nutella into hot milk for Nutella hot chocolate.
5. Layer it with pound cake, whipped cream, and raspberries for a parfait.
6. Use it as a dip for strawberries.
7. Substitute Nutella for chocolate bars when making s'mores.
8. Fold it together with whipped cream for a quick chocolate-hazelnut mousse.
9. Spread that mousse into a graham-cracker pie crust and freeze for a Nutella icebox pie.
10. Make a batch of these Nutella Ribbon Bars.

peanut butter and jelly crumb squares

Makes 16 squares

These moist, flavorful bars borrow the flavors of a favorite lunch box sandwich, but transform them into an absolutely sensational bar cookie. Grape jelly is classic, but substitute any favorite flavor jelly or jam (apricot and raspberry are both great) if you like.

½ cup unbleached all-purpose flour
½ teaspoon baking powder
¼ teaspoon salt
¾ cup smooth or chunky peanut butter
¾ cup firmly packed light brown sugar
½ cup (1 stick) unsalted butter, melted
1 large egg
1 teaspoon pure vanilla extract
1½ cups old-fashioned rolled oats (not instant)
¾ cup grape jelly

1. Preheat the oven to 375°F. Line an 8-inch square baking pan with heavy-duty aluminum foil, making sure the foil is tucked into all the corners and there is at least 1 inch overhanging the top of the pan on all sides.

2. Combine the flour, baking powder, and salt in a small bowl.

3. Combine the peanut butter, brown sugar, and butter together in a medium-size mixing bowl and cream together with an electric mixer until smooth. Stir in the egg. Stir in the vanilla extract. Stir in the flour mixture. Stir in the oats.

4. Sprinkle half the mixture across the bottom of the prepared baking pan and press it with your fingertips into an even layer. Place the other half of the mixture in the freezer for 5 minutes.

5. Spread the jelly in an even layer on top of the crust. Scatter the remaining peanut butter mixture over the jelly, squeezing it into grape-size crumbs as you do so. Bake until the top is golden, 25 to 30 minutes. Let the pan cool completely on a wire rack.

6. Grasping the overhanging foil on either side of the pan, lift out the squares and place them on a cutting board. Cut into 16 squares. Peanut Butter and Jelly Crumb Squares will keep at room temperature in an airtight container for up to 2 days.

jam and shortbread squares

Makes 16 squares Here is one of my favorite recipes in this book. These bars are just the essence of home baking for kids: a few simple ingredients that you probably have on hand, minimally handled, make the best bar cookies ever.

1 cup unbleached all-purpose flour
½ teaspoon baking powder
⅛ teaspoon salt
½ cup (1 stick) unsalted butter, softened
½ cup sugar
1 large egg
½ teaspoon pure vanilla extract
6 tablespoons strawberry, raspberry, or cherry preserves

1. Preheat the oven to 350°F. Place oven racks in the bottom third and top third of the oven. Line an 8-inch square baking pan with heavy-duty aluminum foil, making sure the foil is tucked into all the corners and that there is at least 1 inch overhanging the top of the pan.

2. Combine the flour, baking powder, and salt in a small bowl.

3. Combine the butter and sugar in a medium-size mixing bowl and cream together with an electric mixer until smooth. Stir in the egg. Stir in the vanilla extract. Stir in the flour mixture.

4. Use a spatula to smooth half the mixture in an even layer across the bottom of the pan. Place the pan in the freezer, along with the bowl containing the remaining half of the shortbread dough, for 15 minutes to firm up.

5. Remove the pan from the freezer and spread the preserves in an even layer on top of the dough. Pinch off pieces of the remaining dough and scatter them evenly over the jam.

6. Place the pan on the bottom oven rack and bake for 20 minutes. Transfer the pan to the top rack and bake until the top is light golden, another 5 to 10 minutes. Let the pan cool completely on a wire rack.

7. Grasping the overhanging foil on either side of the pan, lift out the squares and place them on a cutting board. Cut into 16 squares. Jam and Shortbread Squares will keep at room temperature in an airtight container for 2 to 3 days.

blueberry and maple granola bars

Makes 16 bars Blueberries and oats lightly sweetened with maple syrup are my favorite break-fast combination, and they translate beautifully into wholesome granola bars. Dried cranberries, cherries, or raisins may be substituted for the dried blueberries if you like. Look for unsalted sunflower seeds in the natural foods store or the health food section of your supermarket.

¾ cup old-fashioned rolled oats (not instant)
½ cup chopped walnuts
¼ cup unsalted sunflower seeds
½ cup unbleached all-purpose flour
½ teaspoon baking powder
¼ teaspoon salt
½ teaspoon ground cinnamon
Pinch of nutmeg
½ cup canola oil
¼ cup firmly packed light brown sugar
¼ cup pure maple syrup
1 large egg
1 teaspoon pure vanilla extract
½ cup dried blueberries

1. Preheat the oven to 350°F. Line an 8-inch square baking pan with heavy-duty aluminum foil, making sure the foil is tucked into all the corners and there is at least 1 inch overhanging the top of the pan on all sides.

2. Spread the oats, walnuts, and sunflower seeds on a baking sheet and bake until they are lightly toasted, stirring once or twice with a spoon, about 10 minutes. Remove from the oven and let the mixture cool completely.

3. Combine the flour, baking powder, salt, cinnamon, and nutmeg in a small mixing bowl.

4. Combine the canola oil, brown sugar, and maple syrup in a large mixing bowl and mix until smooth. Stir in the egg and vanilla extract. Stir in the flour mixture until it is just combined. Stir in the oat mixture until well combined. Stir in the dried blueberries.

5. Pour the batter into the prepared baking pan. Bake the bars until they are set, 25 to 30 minutes. Let cool completely on a wire rack.

6. Grasping the overhanging foil on either side of the pan, lift out the bars and place them on a cutting board. Cut into 16 squares. Blueberry and Maple Granola Bars will keep at room temperature in an airtight container for up to 5 days.

classic lemon squares and three variations

Makes 16 squares The basic recipe for this sweet-tart classic is from *Mom's Big Book of Baking* (The Harvard Common Press, 2001). The variations are new and irresistible. Make these a day in advance and chill them well for the neatest slicing. But wait until the last minute to dust the squares with powdered sugar, or it will disappear into the lemon custard over time.

For the crust
1 cup unbleached all-purpose flour
⅓ cup confectioners' sugar
2 tablespoons cornstarch
¼ teaspoon salt
7 tablespoons unsalted butter, chilled and cut into 12 pieces

For the lemon filling
1 cup granulated sugar
3 large eggs
3 tablespoons unbleached all-purpose flour
Pinch of salt
1 teaspoon lemon zest
½ cup strained fresh lemon juice

For the topping Confectioners' sugar

1. Preheat the oven to 350°F. Line an 8-inch square baking pan with heavy-duty aluminum foil, making sure the foil is tucked into all the corners and there is at least 1 inch overhanging the top of the pan on all sides.

2. Make the crust: Combine the flour, confectioners' sugar, cornstarch, and salt in a medium-size mixing bowl. With an electric mixer, mix on low speed to combine. Add the chilled butter and mix on low speed until the ingredients just begin to come together in clumps. Sprinkle this mixture evenly across the bottom of the prepared baking pan and press with your fingertips into an even layer. Place the pan in the freezer for 15 minutes, then bake the crust until it is light golden, about 20 minutes.

3. Make the filling: While the crust is baking, whisk together the granulated sugar, eggs, flour, and salt in a medium-size bowl until smooth. Whisk in the lemon zest and juice. When the crust comes out of the oven, reduce the oven temperature to 300°F. Pour the filling on top of the warm crust. Return the pan to the oven and bake until the filling is just set in the center, about 20 minutes. Transfer the pan to a wire rack and let it cool completely. Cover with plastic wrap and refrigerate until well chilled, at least 6 hours and up to 1 day.

4. Grasping the overhanging foil on either side of the pan, lift out the squares and place them on a cutting board. Use a sharp chef's knife to cut 16 squares. Classic Lemon Squares will keep, refrigerated, in an airtight container for up to 2 days. Dust with confectioners' sugar just before serving.

Lemon Squares with Almond Shortbread Crust: Decrease the amount of flour in the crust by 3 tablespoons. Add ¼ cup finely ground blanched almonds and ½ teaspoon almond extract, along with the butter, to the flour mixture for the crust.

Orange Squares: Instead of ½ cup lemon juice, use 1 tablespoon lemon juice and ½ cup minus 1 tablespoon freshly squeezed orange juice. Substitute 1½ tablespoons orange zest for the lemon zest.

Strawberry-Lemon Squares: Whirl ½ cup strawberry preserves in a mini food processor until smooth. Reduce the amount of lemon juice in the recipe to ⅓ cup and eliminate the lemon zest. Whisk the preserves into the filling along with the lemon juice.

pecan pie squares

Makes 16 squares

Here is a nice alternative to pie at Thanksgiving or Christmas, with the same flavors and textures but cut into more manageable portions for small appetites.

For the crust
- **1 cup unbleached all-purpose flour**
- **⅓ cup confectioners' sugar**
- **2 tablespoons cornstarch**
- **1 teaspoon salt**
- **7 tablespoons unsalted butter, chilled and cut into 12 pieces**

For the topping
- **2 large eggs**
- **2 tablespoons unsalted butter, melted and cooled**
- **½ cup granulated sugar**
- **6 tablespoons light corn syrup**
- **1 teaspoon pure vanilla extract**
- **2 cups pecan halves**

1. Preheat the oven to 350°F. Line an 8-inch square baking pan with heavy-duty aluminum foil, making sure the foil is tucked into all the corners and there is at least 1 inch overhanging the top of the pan on all sides.

2. Make the crust: Combine the flour, confectioners' sugar, cornstarch, and salt in a medium-size mixing bowl and, with an electric mixer, mix on low speed to

combine. Add the butter and mix on low speed until the ingredients just begin to come together in clumps. Sprinkle this mixture across the bottom of the prepared pan and press with your fingertips into an even layer. Place in the freezer for 15 minutes, then bake the crust until the edges are just golden, 18 to 20 minutes.

3. Make the topping: When the crust comes out of the oven, reduce the oven temperature to 325°F. Whisk together the eggs, butter, sugar, corn syrup, and vanilla extract. Stir in the pecans.

4. Pour the filling over the hot crust and return to the oven. Bake until the filling is just set, 25 to 30 minutes. Transfer the pan to a wire rack and let cool completely.

5. Grasping the overhanging foil on either side of the pan, lift out the squares and place them on a cutting board. Use a sharp chef's knife to cut 16 squares. Pecan Pie Squares will keep at room temperature in an airtight container for up to 2 days.

almond and honey squares

Makes 16 squares A surplus of honey made by a local beekeeper prompted me to create these sweet, chewy treats. Any nuts may be used, but I like fragrant almonds best with honey. I make these in a large pan because they keep well and are great gift cookies.

For the crust
- **2 cups unbleached all-purpose flour**
- **⅔ cup confectioners' sugar**
- **¼ cup cornstarch**
- **1 teaspoon salt**
- **¾ cup (1½ sticks) unsalted butter, chilled and cut into 12 pieces**

For the topping
- **⅔ cup honey**
- **½ cup firmly packed light brown sugar**
- **¼ teaspoon salt**
- **6 tablespoons cold butter, cut into pieces**
- **2 tablespoons heavy cream**
- **3 cups whole almonds**

1. Preheat the oven to 350°F. Line a 13 x 9-inch baking pan with heavy-duty aluminum foil, making sure the foil is tucked into all the corners and there is at least 1 inch overhanging the top of the pan on all sides.

2. Make the crust: Combine the flour, confectioners' sugar, cornstarch, and salt in a medium-size mixing bowl and, with an electric mixer, mix on low speed to combine. Add the butter and mix on low speed until the ingredients just begin to come together in clumps. Sprinkle this mixture across the bottom of the prepared pan and press with your fingertips into an even layer. Place the dish in the freezer for 15 minutes, and then bake the crust until the edges are just golden, 18 to 20 minutes.

3. Make the topping: When the crust comes out of the oven, reduce the oven temperature to 325°F. Combine the honey, brown sugar, and salt in a medium-size saucepan and bring to a simmer over medium-high heat, stirring once or twice to dissolve the sugar. Let simmer for 2 minutes without stirring. Add the butter and cream and simmer, stirring constantly, for 1 minute. Remove from the heat and stir in the almonds.

4. Pour the hot filling on top of the warm crust. Use the back of a spoon to distribute the nuts evenly across the pan. Return the pan to the oven and bake until the filling is bubbling and slightly browned, 18 to 20 minutes. Transfer the pan to a wire rack and let cool completely.

5. Grasping the overhanging foil on either side of the pan, lift out the squares and place them on a cutting board. Use a sharp chef's knife to cut 16 squares. Almond and Honey Squares will keep at room temperature in an airtight container for 2 to 3 days.

turtle bars

These bars boast the unbeatable combination of chocolate, caramel, and nuts on top of a rich pastry crust. I make multiple batches of these to give to teachers at school holiday parties.

For the crust
1 cup unbleached all-purpose flour
1/3 cup confectioners' sugar
2 tablespoons cornstarch
1 teaspoon salt
7 tablespoons unsalted butter, chilled and cut into 12 pieces
1 cup pecan halves

For the topping
3 tablespoons unsalted butter
6 tablespoons firmly packed light brown sugar
1/4 teaspoon salt
3/4 cup milk chocolate chips

1. Preheat the oven to 350°F. Line an 8-inch square baking pan with heavy-duty aluminum foil, making sure the foil is tucked into all the corners and there is at least 1 inch overhanging the top of the pan on all sides.

2. Make the crust: Combine the flour, confectioners' sugar, cornstarch, and salt in a medium mixing-size bowl and, with an electric mixer, mix on low speed to combine. Add the butter and mix on low speed until the ingredients just begin to come together in clumps. Sprinkle this mixture across the bottom of the prepared pan and press with your fingertips into an even layer. Place in the freezer for 15 minutes.

3. Bake for 10 minutes, then scatter the pecan halves over the crust and bake until the nuts are toasted and the edges of the crust are golden, 10 to 12 minutes more.

4. While the crust is baking, make the topping: Combine the butter, brown sugar, and salt in a small saucepan and heat on low, stirring, until the butter is melted and the sugar has dissolved. Scrape the mixture onto the hot crust and return the pan to the oven. Bake until the caramel is bubbling, about 12 minutes. Transfer the pan to a wire rack and let cool completely.

5. Melt the chocolate chips in a double boiler or in a small bowl in the microwave. Drizzle the chocolate over the cooled bars and let stand until the chocolate has hardened, about 1 hour.

6. Grasping the overhanging foil from either side of the pan, lift out the bars and place them on a cutting board. Use a sharp chef's knife to cut 16 squares. Turtle Bars will keep at room temperature in an airtight container for up to 2 days.

chocolate-caramel candy bars

Makes 16 bars These 10-minute bars have a lot of kid appeal, and grownups like them, too. Vary the ingredients according to your taste: Use chocolate graham crackers instead of plain ones, substitute white or dark chocolate or peanut butter chips for the milk chocolate chips, add mini marshmallows or toasted coconut on top of the chocolate, and try salted peanuts instead of the pecans, walnuts, or almonds.

6 whole graham crackers
6 tablespoons unsalted butter
¼ cup firmly packed light brown sugar
½ teaspoon salt
1 cup milk chocolate chips
½ cup chopped pecans, walnuts, or almonds

1. Preheat the oven to 375°F. Line an 8-inch square baking pan with heavy-duty aluminum foil, making sure the foil is tucked into all the corners and there is at least 1 inch overhanging the top of the pan on all sides.

2. Line the bottom of the pan with the graham crackers, breaking them if necessary to fit tightly.

3. Combine the butter, brown sugar, and salt in a small saucepan and heat on low, stirring, until the butter is melted and the sugar has dissolved. Scrape the mixture onto the graham crackers and smooth with a small offset spatula so that it covers all of the crackers. Bake until the caramel is bubbling, about 10 minutes.

4. Remove from the oven, sprinkle with the chocolate chips, and return to the oven for a minute or two to soften the chocolate. Remove from the oven and smooth the chocolate into an even layer with the spatula. Sprinkle the nuts over the chocolate. Let cool on a wire rack for 30 minutes, then transfer to the freezer to allow the chocolate to harden, another 30 minutes.

5. Grasping the overhanging foil on either side of the pan, lift out the bars and place them on a cutting board. Use a sharp chef's knife to cut 16 squares. Chocolate-Caramel Candy Bars will keep in the refrigerator in an airtight container for up to 1 week.

Kids Can Help

Let your kids fit the graham crackers into the bottom of the pan, as if they're putting together a puzzle.

seven-layer bars

Makes 16 bars

When I first started to make sweets as a kid, I found most of my recipes on the backs of boxes and cans. This one from Eagle sweetened condensed milk was my absolute favorite—I liked it even better than Marshmallow Fluff fudge or Rice Krispies treats. I've added some chopped apricots to balance the sweetness of the other ingredients, but your kids may prefer the bars without fruit. These bars are very sticky, even when cooled. To cut them cleanly, place them in the freezer for 10 minutes to firm them up, and use a sharp chef's knife.

¼ cup (½ stick) unsalted butter, melted
¾ cup graham cracker crumbs
1 cup whole almonds, coarsely chopped
½ cup dried apricots, coarsely chopped (optional)
½ cup semisweet chocolate chips
1½ cups sweetened flaked coconut
One 7-ounce can sweetened condensed milk

A Good Excuse to Make
Chocolate-Caramel Candy Bars or Seven-Layer Bars

Whenever I have a lonely half-dozen graham crackers left in the box, I free up some much-needed space in the cabinet by breaking them into pieces to make Chocolate-Caramel Candy Bars (opposite) or grinding them up to make a batch of Seven-Layer Bars.

1. Preheat the oven to 325°F.

2. Combine the melted butter and graham cracker crumbs in a medium-size bowl and stir until all of the crumbs are moistened. Pour the mixture into the bottom of an 8-inch square baking pan and spread and press firmly with your fingertips to create an even layer.

3. Sprinkle the almonds and the apricots, if you are using them, evenly over the crumbs. Sprinkle the chocolate chips over the almonds and apricots. Sprinkle the coconut over the chocolate chips. Drizzle the sweetened condensed milk evenly over the coconut.

4. Bake until the coconut begins to turn light golden brown, 25 to 27 minutes. Let the pan cool completely on a wire rack.

5. Place in the freezer for 10 minutes before cutting into 16 squares. Seven-Layer Bars will keep at room temperature in an airtight container for up to 1 week.

NO SUCH THING
as too much sugar:
cookie-candy combinations

LEFT TO RIGHT: Spicy Smiley Faces, Snickers Bar Tassies, M&M Biscotti, Sugar Cookie Baseballs

Cookies and candy are often served side by side at birthday parties and other sugar-fests. For true sugar overload, why not actually bake candy right into your cookies? Nothing gets kids more excited than this type of excess. They will thank you—when they take a break from bouncing off the walls, that is.

There is nothing new about combining these two kids' favorites into one over-the-top treat. This chapter eases into the subject with a few of the classics: peanut butter cookies with chocolate kiss centers, iced butter cookies decorated with M&M's, oatmeal cookies studded with Reese's Pieces. It's not such a stretch, then, when we move on to cookie doughs that have been mixed with crushed malted milk balls, butterscotch hard candies, chopped soft caramels, and marshmallows.

Cookie-candy combinations can take other forms. One of my favorite recipes in this chapter is for M&M Biscotti (page 137). A grown-up cookie becomes very kid-friendly when mini candy-coated chocolate pieces are stirred into the dough in place of almonds. Snickers Bar Tassies (page 139) are a clever and time-saving way to make tiny chocolate-caramel-nut tarts. Brownies and blondies can be combined with candy, too. I particularly love the Milky Way Shortbread Bars (page 140). The pastry is patted into the pan and then the candy is melted on top. It's so easy and so delicious.

Even if your kids aren't familiar with the expression "eye candy," they will appreciate the pretty ways that candy is used as a decoration in a bunch of these recipes. Jelly beans, instead of jelly, fill thumbprints (page 145), beautifying as well as sweetening the cookies. Gumdrops are positioned as smiley faces on top of spicy gingerbread rounds (page 146). Red licorice whips make rolled sugar cookies look like baseballs (page 148). Black licorice whips are laced through the holes of anise shortbread "buttons" (page 149).

Approach this chapter as you would a trip to the candy store. Browse the recipes and look for your kids' favorite sugary treats. Then see how their eyes light up when you present them with cookies tailor-made to satisfy their sweet tooth.

peanut butter kisses

I prefer to hide chocolate kiss candies inside peanut butter cookie dough, rather than just plopping a kiss into a shallow thumbprint. This way, the chocolate really becomes part of the cookie instead of just serving as a decoration. These are great eaten right out of the oven, when the chocolate centers are still warm and soft. Or let them cool and wrap them in aluminum foil, just like the chocolate candies, for a fun presentation when you're bringing them to school or to a bake sale.

2 cups unbleached all-purpose flour
½ teaspoon baking soda
½ teaspoon baking powder
½ teaspoon salt
1 cup (2 sticks) unsalted butter, melted and cooled slightly
1 cup firmly packed light brown sugar
½ cup granulated sugar
2 large eggs
1 teaspoon pure vanilla extract
1 cup smooth peanut butter
About 40 chocolate kiss candies

1. Preheat the oven to 350°F. Line baking sheets with parchment paper.

2. Combine the flour, baking soda, baking powder, and salt in a medium-size bowl.

3. Cream the cooled melted butter and sugars together in a large mixing bowl with an electric mixer on medium speed until smooth. Add the eggs, vanilla extract, and peanut butter and beat until smooth. Stir in the flour mixture until just combined. Place the bowl in the refrigerator for 10 minutes (or up to 6 hours) to let the dough firm up.

4. Scoop a heaping tablespoonful of dough and roll it between your palms to form a ball. Place the balls on the baking sheets, leaving about 3 inches between each cookie. Make a deep impression in the center of each cookie with the chocolate candy. Press the cookie dough up and around the chocolate kiss so that just a little bit of the chocolate peeks out of the top of the ball. (Balls of dough may be placed next to each other on parchment paper–lined baking sheets, frozen, transferred to zipper-lock plastic freezer bags, and stored in the freezer for up to 1 month. Frozen cookies may be placed in the oven directly from the freezer and baked as directed.)

5. Bake the cookies until they are lightly colored, about 12 minutes (a minute or two longer for frozen dough). Let them stand on the baking sheet for 5 minutes, and then carefully slide the entire parchment sheet with the cookies from the pan to a wire rack and let them cool completely. Peanut Butter Kisses will keep at room temperature in an airtight container for 2 to 3 days.

mom's from-scratch m&m cookies

Makes about
36 cookies

My older daughter had been raving about a classmate's grandma's M&M cookies for months, so I had to ask for the recipe when I was working on this chapter. As it turned out, Grandma used refrigerated cookie dough and frosting from a tube! Here's my attempt at a from-scratch version that's really not much more difficult. And my daughter and her friends enjoyed them just as much. I like to place the candies in a flower shape, with one color in the center and a contrastingly colored five or six surrounding it. But of course, you and yours will have your own ideas.

2½ cups unbleached all-purpose flour
1 teaspoon baking powder
½ teaspoon salt
1 cup (2 sticks) unsalted butter, softened
1 cup granulated sugar
2 large eggs
2½ teaspoons pure vanilla extract
1½ cups confectioners' sugar, sifted
2 tablespoons milk, plus more if necessary
2½ teaspoons light corn syrup
1 cup M&M's or other candy-coated chocolate

1. Preheat the oven to 375°F.

2. Combine the flour, baking powder, and salt in a medium-size mixing bowl.

3. Cream the butter and granulated sugar together in a large mixing bowl with an electric mixer on medium-high speed, 1 to 2 minutes. Add the eggs and 2 teaspoons of the vanilla extract and beat until smooth. Stir in the flour mixture until just combined. Refrigerate for 10 minutes (or up to 6 hours) to let the dough firm up.

4. Scoop a heaping tablespoonful of dough and roll it between your palms to form a ball. Place the balls on ungreased baking sheets, leaving about 3 inches between each cookie. Flatten each ball slightly with the palm of your hand. (Cookies may be placed next to each other on parchment paper–lined baking sheets, frozen, transferred to zipper-lock plastic freezer bags, and stored in the freezer for up to 1 month. Frozen cookies may be placed in the oven directly from the freezer and baked as directed.)

5. Bake the cookies until they are pale golden around the edges but still soft on top, about 10 minutes (a minute or two longer for frozen dough). Let them stand on the baking sheet for 5 minutes, and then remove them with a metal spatula to a wire rack to cool completely.

6. Place the confectioners' sugar in a medium-size bowl. Whisk in the milk, corn syrup, and the remaining ½ teaspoon vanilla extract until smooth. If necessary, dribble in some more milk, drop by drop, until the frosting is spreadable (it should have the consistency of heavy cream). Spread a thin layer of frosting over the top of each cookie. Press the M&M's into the frosting before it hardens. Mom's From-Scratch M&M Cookies will keep at room temperature in an airtight container for 2 to 3 days.

reese's pieces autumn oatmeal cookies

Makes about 40 cookies

In the fall, when the leaves are turning orange, yellow, and brown, my baker's mind naturally turns to thoughts of oatmeal cookies made with orange, yellow, and brown Reese's Pieces candies. The chewy oatmeal is a great foil for the crispy-sweet candies. Some chopped dry-roasted peanuts added to the dough augment the peanut butter flavor of the candy. Stir in the Reese's Pieces by hand so that their candy shells don't break.

1½ cups unbleached all-purpose flour
1 teaspoon baking powder
½ teaspoon baking soda
1 cup (2 sticks) unsalted butter, melted and cooled slightly
1 cup firmly packed light brown sugar
½ cup granulated sugar
2 large eggs
1 teaspoon pure vanilla extract
3 cups old-fashioned rolled oats (not instant)
½ cup finely chopped dry-roasted peanuts
1½ cups Reese's Pieces candies

1. Preheat the oven to 350°F.

2. Combine the flour, baking powder, and baking soda in a medium-size mixing bowl.

3. Cream the cooled melted butter and sugars together in a large mixing bowl with an electric mixer on medium speed until smooth. Add the eggs and vanilla extract and beat until smooth. Beat in the flour mixture until just combined. Stir in the oats and peanuts. Stir in the Reese's Pieces. Place the bowl in the refrigerator for 10 minutes (or up to 6 hours) to let the dough firm up.

4. Drop the batter by heaping tablespoonfuls onto ungreased baking sheets, leaving about 3 inches between each cookie. (Balls of dough may be placed next to each other on parchment paper–lined baking sheets, frozen, transferred to zipper-lock plastic freezer bags, and stored in the freezer for up to 1 month. Frozen cookies may be placed in the oven directly from the freezer and baked as directed.)

5. Bake the cookies until they are golden around the edges but still soft on top, 15 to 17 minutes (a minute or two longer for frozen dough). Let them stand on the baking sheet for 5 minutes, then remove them with a metal spatula to a wire rack to cool completely. Reese's Pieces Autumn Oatmeal Cookies will keep at room temperature in an airtight container for 2 to 3 days.

A Good Excuse to Make Reese's Pieces Autumn Oatmeal Cookies

Make these for a special home screening of the movie *E.T.* to satisfy the craving that will surely arise when the candy makes its famous cameo appearance.

malted milk cookies with malted milk ball frosting

Malted milk balls are an old-fashioned candy, but well worth introducing to your kids with these wildly chocolatey cookies. Use a food processor to crush the malted milk balls, or put them in a zipper-lock plastic bag and roll over them with a rolling pin to crush them.

2¼ cups unbleached all-purpose flour
¾ cup plus 2 tablespoons Ovaltine or other malted milk powder
1 teaspoon baking powder
½ teaspoon baking soda
½ teaspoon salt
1 cup (2 sticks) unsalted butter, melted and cooled slightly
¾ cup firmly packed light brown sugar
¾ cup firmly packed granulated sugar
2 large eggs
⅓ cup low-fat plain yogurt
1½ teaspoons pure vanilla extract
3 cups confectioners' sugar
¼ cup milk, plus more if necessary
1 cup (two 1.75-ounce packages) Whoppers or other malted milk balls, coarsely crushed

1. Preheat the oven to 375°F.

2. Combine the flour, ½ cup of the Ovaltine, the baking powder, baking soda, and salt in a medium-size mixing bowl.

3. Cream the cooled melted butter and sugars together in a large mixing bowl with a wooden spoon until smooth. Add the eggs, yogurt, and 1 teaspoon of the vanilla extract and beat until smooth. Stir in the flour mixture until just incorporated. Place the bowl in the refrigerator for at least 2 hours (or up to 6 hours) to let the dough firm up.

4. Drop the batter by heaping tablespoonfuls onto ungreased baking sheets, leaving about 3 inches between each cookie. (Balls of dough may be placed next to each other on parchment paper–lined baking sheets, frozen, transferred to zipper-lock plastic freezer bags, and stored in the freezer for up to 1 month. Frozen cookies may be placed in the oven directly from the freezer and baked as directed.)

5. Bake the cookies until golden around the edges but still soft on top, 10 to 12 minutes (a minute or two longer for frozen dough). Let the cookies stand on the baking sheet for 5 minutes, then remove them with a metal spatula to a wire rack to cool completely.

6. Combine the remaining 6 tablespoons Ovaltine, the confectioners' sugar, milk, and the remaining ½ teaspoon vanilla extract in a medium-size mixing bowl and whisk until smooth. If necessary, dribble in some more milk, drop by drop, until the frosting is spreadable (it should have the consistency of heavy cream). Spread a thin layer of frosting over the top of each cookie. Sprinkle a rounded teaspoonful of the crushed malted milk balls on top of each cookie and press lightly with a finger until they adhere. Let stand until the frosting is dry, about 1 hour. Malted Milk Cookies with Malted Milk Ball Frosting will keep at room temperature in an airtight container for 2 to 3 days.

butterscotch crunch cookies

Makes about
42 cookies

These are chewy and crunchy at the same time and full of rich butterscotch flavor. Don't skip the parchment paper, since these cookies get very sticky during baking.

3 ounces (about ⅔ cup) butterscotch
  hard candies
1 cup whole almonds
2¼ cups unbleached all-purpose flour
1 teaspoon baking soda
1 teaspoon salt
1 cup (2 sticks) unsalted butter, melted
  and cooled slightly
1 cup firmly packed light brown sugar
2 large eggs
2 teaspoons pure vanilla extract

1. Preheat the oven to 375°F. Line baking sheets with parchment paper.

2. Place the butterscotch candies and almonds in the work bowl of a food processor and process until finely ground. Combine the flour, baking soda, and salt in a medium-size mixing bowl.

3. Cream the cooled melted butter and sugar together in a large mixing bowl with a wooden spoon until smooth. Add the eggs and vanilla extract and beat until smooth. Stir in the flour mixture until just incorporated. Stir in the butterscotch-nut mixture. Place the bowl in the refrigerator for 10 minutes (or up to 6 hours) to let the dough firm up.

4. Drop the batter by heaping tablespoonfuls onto the lined baking sheets, leaving about 3 inches between each cookie. (Balls of dough may be placed next to each other on parchment paper–lined baking sheets, frozen, transferred to zipper-lock plastic freezer bags, and stored in the freezer for up to 1 month. Frozen cookies may be placed in the oven directly from the freezer and baked as directed.)

5. Bake the cookies until golden around the edges but still soft on top, 9 to 11 minutes (a minute or two longer for frozen dough). Let the cookies stand on the baking sheet for 5 minutes, then remove them with a metal spatula to a wire rack to cool completely. Butterscotch Crunch Cookies will keep at room temperature in an airtight container for 2 to 3 days.

Kids Can Help

Many of the recipes in this chapter call for candies that are individually wrapped—chocolate kisses, butterscotch hard candies, chocolate mints, and so forth. Put your child to work unwrapping the candy. It's a perfect job for small fingers. Just be sure to set out a few more candies than you'll actually need, since they have a tendency to disappear somewhere between the time when they are unwrapped and when they are mixed into your cookie dough.

rocky road cookies

Parchment paper is essential here—melting marshmallows and caramel make for a very sticky batter. Don't worry if some of the caramel oozes out of the cookies as they bake. This just adds to their gooey appeal.

4 ounces (4 squares) unsweetened chocolate, finely chopped
1½ cups semisweet chocolate chips
½ cup (1 stick) unsalted butter, cut into 8 pieces
½ cup unbleached all-purpose flour
½ teaspoon baking powder
½ teaspoon salt
4 large eggs
1½ cups sugar
2 teaspoons pure vanilla extract
1 cup miniature marshmallows
1 cup chopped pecans
15 soft caramel candies, each cut into 4 pieces

1. Preheat the oven to 350°F. Line baking sheets with parchment paper.

2. Put 1 inch of water in the bottom of a double boiler or medium-size saucepan and bring to a bare simmer. Combine the unsweetened chocolate, chocolate chips, and butter in the top of the double boiler or in a stainless steel bowl set on top of the simmering water, making sure that the water doesn't touch the bottom of the bowl. Heat, whisking occasionally, until the chocolate and butter are completely melted. Set aside to cool slightly.

3. Combine the flour, baking powder, and salt in a small bowl.

4. Combine the eggs and sugar in a large mixing bowl and, with an electric mixer, beat on high speed until they are thick and pale, about 5 minutes. Stir in the chocolate mixture and the vanilla extract on low speed until smooth. Stir in the flour mixture until just combined. Stir in the marshmallows, pecans, and caramel pieces. Place the bowl in the refrigerator for 30 minutes (or up to 6 hours) to let the dough firm up.

5. Drop the batter by heaping tablespoonfuls onto the lined baking sheets, leaving about 3 inches between each cookie. (Balls of dough may be placed next to each other on parchment paper–lined baking sheets, frozen, transferred to zipper-lock plastic freezer bags, and stored in the freezer for up to 1 month. Frozen cookies may be placed in the oven directly from the freezer and baked as directed.)

6. Bake the cookies until the tops are cracked and shiny, 10 to 12 minutes (a minute or two longer for frozen dough). Carefully slide the entire parchment sheet with the cookies from the pan to a wire rack and let the cookies cool completely. Rocky Road Cookies will keep at room temperature in an airtight container for 2 to 3 days.

m&m biscotti

Makes about
24 biscotti

I've always thought of biscotti as cookies for grownups, but this changed when I began to stir M&M's into the dough in place of traditional almonds. I don't bake these quite as long as I do traditional biscotti, so they're crisp but not rock-hard, the better for kids to sink their teeth into them. And to soften them up further, kids can always dip their biscotti into tall glasses of milk.

2 cups unbleached all-purpose flour
1 cup sugar
½ teaspoon baking powder
¼ teaspoon salt
½ teaspoon ground cinnamon
4 large eggs
1 teaspoon vanilla extract
One 12-ounce package M&M's Mini Baking Bits
¾ cup chopped walnuts (optional)

1. Preheat the oven to 350°F. Line a baking sheet with parchment paper.

2. Combine the flour, sugar, baking powder, salt, and cinnamon in a large mixing bowl. Add 3 of the eggs and the vanilla extract and mix together with an electric mixer on low speed until just combined. Mix in the M&M's and the walnuts, if you are using them.

3. Turn the dough out onto a lightly floured work surface and divide it in half. Shape each half into a flat log about 12 inches long and 2½ inches wide. Place the logs on the lined baking sheet several inches apart.

4. Beat the remaining egg and brush it over the dough. Bake the logs until they are firm to the touch, about 35 minutes. Remove them from the oven and allow them to cool completely.

5. Reduce the oven temperature to 325°F. Transfer the logs to a cutting board and cut them into 1-inch-thick slices. Lay the slices cut side down on the baking sheet and return them to the oven. Bake them until they are just crisping up, about 8 minutes. Transfer the sliced cookies to wire racks and let them cool completely. M&M Biscotti will keep at room temperature in an airtight container for 1 to 2 weeks.

 A Good Excuse to Make M&M Biscotti

Serve these Italian-style cookies at the end of a take-out pizza party for your kids and their friends. Make sure to throw in a salad and pour lots of milk with the cookies, for a fun but balanced meal.

chocolate biscotti with chocolate-covered raisins

A combination of chocolate-covered raisins and chocolate morsels makes these biscotti extra fudgy.

1⅔ cups unbleached all-purpose flour
⅓ cup unsweetened Dutch-processed cocoa powder
1 teaspoon baking soda
½ teaspoon salt
1 cup sugar
3 large eggs
2 large egg yolks
1 teaspoon pure vanilla extract
1 cup chocolate-covered raisins
½ cup semisweet chocolate chips

1. Preheat the oven to 350°F. Line a baking sheet with parchment paper.

2. Sift together the flour, cocoa powder, baking soda, and salt in a large mixing bowl. Stir in the sugar. Add 2 of the whole eggs, the egg yolks, and the vanilla extract and mix with in an electric mixer on low speed until just combined. Mix in the chocolate-covered raisins and chocolate chips on low speed.

3. Turn the dough out onto a lightly floured work surface and divide it in half. Shape each half into a flat log about 12 inches long and 2½ inches wide. Place the logs on the lined baking sheet several inches apart.

4. Beat the remaining whole egg and brush it over the dough. Bake the logs until they are firm to the touch, about 35 minutes. Remove them from the oven and allow them to cool completely.

5. Reduce the oven temperature to 325°F. Transfer the logs to a cutting board and cut them into 1-inch-thick slices. Lay the slices cut side down on the baking sheet and return the cookies to the oven. Bake them until they are crisp, about 10 minutes. Transfer the cookies to wire racks and let them cool completely. Chocolate Biscotti with Chocolate-Covered Raisins will keep at room temperature in an airtight container for 1 to 2 weeks.

snickers bar tassies

Makes 24 tassies Tassies, miniature tarts baked in mini muffin tins, are usually filled with a pecan pie–type mixture. Here I simplify the recipe by using a popular candy bar instead. The peanuts, caramel, and chocolate make a fun and simple filling, and the result is a cookie pretty enough to pack up and give as a gift to a favorite teacher for the holidays or at the end of the school year.

For the dough
1¼ cups unbleached all-purpose flour
½ cup sugar
¼ teaspoon baking powder
Pinch of salt
½ cup (1 stick) unsalted butter, chilled
    and cut into 8 pieces
1 large egg

For the filling
Three 2.07-ounce Snickers bars,
    coarsely chopped
2 tablespoons heavy cream
1 large egg yolk
1 tablespoon sugar

1. Make the dough: Combine the flour, sugar, baking powder, salt, and butter in the work bowl of a food processor and process until the mixture resembles coarse meal. Add the egg and process until the dough just comes together in a ball. Do not overprocess. Press the dough into a disk, wrap in plastic wrap, and refrigerate until well chilled, at least 2 hours and up to 1 day.

2. Preheat the oven to 350°F.

3. Make the filling: Put 1 inch of water in the bottom of a double boiler or medium-size saucepan and bring to a bare simmer. Combine the candy and heavy cream in the top of the double boiler or in a stainless-steel bowl set on top of the simmering water, making sure that the water doesn't touch the bottom of the bowl. Heat, stirring occasionally, until the chocolate is completely melted. Remove from the heat. Set aside to cool slightly.

4. Place the egg yolk and sugar in a medium-size mixing bowl and whisk until pale yellow and thickened. Stir the melted candy mixture into the egg mixture.

5. Remove the dough from the refrigerator and divide into 24 equal pieces. Roll each portion into a ball. Place each ball into a cup of a mini muffin tin, pressing the dough into the bottom and sides of the pan with your thumb in an even layer. Spoon the candy mixture into the muffin cups so that it almost but doesn't quite reach the top of the pastry. Do not overfill.

6. Bake until the filling is puffed and the pastry is light golden, about 25 minutes. Cool in the pans on a wire rack for 10 minutes, then carefully lift the tassies from the pans and cool completely on the wire rack. Snickers Bar Tassies will keep at room temperature in an airtight container for up to 1 week.

milky way shortbread bars

Makes 20 bars No one will ever guess that you made these incredibly rich bar cookies by spreading melted candy bars on top of a shortbread crust.

1 cup unbleached all-purpose flour
⅓ cup confectioners' sugar
2 tablespoons cornstarch
¼ teaspoon salt
7 tablespoons unsalted butter, chilled, cut into 14 pieces
20 Fun Size Milky Way bars

1. Preheat the oven to 350°F. Line an 8-inch square baking pan with heavy-duty aluminum foil, making sure that the foil is tucked into all the corners and that there is at least 1 inch overhanging the top of the pan on all sides.

2. Combine the flour, confectioners' sugar, cornstarch, and salt in a medium-size mixing bowl and, with an electric mixer, mix on low speed to combine. Add the butter and mix on low speed until the ingredients just begin to come together in clumps. Sprinkle this mixture across the bottom of the prepared pan and press with your fingertips into an even layer. Place the dish in the freezer for 15 minutes, then bake the crust until the edges are just golden, 18 to 20 minutes.

3. Place the Milky Way bars in 4 rows of 5 over the hot crust and return the pan to the oven. Bake for 10 more minutes, remove the pan from the oven, and then spread the melted candy into an even layer with an offset spatula. Bake an additional 5 minutes until the candy is melted and bubbly. Transfer the pan to a wire rack and let it cool completely.

4. Grasping the overhanging foil on either side of the pan, lift the bars from the pan and place on a cutting board. Use a sharp chef's knife to cut into 20 pieces. Milky Way Shortbread Bars will keep at room temperature in an airtight container for up to 3 days.

A Good Excuse to Make Milky Way Shortbread Bars

I never know how many trick-or-treaters I'm going to have knocking on my front door. Some years I have 50 kids demanding candy; some years I just see five. I always have a bowl of miniature Milky Way bars on hand. If I have a lot left over, I'll make a batch of these super-easy bar cookies.

s'mores in a pan

Makes 6 big bars

In the winter or when it's raining, you've got to love classic s'mores made in a pan rather than over an open fire.

1⅓ cups unbleached all-purpose flour
¾ cup graham cracker crumbs
1 teaspoon baking powder
¼ teaspoon salt
½ cup (1 stick) unsalted butter, melted and cooled slightly
¾ cup sugar
1 egg
1 teaspoon pure vanilla extract
Three 1.55-ounce Hershey's Milk Chocolate Bars or other milk chocolate bars, broken into 8 pieces each
1½ cups miniature marshmallows

1. Preheat the oven to 375°F. Line an 8-inch square baking pan with heavy-duty aluminum foil, making sure that the foil is tucked into all the corners and that there is at least 1 inch overhanging the top of the pan on all sides.

2. Combine the flour, graham cracker crumbs, baking powder, and salt in a medium-size mixing bowl. Cream the cooled melted butter and sugar together in a large mixing bowl with a wooden spoon until smooth. Add the egg and vanilla extract and beat until smooth. Stir in the flour mixture until just incorporated.

3. Transfer half the batter to the prepared pan and press it into an even layer with your fingertips. Place the chocolate bar pieces on top of the dough. Sprinkle the miniature marshmallows in a single layer over the chocolate. Drop teaspoonfuls of the remaining batter over the marshmallows and press it into a layer over the marshmallows. Try to cover most of the marshmallows, but don't worry if they poke through here and there.

4. Bake until set and just beginning to brown around the edges, about 30 minutes. Let the pan cool completely on a wire rack. Refrigerate the bars for 10 minutes.

5. Grasping the overhanging foil on either side of the pan, lift out the bars and place them on a cutting board. Cut into bars. S'mores in a Pan will keep at room temperature in an airtight container for 4 to 5 days.

peppermint surprise brownie bites

Peppermint patties placed between layers of chocolate batter become a meltingly delicious filling for these rich brownies. I like to cut them into small pieces so that you can see the creamy peppermint in every bite.

½ cup (1 stick) unsalted butter
2 ounces (2 squares) unsweetened chocolate
¾ cup unbleached all-purpose flour
½ teaspoon baking powder
¼ teaspoon salt
1 cup sugar
2 large eggs
1 teaspoon pure vanilla extract
16 small (1½-inch) York Peppermint Patties or other chocolate-covered peppermint candies

1. Preheat the oven to 350°F. Line an 8-inch square baking pan with heavy-duty aluminum foil, making sure that the foil is tucked into all the corners and that there is at least 1 inch overhanging the top of the pan on all sides.

2. Put 1 inch of water in the bottom of a double boiler or medium-size saucepan and bring to a bare simmer. Combine the butter and chocolate in the top of the double boiler or in a stainless-steel bowl set on top of the simmering water, making sure that the water doesn't touch the bottom of the bowl. Heat, whisking occasionally, until the chocolate and butter are completely melted. Set aside to cool slightly.

3. Combine the flour, baking powder, and salt in a small mixing bowl.

4. Whisk together the sugar and eggs in a large mixing bowl. With a wooden spoon, stir in the chocolate mixture and vanilla extract. Stir in the flour mixture until just incorporated.

5. Set aside 1 cup batter and pour the remaining batter into the prepared baking pan. Arrange the peppermint patties on top of the batter, with about ½ inch between each patty. Smooth the reserved 1 cup batter over the candy.

6. Bake the brownies until they are just set in the center, 30 to 35 minutes. Let them cool completely on a wire rack.

7. Grasping the overhanging foil on either side of the pan, lift out the brownies and place them on a cutting board. Cut into 32 pieces. Peppermint Surprise Brownie Bites will keep at room temperature in an airtight container for up to 3 days.

peanut butter surprise blondies

Makes 16 blondies

This idea worked so well when I tried it with peppermint patties and brownie batter that I thought I'd give it a try with peanut butter cups and blondies. I was not disappointed.

1½ cups unbleached all-purpose flour
1½ teaspoons baking powder
¼ teaspoon salt
¾ cup (1½ sticks) unsalted butter
1½ cups firmly packed light brown sugar
1 large egg
1 large egg yolk
1 teaspoon pure vanilla extract
16 miniature peanut butter cup candies

1. Preheat the oven to 350°F. Line an 8-inch square baking pan with heavy-duty aluminum foil, making sure that the foil is tucked into all the corners and that there is at least 1 inch overhanging the top of the pan on all sides.

2. Combine the flour, baking powder, and salt in a small mixing bowl.

3. Melt the butter in a medium-size saucepan over low heat. Remove it from the heat and, with a wooden spoon, stir in the brown sugar until it is dissolved. Quickly whisk in the egg, egg yolk, and vanilla extract. Stir in the flour mixture until just incorporated.

4. Set aside 1 cup batter and spread the remaining batter into the prepared baking dish. Arrange the peanut butter cups on top of the batter in the pan, with about ½ inch between each candy. Smooth the reserved 1 cup batter over the candy.

5. Bake the blondies until they are just set in the center, 30 to 35 minutes. Let them cool completely on a wire rack.

6. Grasping the overhanging foil on either side of the pan, lift out the blondies and place them on a cutting board. Cut into 16 pieces. Peanut Butter Surprise Blondies will keep at room temperature in an airtight container for up to 3 days.

andes mint shortbread sandwiches

Makes 16 squares Shortbread cookie dough encases a layer of thin mints in this simple recipe. You will be amazed at the brownie-like richness of the cookies, considering that there are no eggs in the recipe.

1½ cups unbleached all-purpose flour
½ cup unsweetened Dutch-processed cocoa powder
¼ teaspoon salt
1 cup (2 sticks) unsalted butter, softened
1 cup sugar
½ teaspoon pure vanilla extract
28 Andes Crème de Menthe Thins or other chocolate mint candies

1. Preheat the oven to 325°F. Sift together the flour, cocoa powder, and salt in a medium-size mixing bowl.

2. Cream the butter, sugar, and vanilla extract together in a large mixing bowl with an electric mixer on medium speed until fluffy, 2 to 3 minutes. Add the flour mixture and beat on low speed until the dough just comes together. Do not overmix.

3. Divide the dough into 2 equal portions. Press half of the dough into an ungreased 8-inch square baking pan. Place the chocolate mint candies in rows over the dough and gently press to embed them. Break the remaining half of the dough into small pieces and scatter over the candy layer. Press with your fingers to flatten the dough and cover the candy evenly.

4. Bake until the shortbread is firm at the edges but still soft in the center, 40 to 45 minutes. Let the shortbread cool completely on a wire rack and then cut into 16 squares with a sharp paring knife. Andes Mint Shortbread Sandwiches will keep at room temperature in an airtight container for 2 to 3 days.

jelly bean thumbprint cookies

Makes about 32 cookies

Instead of filling thumbprints with jelly, why not use jelly beans? If you can find them, try intensely flavored Jelly Bellies in these cookies.

1 cup (2 sticks) plus 2 tablespoons unsalted butter, softened
⅔ cup sugar
½ teaspoon salt
2 large eggs
2 teaspoons pure vanilla extract
3⅓ cups unbleached all-purpose flour
About 100 small jelly beans

1. Preheat the oven to 350°F.

2. Combine the butter, sugar, and salt in a large mixing bowl and beat with an electric mixer until fluffy, 2 to 3 minutes. Add the eggs and vanilla extract and beat until smooth. Stir in the flour until just combined.

3. Drop the batter by heaping tablespoon-fuls onto ungreased baking sheets, leaving about 3 inches between each cookie. (Balls of dough may be placed next to each other on parchment paper–lined baking sheets, frozen, transferred to zipper-lock plastic freezer bags, and stored in the freezer for up to 1 month. Frozen cookies may be placed in the oven directly from the freezer and baked as directed.)

4. Bake for 7 minutes (a minute or two longer for frozen dough), remove the baking sheets from the oven, and make an indentation in each cookie with the back of a small measuring spoon. Drop 3 small jelly beans into each indentation. Return the baking sheets to the oven and bake until the edges of the cookies are pale golden, 5 to 7 minutes longer. Let them stand on the baking sheet for 5 minutes, then remove them with a metal spatula to a wire rack to cool completely. Jelly Bean Thumbprint Cookies will keep at room temperature in an airtight container for 2 to 3 days.

Kids Can Help

After your kids have cataloged and sorted their Easter candy, see if you can persuade them to fill thumbprint cookies with their choice of jelly beans.

spicy smiley faces

Makes about
30 cookies

Spicy gumdrops are the perfect match for molasses-flavored gingerbread. My kids love cookies with faces, so that's the way I arrange the candy. Plain polka dots are cute, too.

½ cup (1 stick) unsalted butter, softened
½ cup sugar
1 teaspoon ground ginger
1 teaspoon ground cinnamon
¼ teaspoon ground cloves
¼ teaspoon salt
1 teaspoon baking soda
1 tablespoon hot tap water
½ cup dark (not blackstrap) molasses
2¾ cups unbleached all-purpose flour
About 210 small gumdrops

1. Combine the butter, sugar, ginger, cinnamon, cloves, and salt in a large mixing bowl with an electric mixer on medium-high speed until well combined, 1 to 2 minutes.

2. Whisk together the baking soda and hot water in a small bowl until smooth. Whisk in the molasses. Add the molasses mixture to the butter mixture and beat until well combined.

3. Stir in the flour and mix on low speed until the dough is smooth. Divide the dough into 2 balls, wrap in plastic wrap, and refrigerate until firm, about 1 hour.

4. Preheat the oven to 350°F. Line baking sheets with parchment paper.

5. With a lightly floured rolling pin, roll out 1 dough ball to a ¼-inch thickness. Use a 3-inch biscuit cutter to cut it into circles, and place the circles on the prepared baking sheets. Refrigerate the scraps. Arrange 7 gumdrops on each round: 2 for the eyes, 1 for the nose, and 4 for the smile. Repeat with the remaining dough ball and then with the chilled scraps.

6. Bake until the cookies are firm on top, 5 to 7 minutes. Lightly press on the gumdrops to embed them further into the hot cookies. Slide the entire parchment sheet with the cookies onto a wire rack and let the cookies cool completely. Spicy Smiley Faces will keep at room temperature in an airtight container for several days.

white chocolate–orange nonpareil cookies

Makes 24 cookies This recipe was inspired by one from Carole Walter's wonderful book *Great Cookies* (Clarkson Potter, 2003). I saw the photo of her chocolate shortbread cookies topped with semisweet chocolate nonpareil candies, and I thought that the white chocolate and multicolored nonpareil candies at my favorite local candy store would make a great kid-friendly variation. Here I use an orange-flavored dough and affix the candy disks to the cookies with a dab of orange marmalade. They are colorful and delicious.

1 cup (2 sticks) unsalted butter, softened
1 cup confectioners' sugar
1 teaspoon pure vanilla extract
1½ teaspoons grated orange zest
2¼ cups unbleached all-purpose flour
¼ teaspoon salt
1½ teaspoons orange marmalade
Twenty-four 1-inch white chocolate multicolored nonpareils

1. Cream the butter and sugar together in a large mixing bowl with an electric mixer on medium speed until fluffy, 3 to 4 minutes. Stir in the vanilla extract and orange zest. Stir in the flour and salt on low speed until the dough just comes together.

2. Turn the dough onto a sheet of waxed paper and shape it, rolling it inside the paper, into a log about 10 inches long and 2 inches in diameter. Wrap the dough in plastic wrap and refrigerate it for at least 2 hours and up to 1 day.

3. Preheat the oven to 350°F.

4. Slice the dough into ⅓-inch-thick rounds and place them on ungreased baking sheets, leaving 1 inch between each cookie. Dab the bottom of each nonpareil candy with a little bit of marmalade and press the candies, nonpareil-side-up, into the center of each cookie.

5. Bake until the cookies are dry on top, 11 to 13 minutes. Let them stand on the baking sheet for 5 minutes, then remove them with a metal spatula to a wire rack and let them cool completely. White Chocolate–Orange Nonpareil Cookies will keep at room temperature in an airtight container for 3 to 4 days.

sugar cookie baseballs

Makes about 24 cookies

I've taken a favorite quick cake decoration—white buttercream frosting and red licorice arranged to resemble the lacings on a baseball—and transferred it to cookies. Because the frosting is made with butter, these should be served within several hours of being made. Or you can make the frosting and cookies ahead of time, refrigerate the frosting for up to 2 days, let it come to room temperature, and rewhip before using.

½ recipe Rolled Sugar Cookie dough
  (page 236), chilled
7 tablespoons unsalted butter, softened
¼ teaspoon pure vanilla extract
Pinch of salt
2⅓ cups confectioners' sugar
2 teaspoons whole or low-fat milk
Forty-eight 2-inch lengths red licorice
  laces plus 288 ⅛-inch lengths

1. Preheat the oven to 375°F. Line baking sheets with parchment paper.

2. Knead the sugar cookie dough 4 or 5 times on a lightly floured work surface to soften it. With a lightly floured rolling pin, roll out the dough to a ¼-inch thickness. Use a 3-inch biscuit cutter to cut it into circles, and place the circles on the prepared baking sheets. Re-roll the scraps until you have used all of the dough.

3. Bake the cookies until they are firm and golden around the edges, about 10 minutes. Slide the entire parchment sheet with the cookies onto a wire rack and let the cookies cool completely.

4. Combine the butter, vanilla extract, and salt in a large mixing bowl. With an electric mixer on medium-high speed, beat until the mixture is fluffy, scraping down the sides of the bowl several times as necessary.

5. Add the confectioners' sugar ⅓ cup at a time, mixing on low speed after each addition so that the sugar doesn't fly out of the bowl. When all the sugar has been mixed into the butter, add the milk. Beat on high speed, scraping down the sides of the bowl as necessary, until the frosting is light and fluffy, about 5 minutes.

6. Use an offset spatula to spread a thin layer of frosting on each cookie. Arrange two 2-inch lengths of red licorice in opposing arcs equidistant from the center of the cookie. Arrange six ⅛-inch pieces of licorice alongside each arc so that they look like three stitches perpendicular to each arc. Sugar Cookie Baseballs are best eaten on the day they're made.

A Good Excuse to Make Sugar Cookie Baseballs

Serve these cute cookies with pink lemonade to your T-ball players as an end-of-the-season-party treat.

Kids Can Help

Put kids to work cutting the red licorice laces to the proper lengths and decorating the frosted cookies with the licorice.

anise-flavored shortbread buttons with licorice lacing

Makes 24 cookies

I am a fiend for black licorice, so I developed this recipe for myself. The buttery shortbread cookie is far from bland, since it is spiked with ground anise. The licorice laces look like thread and taste great as an accompaniment. If you and your family prefer, substitute a teaspoon of vanilla for the anise seeds and lace the cookies with red licorice.

1 cup (2 sticks) unsalted butter, chilled, cut into 16 pieces
½ cup sugar
2 cups unbleached all-purpose flour
1 teaspoon anise seeds, finely ground with a mortar and pestle or in a spice grinder
Twenty-four 6-inch lengths black licorice laces

1. Cream the butter and sugar together in a large mixing bowl with an electric mixer on medium speed until fluffy, 3 to 4 minutes. Stir in the flour and ground anise on low speed until the dough just comes together.

2. Turn the dough onto a sheet of waxed paper and shape it, rolling it inside the paper, into a log about 8 inches long and 2½ inches in diameter. Wrap the dough in plastic wrap and refrigerate it for at least 2 hours and up to 24 hours. (Dough logs may be wrapped tightly in plastic and frozen for up to 1 month. Defrost the dough in the refrigerator overnight before proceeding with the recipe.)

3. Preheat the oven to 250°F.

4. Slice the dough into ⅓-inch-thick rounds and place them on ungreased baking sheets, leaving 1 inch between each cookie. Using a metal skewer, pierce each cookie with 4 holes in the center so that it looks like a button. The holes should be large enough so that the licorice laces will fit through. Bake the cookies until they are dry and firm but have not changed color, 45 to 50 minutes. Let them stand on the baking sheet for 5 minutes, then remove them with a metal spatula to a wire rack and let them cool completely.

5. Lace the licorice through the holes, crisscrossing them and leaving the loose ends on the undersides of the cookies. Anise-Flavored Shortbread Buttons with Licorice Lacing will keep at room temperature in an airtight container for 3 to 4 days.

chocolate butterfingers

Makes about 30 cookies

Here's yet another way to enjoy chocolate and peanut butter together. You stir chopped Butterfinger candy bars into chocolate cookie dough and then shape the dough into "fingers."

1½ cups unbleached all-purpose flour

½ cup unsweetened Dutch-processed cocoa powder

½ teaspoon baking powder

½ teaspoon salt

1 cup (2 sticks) unsalted butter, softened

½ cup firmly packed light brown sugar

¼ cup granulated sugar

1 large egg

2 teaspoons pure vanilla extract

Four 2.1-ounce Butterfinger candy bars, finely chopped

1. Preheat the oven to 350°F. Line baking sheets with parchment paper.

2. Sift together the flour, cocoa powder, baking powder, and salt in a medium-size mixing bowl. Set aside.

3. Combine the butter and sugars in a large mixing bowl and cream together with an electric mixer on medium-high speed until fluffy, 2 to 3 minutes. Add the egg and vanilla extract and beat until smooth. Stir in the flour mixture until just incorporated. Stir in the chopped Butterfingers.

4. Scoop up heaping tablespoonfuls of dough and roll between your palms to form 2½-inch-long logs. Place the logs on the baking sheets, leaving about 3 inches between each. Bake until they are firm around the edges but still soft on top, 14 to 16 minutes.

5. Let the cookies stand on the baking sheet for 5 minutes, then remove them with a metal spatula to a wire rack to cool completely. Chocolate Butterfingers will keep at room temperature in an airtight container for 2 to 3 days.

caramel turtles

Makes 12 turtles Even the smallest kids will be able to arrange 3 ingredients into simple turtle shapes. I like to use a Hershey bar for these, because it is conveniently divided into 12 squares.

60 pecan halves
12 soft caramel candies
One 1½-ounce milk chocolate bar,
**   broken into 12 equal squares**

1. Preheat the oven to 350°F. Place the pecans on a rimmed baking sheet and toast until fragrant, 7 to 9 minutes. Remove from the oven and let cool completely on the sheet.

2. Line baking sheets with parchment paper. Arrange the pecans on the baking sheets in clusters of 5: 1 for the head, 2 for the arms, and 2 for the legs. Flatten each caramel piece with the palm of your hand so that it measures 1¼ inches square. Place a flattened caramel on top of each pecan cluster. Bake until the caramel is soft and shiny but not yet runny, 3 to 4 minutes.

3. Remove the sheets from the oven and place a piece of chocolate on top of each caramel. Return the baking sheet to the oven and heat until the chocolate begins to melt, about 30 seconds. Remove from the oven and smooth the chocolate over the caramel with a small offset spatula. Cool completely on the baking sheet. Transfer to the refrigerator until the chocolate hardens, about 15 minutes. Caramel Turtles will keep at room temperature in an airtight container for 2 to 3 days.

the greatest thing since `sliced bread: SCRUMPTIOUS sandwich cookies

LEFT TO RIGHT: Crunchy Peanut Butter Ice Cream Sandwiches, Whoopie Pies, Hazelnut Cookies with Nutella and Raspberry Filling, Raspberry-Almond Icebox Thumbprints (page 70)

When you sandwich two freshly baked cookies

together with a complementary filling, you are taking those cookies to another level. First, there is the visual component. Sandwich cookies are undoubtedly more exciting to look at than simple drop cookies or slice-and-bakes. And then there is the matter of flavor. A well-chosen filling will add new dimensions to the taste and texture of a cookie. Tart apricot jam perks up poppy seed shortbreads (page 160); maple buttercream softens the crunch and sweetens the spice of molasses spice rounds (page 161). Finally, there's the fun quotient. The sandwich tempts children and parents to un-sandwich it, lick the filling from the middle, and then eat the cookies separately, thus prolonging enjoyment, if creating a bit of a mess. Are you sold yet?

There's really not much extra work involved in making sandwich cookies. The cookies themselves are either of the drop or slice-and-bake variety. The fillings are simple, too—jelly, melted chocolate, butter whipped with sugar and other flavorings. There *are* a few tricks to making perfect sandwich cookies. Here are some tips I've gathered, often the hard way, when putting together my own sandwich cookies:

* It's important to bake cookies that are uniform in size. They'll be easier to sandwich, and will look better when finished, than unevenly sized cookies. Use a small ice cream scoop for drop cookies to get uniform results. For slice-and-bake cookies, take some extra time when rolling your dough into logs to make sure that they are perfectly round.

* That said, all of your cookies are not going to look exactly alike. Match up tops and bottoms that most closely resemble each other before you begin to sandwich. This way you won't wind up with several mismatched pairs at the end.

* Make sure to let the cookies cool completely before you fill them, or you'll risk melting the filling or making it runny. This is especially important when the filling is made with butter or chocolate.

* Don't use more than the recommended amount of filling. It's tempting to put a little extra chocolate ganache between your mocha shortbreads, but if you do, it will just squish out the sides when you take your first bite.

* It is possible to substitute vegetable shortening for butter in some of the filling recipes, but I don't recommend it. It's true that vegetable-shortening fillings can be left out at room temperature for several days, while butter fillings need to be refrigerated, but the tradeoff in flavor is huge. If you want to make your buttercream ahead of time, refrigerate and rewhip it the day you'll be filling and serving your cookies.

* Most sandwich cookies are best eaten on the day they are made. Fillings tend to soften the cookies to the point of sogginess after more than a day. (The exceptions are jelly-filled cookies, which will hold for 2 to 3 days.) But you can certainly prepare the separate components and simply sandwich them just before serving. Individual recipes specify how to freeze unbaked dough and how long baked cookies will keep in an airtight container before they are filled.

Of course, even imperfectly matched or overfilled cookies will taste great and be fun to eat. Sandwich cookies are good to put together with kids, and mine certainly don't stress out when their vanilla cookies aren't perfectly symmetrical or they've loaded too much marshmallow cream into their whoopie pies.

The recipes in this chapter can be broken down into three types. First come the cakey cookies. Vanilla Sandwich Cookies (page 156), Peanut Butter and Banana Sandwich Cookies (page 157), and Carrot Cookies with Cream Cheese Filling (page 158) are all soft, oversized snack cake–type cookies with creamy fillings. The yields are on the small side, but one of these cookies will be more than enough for even the hungriest kid. These batters are too soft to form into perfect balls by hand. I highly recommend using a small ice cream or cookie scoop (see Resources, page 257, if you can't find one at your local cookware shop) for making uniform cookies. If you don't have an ice cream scoop, be sure to measure out the portions carefully, and shape the dough balls into neat rounds with your fingers once you've dropped them onto the cookie sheet.

Next come the slice-and-bake cookies, which make great sandwiches because they are very easily cut into uniform shapes. To make sure that the dough keeps its shape when cut, chill it well before slicing. Be sure to rotate it frequently as you slice, so one side doesn't become flattened from the repeated pressure of the knife. These doughs bake up crispy rather than cakey. For this reason, its best to slice most of the doughs as thin as you can (exceptions are noted in recipes). I recommend slices of $\frac{1}{8}$ of an inch. If the cookies are cut much thicker, the ratio between cookies and filling will be off, and the resulting sandwich will be too dry.

The ultimate filling for sandwich cookies is ice cream, so this chapter ends with three ice cream sandwich recipes, very different from each other but each delectable in its own way.

vanilla sandwich cookies with chocolate ganache filling

Makes about 15 cookies

A good dose of vanilla extract gives these plain cookies a wonderful aroma and flavor. To get evenly sized cookies, use a small ice cream scoop to portion out the dough. Best-quality chocolate (I buy Ghirardelli, Lindt, or Callebaut) will give the filling a truffle-like flavor and texture.

For the cookies

- 1½ cups unbleached all-purpose flour
- 1½ teaspoons baking powder
- ½ teaspoon salt
- ¾ cup (1½ sticks) unsalted butter, softened
- 1 cup sugar
- 3 large eggs
- 2 tablespoons pure vanilla extract

For the filling

- 6 ounces bittersweet or semisweet chocolate, finely chopped
- ½ cup heavy cream

1. Make the cookies: Preheat the oven to 375°F. Line baking sheets with parchment paper.

2. Combine the flour, baking powder, and salt in a medium-size mixing bowl.

3. Cream the butter and sugar together in a large mixing bowl with an electric mixer on medium speed until fluffy, 2 to 3 minutes. Add the eggs and vanilla extract and beat until smooth. Stir in the flour mixture until just combined. Place the bowl in the refrigerator for 10 minutes (or up to 6 hours) to let the dough firm up.

4. Use a small ice cream scoop to drop the batter by tablespoonfuls onto the lined baking sheets, leaving about 2 inches between each cookie. (Cookies may be placed next to each other on parchment paper–lined baking sheets, frozen, transferred to zipper-lock plastic freezer bags, and stored in the freezer for up to 1 month. Frozen cookies may be placed in the oven directly from the freezer and baked as directed.) Bake until the edges have browned and the tops of the cookies are set, 8 to 10 minutes (a minute or two longer for frozen dough). Remove the sheets from the oven and let the cookies firm up on the baking sheets for 2 minutes. With a metal spatula, transfer the cookies to a wire rack to cool completely.

5. Make the filling: Place the chopped chocolate in a small bowl. Bring the heavy cream just to a boil in a small saucepan over medium-low heat. Pour the hot cream into the bowl and let the mixture stand for 5 minutes. Whisk until smooth.

6. Let the ganache come to room temperature and thicken slightly, about 1 hour. Then whip it with an electric mixer on medium-high speed until it holds soft peaks, 2 to 3 minutes. Spoon 1 teaspoon of the filling onto the flat side of a cookie. Sandwich with another cookie. Repeat with the remaining cookies. Vanilla Sandwich Cookies with Chocolate Ganache Filling will keep at room temperature in an airtight container for 2 to 3 days.

peanut butter and banana sandwich cookies

Makes about 14 large cookies

These were inspired by a favorite sandwich combination. The cake-like cookies are soft and moist, with a little bit of crunch from chopped peanuts. Use a very ripe banana (all brown is just right) for the best banana flavor.

For the cookies

1½ cups unbleached all-purpose flour
1½ teaspoons baking powder
½ teaspoon salt
½ cup (1 stick) unsalted butter, softened
1 cup granulated sugar
2 large eggs
1 very ripe banana, peeled and mashed (about ½ cup)
1 teaspoon pure vanilla extract
½ cup roasted peanuts, finely chopped

For the filling

3 tablespoons unsalted butter, softened
¾ cup smooth peanut butter
1½ cups confectioners' sugar
1 tablespoon water

1. Make the cookies: Preheat the oven to 375°F. Line baking sheets with parchment paper.

2. Combine the flour, baking powder, and salt in a medium-size mixing bowl. Cream the butter and sugar together in a large mixing bowl with an electric mixer on medium speed until fluffy, 2 to 3 minutes. Add the eggs, banana, and vanilla extract and beat until smooth. Stir in the flour mixture until just combined. Stir in the chopped peanuts. Place the bowl in the refrigerator for 10 minutes (or up to 6 hours) to let the dough firm up.

3. Use a small ice cream scoop to drop the batter by tablespoonfuls onto the lined baking sheets, leaving about 2 inches between each cookie. (Cookies may be placed next to each other on parchment paper–lined baking sheets, frozen, transferred to zipper-lock plastic freezer bags, and stored in the freezer for up to 1 month. Frozen cookies may be placed in the oven directly from the freezer and baked as directed.) Bake until the edges have browned and the tops of the cookies are set, 8 to 10 minutes (a minute or two longer for frozen dough). Remove the sheets from the oven and let the cookies firm up on the baking sheets for 2 minutes. With a metal spatula, transfer the cookies to a wire rack to cool completely.

4. Make the filling: Cream the butter, peanut butter, and confectioners' sugar together in a large mixing bowl with an electric mixer on low speed until combined. Add the water and beat on high until light and fluffy, about 5 minutes. Use the filling immediately, or cover the surface of the filling with plastic wrap and store in the refrigerator for up to 1 day (rewhip it before using).

5. Spoon 1½ teaspoons of the filling onto the flat side of a cookie. Sandwich with another cookie. Repeat with the remaining cookies. Peanut Butter and Banana Sandwich Cookies are best eaten on the day they are made. Store at room temperature in an airtight container.

carrot cookies with cream cheese filling

Makes about 12 large cookies

These are for carrot cake lovers, big and small. The cream cheese and honey filling couldn't be simpler. The recipe yields only about 12 cookies, but they are large—the size of muffins. In addition to making great after-school snacks, they are also a fun addition to a special breakfast or brunch.

For the cookies

1¼ cups unbleached all-purpose flour
½ teaspoon baking powder
½ teaspoon ground cinnamon
¼ teaspoon salt
1 stick (½ cup) unsalted butter, softened
¾ cup firmly packed light brown sugar
1 large egg
1 teaspoon pure vanilla extract
1 cup peeled and grated carrots (about 2 medium-size carrots)
¾ cup chopped walnuts

For the filling

6 ounces (¾ package) cream cheese, softened
3 tablespoons honey

1. Make the cookies: Preheat the oven to 375°F. Line baking sheets with parchment paper.

2. Combine the flour, baking powder, cinnamon, and salt in a medium-size mixing bowl. Cream the butter and sugar together in a large mixing bowl with an electric mixer on medium speed until fluffy, 2 to 3 minutes. Add the egg and vanilla extract and beat until smooth. Beat in the carrots. Stir in the flour mixture until just combined. Stir in the chopped walnuts. Place the bowl in the refrigerator for 10 minutes (or up to 6 hours) to let the dough firm up.

3. Use a small ice cream scoop to drop the batter by tablespoonfuls onto the baking sheets, leaving about 2 inches between each cookie. (Cookies may be placed next to each other on parchment paper–lined baking sheets, frozen, transferred to zipper-lock plastic freezer bags, and stored in the freezer for up to 1 month. Frozen cookies may be placed in the oven directly from the freezer and baked as directed.) Bake until the edges have browned and the tops of the cookies are set, 10 to 12 minutes (a minute or two longer for frozen dough). Remove the sheets from the oven and let the cookies firm up on the baking sheets for 2 minutes. With a metal spatula, transfer the cookies to a wire rack to cool completely.

4. Make the filling: Place the cream cheese in a medium-size mixing bowl. With an electric mixer, beat the cream cheese on medium-high speed until light and fluffy, 2 to 3 minutes, scraping down the sides of the bowl once or twice as necessary. Add the honey and beat again until combined.

5. Spoon a scant tablespoon of the filling onto the flat side of a cookie and sandwich with another cookie. Repeat with the remaining cookies and filling. Carrot Cookies with Cream Cheese Filling are best eaten on the day they are made. Store at room temperature in an airtight container.

chocolate sandwich cookies

Makes about
36 cookies

These buttercream-filled cookies will be a revelation to anyone who enjoys Oreos. Yes, they resemble the commercial cookies, but in taste and texture they are so far superior that they belong in a different category.

For the cookies

1 cup unbleached all-purpose flour
6 tablespoons unsweetened Dutch-processed cocoa powder, sifted
½ teaspoon baking soda
½ teaspoon salt
10 tablespoons (1¼ sticks) unsalted butter, softened
1 cup granulated sugar
1 large egg
1 teaspoon pure vanilla extract

For the filling

½ cup (1 stick) unsalted butter, softened
2½ cups confectioners' sugar
1 teaspoon pure vanilla extract
Pinch of salt
1½ teaspoons water

1. Make the cookies: Combine the flour, cocoa powder, baking soda, and salt in a medium-size mixing bowl. Cream the butter and granulated sugar together in a large mixing bowl with an electric mixer on medium speed until fluffy, 2 to 3 minutes. Add the egg and vanilla extract and beat until smooth. Stir in the flour mixture until just combined.

2. Divide the dough into 2 equal portions. Shape each portion into a log about 9 inches long and 1½ inches in diameter. Wrap in plastic wrap and refrigerate for at least 2 hours or up to 24 hours. (Dough logs may be wrapped tightly in plastic and

frozen for up to 1 month. Defrost the dough on the counter for 15 minutes before proceeding.)

3. Preheat the oven to 350°F.

4. Slice the dough into ¼-inch-thick rounds and place the cookies on ungreased baking sheets, leaving about 2 inches between each cookie. Bake the cookies until they are dry on top, 6 to 8 minutes (a minute or two longer for partially frozen dough). Let them stand on the baking sheets for 5 minutes, then remove them from the sheets with a metal spatula to a wire rack and let them cool completely.

5. Make the filling: Cream the butter and confectioners' sugar together in a large mixing bowl with an electric mixer on low speed until combined. Stir in the vanilla extract and salt. Add the water and beat on high until light and fluffy, about 5 minutes. Use the filling immediately, or cover the surface of the filling with plastic wrap and store in the refrigerator for up to 1 day (rewhip it before using).

6. Spoon 1 teaspoon of the filling onto the flat side of a cookie. Sandwich with another cookie. Repeat with the remaining cookies. Chocolate Sandwich Cookies are best eaten on the day they are made. Store at room temperature in an airtight container.

poppy seed sandwich cookies

Makes about 36 cookies

I have one daughter who absolutely is afraid of poppy seeds, and one daughter who absolutely loves them. I love them, too, so when we both get a craving, we send the big sister out with her dad and make a batch of these. The dough is quite soft, so I shape it into a squared-off log rather than attempting to roll it into a perfect cylinder. Feel free to use whatever jam you like best.

1½ cups unbleached all-purpose flour
¼ teaspoon salt
2 tablespoons poppy seeds
¾ cup (1½ sticks) unsalted butter, softened
½ cup sugar
1 large egg
1 large egg yolk
1 teaspoon pure vanilla extract
¼ cup apricot jam

1. Combine the flour, salt, and poppy seeds in a medium-size mixing bowl. Cream the butter and sugar together in a large mixing bowl with an electric mixer on medium speed until fluffy, 2 to 3 minutes. Add the egg, egg yolk, and vanilla extract and beat until smooth. Stir in the flour mixture until just combined.

2. Shape the dough into a log 12 inches long and 1½ inches in diameter. Wrap the log in parchment paper and shape into a rectangle by flattening the top and sides with your hands. Wrap in plastic wrap and refrigerate for at least 2 hours or up to 24 hours. (Dough logs may be wrapped tightly in plastic and frozen for up to 1 month. Defrost the dough on the counter for 15 minutes before proceeding.)

3. Preheat the oven to 350°F.

4. Slice the dough into ⅛-inch-thick rounds and place the cookies on un-greased baking sheets, leaving about 2 inches between each cookie. Bake the cookies until they are dry on top, 12 to 15 minutes. Let them stand on the baking sheets for 5 minutes, then remove them from the sheets with a metal spatula to a wire rack and let them cool completely.

5. Place the jam in a food processor or blender and process until smooth. Spoon about ½ teaspoon of jam onto the flat side of a cookie. Sandwich with another cookie. Repeat with the remaining cookies. Poppy Seed Sandwich Cookies will keep at room temperature in an airtight container for 2 to 3 days.

Jelly-Filled Icebox Cookies

Several recipes from chapter 2 are good candidates for this treatment. Slice the cookies ⅛ inch thick before baking, and bake until the centers are just set and dry. Let cool, and sandwich with ½ teaspoon of jam or jelly filling.

* Chocolate-Walnut Slice-and-Bakes (page 64) with raspberry jam
* Hazelnut Biscuits (page 69) with orange marmalade
* Slice-and-Bake Peanuts (page 74) with grape jelly

molasses sandwich cookies with maple cream filling

Makes about 48 cookies

This is a nice combination of spicy cookie and smooth, sweet filling. The dough bakes up very firm, so slice it thin for crisp, but not overly hard, sandwiches.

For the cookies
2¼ cups unbleached all-purpose flour
1 teaspoon baking powder
1 teaspoon ground cinnamon
½ teaspoon ground ginger
6 tablespoons unsalted butter, melted and cooled
⅔ cup dark (not light or blackstrap) molasses

For the filling
6 tablespoons unsalted butter, softened, or 6 tablespoons vegetable shortening
1 cup confectioners' sugar
¼ cup pure maple syrup
½ teaspoon maple extract

1. Make the cookies: Combine the flour, baking powder, cinnamon, and ginger in a medium-size mixing bowl.

2. Combine the butter and molasses in a large mixing bowl with an electric mixer on medium speed until smooth, 2 to 3 minutes. Stir in the flour mixture until just combined.

3. Divide the dough into 2 equal portions. Shape each portion into a log about 8 inches long and 1½ inches in diameter. Wrap in plastic wrap and refrigerate for at least 2 hours or up to 24 hours. (Dough logs may be wrapped tightly in plastic and frozen for up to 1 month. Defrost the dough on the counter for 15 minutes before proceeding.)

4. Preheat the oven to 350°F.

5. Slice the dough into ⅛-inch-thick rounds and place the cookies on ungreased baking sheets, leaving about 2 inches between each cookie. Bake the cookies until they are dry on top, 10 to 12 minutes. Let them stand on the baking sheets for 5 minutes, then remove them from the sheets with a metal spatula to a wire rack and let them cool completely.

6. Make the filling: Cream the butter and confectioners' sugar together in a large mixing bowl with an electric mixer on low speed until combined. Stir in the maple syrup and maple extract on low. Beat on high until light and fluffy, about 5 minutes. Use the filling immediately, or cover the surface of the filling with plastic wrap and store in the refrigerator for up to 1 day (rewhip it before using).

7. Spoon ½ teaspoon of the filling onto the flat side of a cookie. Sandwich with another cookie. Repeat with the remaining cookies. Molasses Sandwich Cookies with Maple Cream Filling are best eaten on the day they are made. Store at room temperature in an airtight container.

hazelnut cookies with nutella and raspberry filling

These hazelnut slice-and-bakes are simple to make, but they have a sophisti-cated flavor that reminds me of cookies from French pastry shops. The filling is also simple and sophisticated: Nutella, the European hazelnut-chocolate spread, becomes absolutely out of this world when mixed with a little raspberry jam.

For the cookies

½ cup whole hazelnuts
1 cup (2 sticks) unsalted butter, softened
½ cup sugar
2¼ cups unbleached all-purpose flour
¼ teaspoon salt

For the filling

6 tablespoons Nutella
3 tablespoons seedless raspberry jam

1. Make the cookies: Preheat the oven to 350°F. Place the nuts on a baking sheet and bake until fragrant, about 10 minutes. Remove the pan from the oven, wrap the nuts in a clean kitchen towel, and allow to cool for 10 to 15 minutes. Rub the nuts with the towel to remove the skins (it's okay if bits of skin stick to some of the nuts). Let cool completely and finely chop.

2. Cream the butter and sugar together in a large mixing bowl with an electric mixer on medium speed until fluffy, 2 to 3 minutes. Stir in the flour and salt until just combined. Stir in the nuts.

3. Divide the dough into 2 equal portions. Shape each portion into a log about 8 inches long and 1½ inches in diameter. Wrap in plastic wrap and refrigerate for at least 2 hours or up to 24 hours. (Dough logs may be wrapped tightly in plastic and frozen for up to 1 month. Defrost the dough on the counter for 15 minutes before proceeding.)

4. Preheat the oven to 350°F.

5. Slice the dough into ⅙-inch-thick rounds and place the cookies on un-greased baking sheets, leaving about 2 inches between each cookie. Bake the cookies until they are dry on top, 8 to 10 minutes. Let them stand on the baking sheets for 5 minutes, then remove them from the sheets with a metal spatula to a wire rack and let them cool completely.

6. Make the filling: Combine the Nutella and raspberry jam in a small bowl and stir until smooth. Spoon about ½ teaspoon of the mixture onto the bottom of a cookie. Sandwich with another cookie. Repeat with the remaining cookies. Hazelnut Cookies with Nutella and Raspberry Filling will keep at room temperature in an airtight container for 2 to 3 days.

cashew and caramel rounds

Makes about
48 cookies

These cookies are one reason why my family quickly goes through the giant cans of cashews that I buy at the local warehouse club. Caramel is not difficult to make, but there are a few tricks you need to know. Don't stir the mixture as it cooks, or you may deposit undissolved sugar crystals onto the sides of the pan, causing crystallization of your caramel. Watch it carefully when it begins to color, because caramel will burn quickly. Remove the pan from the heat as soon as the mixture is light amber. And be very careful when you stir in the cream, because the molten sugar may bubble up to the top of the pan.

For the cookies

1 cup (2 sticks) unsalted butter, softened
½ cup firmly packed light brown sugar
2¼ cups unbleached all-purpose flour
⅛ teaspoon salt
½ cup finely chopped salted cashews

For the filling

¾ cup granulated sugar
3 tablespoons water
⅓ cup heavy cream
2 tablespoons unsalted butter

1. Make the cookies: Cream the butter and the brown sugar together in a large mixing bowl with an electric mixer on medium speed until fluffy, 2 to 3 minutes. Stir in the flour and salt until just combined. Stir in the nuts.

2. Divide the dough into 2 equal portions. Shape each portion into a log about 8 inches long and 1½ inches in diameter. Wrap in plastic wrap and refrigerate for at least 2 hours or up to 24 hours. (Dough logs may be wrapped tightly in plastic and frozen for up to 1 month. Defrost the dough on the counter for 15 minutes before proceeding.)

3. Preheat the oven to 350°F.

4. Slice the dough into ⅙-inch-thick rounds and place the cookies on un-greased baking sheets, leaving about 2 inches between each cookie. Bake the cookies until they are dry on top, 8 to 10 minutes. Let them stand on the baking sheets for 5 minutes, then remove them from the sheets with a metal spatula to a wire rack and let them cool completely.

5. Make the filling: Combine the granulated sugar and water in a small saucepan. Bring to a boil and let boil until the mixture turns a light amber color, 5 to 7 minutes. Do not stir. If parts of the syrup are turning darker than others, gently tilt the pan to even out the cooking. As soon as the syrup is a uniform amber color, remove from the heat. At arm's length, pour the heavy cream into the pot. Stir with a wooden spoon until combined. Be careful; the cream may splatter. Stir in the butter until it is melted. Pour the caramel into a heatproof glass bowl and let cool until spreadable, about 20 minutes.

6. Spoon a generous ½ teaspoon of the filling over one cookie and top with another cookie. Repeat with the remaining cookies and filling. Cashew and Caramel Rounds are best eaten on the day they are made. Store at room temperature in an airtight container.

mocha shortbread sandwiches with milk chocolate filling

Makes about 30 cookies

Even though kids don't drink coffee, many of them like the flavor in their cookies. The slight bitterness of espresso powder in these shortbread rounds is offset by a mild milk chocolate filling. These cookies turn out rather delicate, almost lacy, so handle them carefully while filling and sandwiching them.

For the cookies
1½ cups unbleached all-purpose flour
½ cup unsweetened Dutch-processed cocoa powder
¼ teaspoon salt
1 tablespoon instant espresso powder
1 cup (2 sticks) unsalted butter, softened
1 cup firmly packed light brown sugar

For the filling
6 ounces milk chocolate, finely chopped
⅓ cup heavy cream
1 tablespoon unsalted butter
1 tablespoon light corn syrup
⅛ teaspoon salt

1. Make the cookies: Sift together the flour, cocoa powder, salt, and espresso powder into a medium-size mixing bowl.

2. Cream the butter and brown sugar together in a large mixing bowl with an electric mixer on medium speed until fluffy, 2 to 3 minutes. Add the flour mixture and beat on low speed until the dough just comes together. Do not overmix.

3. Shape the dough into a log about 12 inches long and 1½ inches in diameter. Wrap in plastic wrap and freeze for at least 2 hours or up to 1 month.

4. Preheat the oven to 325°F.

5. Slice the dough into ⅛-inch-thick rounds and place the cookies on ungreased baking sheets, leaving about 2 inches between each cookie. Bake the cookies until they are dry on top, 8 to 10 minutes. Let them stand on the baking sheets for 5 minutes, then remove them from the sheets with a metal spatula to a wire rack and let them cool completely.

6. Make the filling: Place the chopped chocolate in a small heatproof bowl. Combine the cream, butter, corn syrup, and salt in a small saucepan and bring just to a boil. Pour over the chocolate, cover the bowl with plastic wrap, and let stand for 5 minutes. Whisk until smooth. Let cool to room temperature.

7. Spoon about ½ teaspoon of the mixture onto the bottom of a cookie. Sandwich with another cookie. Repeat with the remaining cookies. Mocha Shortbread Sandwiches with Milk Chocolate Filling are best eaten on the day they are made. Store at room temperature in an airtight container.

whoopie pies

Makes about 20 large cookies

I couldn't resist trying my hand at this classic sandwich cookie, if only because my kids love the name so much. These rich devil's food cakes sandwiched together with marshmallow filling have become family favorites, almost as much for their irresistible good looks as for their moist, chocolatey flavor. Resist the temptation to overfill them. A teaspoonful of filling is all you need here. Any more will ooze out the sides and make a mess.

For the cookies
- 1 cup unsweetened natural cocoa powder
- 1 cup boiling water
- ½ cup full-fat or low-fat sour cream
- 1 large egg yolk
- 1 teaspoon pure vanilla extract
- 2 cups unbleached all-purpose flour
- 1 cup firmly packed light brown sugar
- 1 teaspoon baking soda
- ½ teaspoon salt
- ½ cup (1 stick) unsalted butter, softened

For the filling
- 5 tablespoons unsalted butter, softened
- ½ cup confectioners' sugar
- 1 tablespoon light corn syrup
- ½ teaspoon pure vanilla extract
- Pinch of salt
- ¾ cup Marshmallow Fluff

1. Make the cookies: Preheat the oven to 375°F. Line baking sheets with parchment paper.

2. Whisk together the cocoa powder and boiling water in a small bowl until smooth. Set aside to cool. Combine the sour cream, egg yolk, and vanilla extract in a medium-size mixing bowl and beat lightly with a fork. Set aside.

3. Combine the flour, brown sugar, baking soda, and salt in a large mixing bowl. Add the butter and, with an electric mixer fitted with the paddle attachment, mix on low speed until the butter pieces are no larger than small peas. Stir in the sour cream mixture and mix on low speed until all the ingredients are moistened. Add the cocoa mixture and beat on medium-high speed until combined, scraping down the sides of the bowl once or twice as necessary.

4. Use a small ice cream scoop to drop the batter by tablespoonfuls onto the lined baking sheets, leaving about 2½ inches between each cookie. Bake until the tops are cracked, 8 to 9 minutes. Remove the sheets from the oven and let the cookies firm up on the baking sheets for 5 minutes. With a metal spatula, transfer the cookies to a wire rack to cool completely.

5. Make the filling: Cream the butter and confectioners' sugar together in a large mixing bowl with an electric mixer on low speed until combined. Stir in the corn syrup, vanilla extract, and salt. Stir in the Marshmallow Fluff. Beat on high until light and fluffy, about 3 minutes. Refrigerate until slightly thickened, about 20 minutes.

6. Spoon 1 teaspoon of the filling onto the flat side of a cookie. Sandwich with another cookie. Repeat with the remaining cookies. Whoopie Pies are best eaten on the day they are made. Store at room temperature in an airtight container.

A Good Excuse to Make Whoopie Pies

These are as fun and satisfying as cupcakes, and my kids often request them instead of cupcakes for school birthdays and other classroom parties. Novelty toothpicks (a heart toothpick for Valentine's Day, a four-leaf clover for St. Patrick's Day) make quick and festive decorations.

brownie ice cream sandwiches

Makes 8 large ice cream sandwiches

The brownie sundae is one of my favorite desserts, so I thought it would be great to sandwich a layer of ice cream between brownies, eliminating the need for a spoon. Here basic brownie batter is spread thinly in two baking pans to make thin, cookie-like brownies. One of the pans is then used to mold the ice cream. When the brownies and ice cream are nice and cold, they are sandwiched together, cut into small bars, and wrapped up and frozen until you need them. Make sure that your ice cream is thoroughly frozen, or it will ooze out of the sides of the brownies when you cut them. If some ice cream does ooze out, just smooth it back in with the side of your knife. I like mint chocolate chip ice cream with my brownies, but any favorite flavor is great.

6 tablespoons unsalted butter
1½ ounces (1½ squares) unsweetened chocolate
½ cup unbleached all-purpose flour
¼ teaspoon baking powder
⅛ teaspoon salt
¾ cup sugar
1 large egg
1 large egg yolk
1 teaspoon pure vanilla extract
2 pints ice cream, softened

1. Preheat the oven to 350°F. Line two 8-inch square baking pans with heavy-duty aluminum foil, making sure that the foil is tucked into all the corners and that there is at least 1 inch overhanging the tops of the pans on all sides.

2. Put 1 inch of water in the bottom of a double boiler or medium-size saucepan and bring to a bare simmer. Combine the butter and chocolate in the top of the double boiler or in a stainless-steel bowl set on top of the simmering water, making sure that the water doesn't touch the bottom of the bowl. Heat, whisking occasionally, until the chocolate and butter are completely melted. Set aside to cool slightly.

3. Combine the flour, baking powder, and salt in a small mixing bowl.

4. Whisk together the sugar, egg, and egg yolk in a large mixing bowl. With a wooden spoon, stir in the chocolate mixture and the vanilla extract. Stir in the flour mixture until just incorporated. Pour half of the batter into each of the prepared baking pans. Spread to the edges with a small offset spatula. Bake until the brownies are just set in the center, 15 to 20 minutes. Let cool completely on a wire rack.

5. Grasping the overhanging foil on either side of the pans, lift out each pan of brownies. Place the uncut brownies, still in their foil, on a baking sheet, cover the baking sheet with plastic wrap, and freeze until firm, at least 3 hours and up to 1 day.

6. Line one of the empty baking pans with a square of parchment or waxed paper. Use an offset spatula to spread the ice cream in an even layer over the bottom of the pan. Cover with plastic wrap and freeze until very firm, at least 6 hours and up to 1 day.

7. Invert one of the brownie squares onto a cutting board and peel away the foil. Run a sharp paring knife around the edges of the ice cream and invert onto the brownie. Peel the aluminum foil from the remaining brownie square and place it, top side up, on top of the ice cream. With a sharp chef's knife, cut into 8 rectangles. Wrap each rectangle in plastic wrap and freeze until ready to serve, at least 1 hour and up to 3 days.

Cookie-wiches

There are plenty of drop cookies that make superb ice cream sandwiches. Here are some of my favorite cookie and ice cream combinations. Follow the directions in Gingersnap Ice Cream Sandwiches (page 168) for scooping and sandwiching the ice cream.

* Mom's Chocolate Chip Cookies (page 24) with chocolate or vanilla ice cream
* Coffee Heath Bar Crunch–Chip Cookies (page 28) with coffee ice cream
* Black Forest Chocolate Chip Cookies (page 35) with cherry vanilla ice cream
* Orange-Pecan Oatmeal Cookies (page 42) with butter pecan ice cream
* Trail Mix Cookies (page 52) with vanilla frozen yogurt

gingersnap ice cream sandwiches

**Makes 7
ice cream sandwiches**

I love ginger in all its forms. Here I use a generous portion of ground ginger to make these sturdy cookies, and then stir some chopped crystallized ginger into the vanilla ice cream that I sandwich between them. For milder sandwiches, skip that step and use plain vanilla ice cream. Put the sandwiches together just before serving, so that the cookies are not freezing cold but the ice cream is still very firm from the freezer.

1 cup unbleached all-purpose flour
¼ teaspoon baking soda
½ teaspoon salt
1½ teaspoons ground ginger
¼ teaspoon ground cinnamon
6 tablespoons unsalted butter, softened
½ cup firmly packed light brown sugar
1 egg yolk
2 tablespoons dark (not light or blackstrap) molasses
2 pints vanilla ice cream, slightly softened
¼ cup crystallized ginger, finely chopped (optional)

1. Make the cookies: Combine the flour, baking soda, salt, ginger, and cinnamon in a medium-size mixing bowl.

2. Cream the butter and sugar together in a large mixing bowl with an electric mixer on medium speed until fluffy, 2 to 3 minutes. Add the egg yolk and molasses and beat until smooth. Stir in the flour mixture until just combined. Place the bowl in the refrigerator for 1 hour (or up to 6 hours) to let the dough firm up.

3. Preheat the oven to 350°F. Line baking sheets with parchment paper.

4. Use a small ice cream scoop to drop the batter by tablespoonfuls onto the lined baking sheets, leaving about 2 inches between each cookie. (Cookies may be placed next to each other on parchment paper–lined baking sheets, frozen, transferred to zipper-lock plastic freezer bags, and stored in the freezer for up to 1 month. Frozen cookies may be placed in the oven directly from the freezer and baked as directed.) Bake until the edges have browned and the tops of the cookies are set, 12 to 14 minutes (a minute or two longer for frozen dough). Remove the sheets from the oven and let the cookies firm up on the baking sheets for 2 minutes. With a metal spatula, transfer the cookies to a wire rack to cool completely.

5. Place a rimmed baking sheet in the freezer to chill for 15 minutes. Place the ice cream in a large mixing bowl and sprinkle with the crystallized ginger, if you are using it. Mash with a spoon to distribute evenly. Use a ¼-cup ice cream scoop to scoop 7 scoops of ice cream onto the chilled baking sheet. Press on each scoop with the back of a glass to flatten slightly. If at any point the ice cream becomes too soft, return it to the freezer for 20 minutes before proceeding. Loosely cover the ice cream rounds with plastic wrap and place in the freezer until the ice cream is firm, at least 3 hours and up to 1 day. When ready to serve, sandwich each portion of ice cream between 2 cookies and serve immediately.

crunchy peanut butter ice cream sandwiches

**Makes 8
ice cream sandwiches**

This is an especially simple and cool addition to your ice cream sandwich repertoire, since the "cookies" sandwiching the ice cream here are actually a no-bake type of Rice Krispies treat. I like to layer chocolate and vanilla ice cream, but you may choose one or the other if you like.

½ cup light corn syrup
½ cup smooth peanut butter
3 cups Rice Krispies or other crispy rice cereal
1 pint vanilla ice cream, slightly softened
1 pint chocolate ice cream, slightly softened

1. Line an 8-inch square baking pan with heavy-duty aluminum foil, making sure that the foil is tucked into all the corners and that there is at least 1 inch overhanging the top of the pan on all sides.

2. Combine the corn syrup and peanut butter in the bowl of an electric mixer fitted with a whisk attachment. Add the rice cereal and continue to mix until all of the cereal is moistened but not completely crushed. Spread half of the cereal mixture into the bottom of the prepared pan and press it into a thin, even layer with your fingertips. Place in the freezer for 15 minutes.

3. Spoon the vanilla ice cream in tablespoonfuls across the cereal layer. Use an offset spatula to smooth the ice cream into an even layer. Place in the freezer for 20 minutes to firm up.

4. Spoon and smooth the chocolate ice cream over the vanilla ice cream, and place back in the freezer for another 20 minutes.

5. Spread the remaining cereal mixture over the top of the chocolate ice cream and press it into a thin, even layer with your fingertips. Freeze until very firm, at least 6 hours.

6. Grasping the overhanging foil on either side of the pan, lift out the bars and place them on a cutting board. Remove the foil and cut into 8 bars. Serve immediately, or wrap individually in plastic wrap and freeze until ready to serve, up to 1 day.

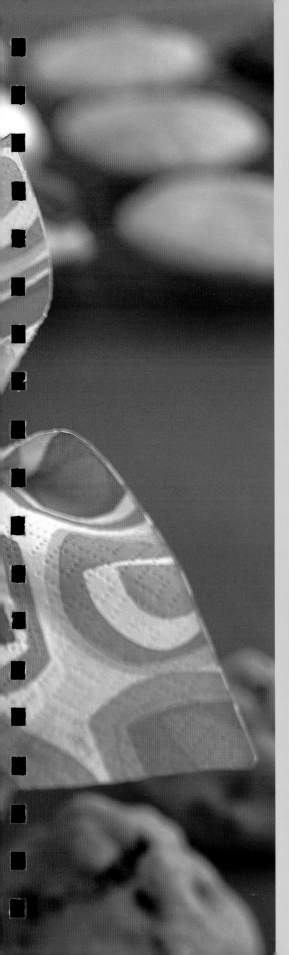

heirloom cookies: OLD-FASHIONED recipes for today's moms

CLOCKWISE FROM TOP LEFT: Black and White Cookies, Grandma Rose's Sour Cream Icebox Cookies, Chocolate Jumbles, Raisin Hermits

"Heirloom" is a difficult concept to explain to

little kids, whose sense of history may only go back to their early days of preschool. But mothers who bake know very well that recipes come from somewhere, and many of the best cookie recipes are passed down from baker to baker, sometimes across several generations. This chapter contains my own personal collection of heirloom recipes, given to me by friends and family, collected from old cookbooks and magazines, clipped from the backs of boxes and bags by my own mom when I was a kid. These cookies are not relics, historical oddities, or exercises in nostalgia. They are time-tested treats that have pleased kids for years and continue to do so.

Some of the recipes are truly old. American moms have been baking snickerdoodles, jumbles, and hermits since at least the middle of the nineteenth century (see my versions on pages 174, 175, and 180). Some of my favorite heirloom recipes are of foreign origin. Fregolata and Biscotti (pages 186 and 188) are traditional Italian cookies, Kourabiethes (page 185) are Greek, and Madeleines (page 184) are, of course, from France. But in my opinion, a recipe doesn't have to be a hundred years old or have crossed an ocean to qualify as an heirloom. I was a kid in the 1960s, when cooking with convenience foods was new and exciting, and so some of my favorite heirloom cookies are made with ingredients like Special K cereal (page 181) and crushed potato chips (page 182).

I've never been a purist when it comes to cookies. If I think an old recipe would taste better with more sugar, or butter instead of shortening, I won't hesitate to make the change. I know very well that the typical black and white cookies found in New York delis are not frosted with chocolate ganache, but I also know that my version (page 178) tastes a lot better than the black and white cookie my mom used to buy me as a treat while she ordered cold cuts from the counterman at the deli. The important thing in updating heirloom recipes is to capture the magic of the original—chocolate and vanilla on the same cookie!—while changing anything that might not mesh with today's tastes.

The chapter ends with two bona fide heirlooms, one a recipe from my great-grandma Rose (page 190) and one from my friend Tom's grandma (page 191). When I was growing up, my great-grandmother, an excellent cook and baker, used only one cookie recipe. Packed in an empty Martinson's coffee tin saved for this purpose, her marvelously light sour cream refrigerator cookies dusted with cinnamon sugar became her calling card. Whenever she came to visit me and my sisters or any of my cousins, she brought them along, and we couldn't wait to eat them. Tom says that his grandma baked only one type of cookie, too. He and all the kids in his family made a beeline for the large jar of long-keeping molasses rounds she always had under the sink in her kitchen.

That Tom and I still remember these cookies so vividly and with so much pleasure after all these years makes me want to bake memorable cookies for my own children. I have a bunch of favorites in rotation, including Grandma Rose's Sour Cream Icebox Cookies, and I'm curious to find out which cookie is the one that reminds them of me when they're all grown up, which is the one that they'll make for their own kids.

snickerdoodles

Snickerdoodles get their funny name from the German word *Schneckennudeln*, which translates as "crinkly noodles." These old-fashioned cinnamon sugar cookies have been popular in New England since the nineteenth century. Although they are plain enough for the pickiest kids, they are not at all bland because the cream of tartar gives them a slight tang.

2¼ cups unbleached all-purpose flour
2 teaspoons cream of tartar
1 teaspoon baking soda
½ teaspoon salt
1 cup (2 sticks) unsalted butter, softened
1¾ cups sugar
2 large eggs
2 teaspoons ground cinnamon

1. Preheat the oven to 400°F. Line baking sheets with parchment paper.

2. Combine the flour, cream of tartar, baking soda, and salt in a medium-size mixing bowl.

3. Cream the butter and 1½ cups of the sugar together in a large mixing bowl with an electric mixer on medium-high speed until fluffy, 2 to 3 minutes. Add the eggs and beat until smooth. Beat in the flour mixture until just combined.

4. Combine the cinnamon and the remaining ¼ cup of sugar in a small bowl. Scoop up a heaping tablespoon of dough and roll it between your palms to form a ball. Roll each ball in the cinnamon sugar to coat it completely. Place the balls on the lined baking sheets, leaving about 3 inches between each cookie. (Cookies may be placed next to each other on parchment paper–lined baking sheets, frozen, transferred to zipper-lock plastic freezer bags, and stored in the freezer for up to 1 month. Frozen cookies may be placed in the oven directly from the freezer and baked as directed.)

5. Bake the cookies until they are pale golden around the edges but still soft on top, about 10 minutes (a minute or two longer for frozen dough). Let them stand on the baking sheets for 5 minutes, then carefully slide the entire parchment sheet with the cookies from the pan to a wire rack to cool completely. Snickerdoodles will keep at room temperature in an airtight container for 2 to 3 days.

chocolate jumbles

Makes about
20 cookies

Ring-shaped jumble cookies date back to the nineteenth century, and every home baker had her own specialty. There are recipes for cinnamon, coconut, lemon, and candied fruit jumbles in community cookbooks from the period. Here's my chocolate version, puffy and doughnut-like, perfect for dunking into milk.

1½ cups unbleached all-purpose flour
½ cup unsweetened natural cocoa
  powder, sifted, plus more for dusting
½ teaspoon baking soda
½ teaspoon salt
½ cup (1 stick) unsalted butter,
  softened
⅔ cup sugar
1 large egg
1 teaspoon pure vanilla extract
½ cup buttermilk
2 ounces bittersweet or semisweet
  chocolate, melted (optional)

1. Preheat the oven to 375°F. Line a baking sheet with parchment paper.

2. Combine the flour, cocoa powder, baking soda, and salt in a small bowl.

3. Cream the butter and sugar together in a large mixing bowl with a wooden spoon until smooth. Add the egg and vanilla extract and beat until smooth. Stir in half the flour mixture until just incorporated. Stir in the buttermilk. Stir in the remaining flour mixture and beat until smooth, scraping down the sides of the bowl once or twice as necessary. Place the bowl in the refrigerator for 15 minutes (or up to 6 hours) to let the dough firm up.

4. Lightly dust your hands with a little cocoa powder, scoop up a walnut-size piece of the dough, and roll it between your palms to form a short, thick log. Place the log on a clean countertop and roll back and forth until the log is 5 inches long. Pinch the two ends together to form a ring and place on the lined baking sheet. Repeat with the remaining dough, redusting your hands with cocoa powder as necessary. Place cookies about 2 inches apart on the baking sheet.

5. Bake until the cookies are slightly puffed and firm, 10 to 12 minutes. Slide the entire parchment sheet with the cookies onto a wire rack and let the cookies cool completely.

6. Dip a fork into the melted chocolate, if you are using it, and wave it over the cookies to form decorative stripes. Let the chocolate harden, about 15 minutes, before serving. Chocolate Jumbles will keep at room temperature in an airtight container for 3 to 4 days.

Kids Can Help

Waving a fork dipped in chocolate is definitely a job for a kid. Just put on an apron, or get out of the way, before the waving begins.

benne wafers

Makes about
22 cookies

Benne Wafers are traditional in South Carolina, where sesame seeds are called benne seeds. I had never made these sesame seed cookies until I was developing recipes for this book. I went crazy for them and so did my family. In spite of their all-American pedigree, they have an exotic flavor and creamy texture reminiscent of halvah, the Middle Eastern sesame seed candy.

1 cup sesame seeds
1 cup unbleached all-purpose flour
½ teaspoon salt
½ teaspoon baking powder
½ cup (1 stick) unsalted butter, softened
⅔ cup firmly packed light brown sugar
1 large egg
1 teaspoon pure vanilla extract

1. Preheat the oven to 350°F.

2. Pour the sesame seeds onto a rimmed baking sheet and toast until light golden, 6 to 8 minutes. Watch them carefully and remove them from the oven before they become too dark. Cool completely.

3. Line baking sheets with parchment paper. Combine the flour, salt, and baking powder in a small bowl.

4. Combine the butter and brown sugar in a large mixing bowl and cream together with an electric mixer on medium-high speed until fluffy, 2 to 3 minutes. Add the egg and vanilla extract and beat until smooth. Beat in the flour mixture until just incorporated. Stir in the sesame seeds.

5. Shape the dough into 1-inch balls and place on the lined baking sheets, leaving about 3 inches between each cookie. Flatten each cookie slightly with the palm of your hand. (Balls of dough may be placed next to each other on parchment paper–lined baking sheets, frozen, transferred to zipper-lock plastic freezer bags, and stored in the freezer for up to 1 month. Frozen cookies may be thawed slightly on cookie sheets, flattened, and baked as directed.)

6. Bake the cookies until golden, 9 to 11 minutes (a minute or two longer for frozen dough). Let the cookies stand on the baking sheets for 5 minutes, then remove them with a metal spatula to a wire rack to cool completely. Benne Wafers will keep at room temperature in an airtight container for 2 to 3 days.

chocolate raisin pockets

Makes about
36 cookies

These are my version of a traditional Pennsylvania Dutch recipe for simple pastry dough filled with raisins. I like some cream cheese in the dough for tenderness and tang, and I put some mini chocolate chips in with the raisins, which I think makes the filling deliciously rich. To get a good seal, press the tines of a fork into the dough and then drag the fork to the edges of the cookie. Here's a kid-tested variation: My daughter likes to substitute pieces of cut-up candy bars (Snickers and Milky Way work best) for the filling.

For the filling

- **1 cup dark raisins**
- **½ cup water**
- **½ cup firmly packed light brown sugar**
- **1 tablespoon unbleached all-purpose flour**
- **½ teaspoon orange zest**
- **3 tablespoons mini chocolate chips**

For the cookie dough

- **2½ cups unbleached all-purpose flour**
- **1 teaspoon baking powder**
- **½ teaspoon cinnamon**
- **¼ teaspoon salt**
- **1 cup (2 sticks) unsalted butter, softened**
- **8 ounces cream cheese, softened**
- **¾ cup granulated sugar, plus more for sprinkling**
- **1 teaspoon pure vanilla extract**

1. Make the filling: Combine the raisins, water, brown sugar, flour, and orange zest in a small saucepan and bring to a boil. Lower the heat and simmer until the raisins have absorbed most of the liquid, 10 to 12 minutes. Transfer to a bowl and let cool completely. Stir in the chips.

2. Make the dough: Combine the flour, baking powder, cinnamon, and salt in a medium-size bowl. Combine the butter, cream cheese, and sugar in a large mixing bowl and beat with an electric mixer until fluffy. Add the vanilla extract and beat until incorporated, scraping down the sides of the bowl as necessary. Add the flour mixture and mix on low until the dough comes together in a ball.

3. Divide the dough into 2 equal-size balls, wrap each tightly in plastic wrap, and refrigerate until firm, at least 2 hours and up to 1 day.

4. Preheat the oven to 375°F. Line baking sheets with parchment paper.

5. Remove one ball of dough from the refrigerator and place on a lightly floured work surface. Roll it out to a ⅛-inch thickness between 2 sheets of parchment paper. Using a biscuit cutter, cut out as many 2-inch rounds as you can. Reroll the scraps and cut more rounds.

6. Place half of the rounds on the lined baking sheets. Place a heaping ½-teaspoon of the raisin mixture into the center of each round. Place another pastry round on top of the filling. Flour the tines of a fork and seal the cookies together by pressing the tines all around the edges of each cookie. Sprinkle each cookie with sugar.

7. Bake until the cookies are golden brown around the edges and pale golden on top, 12 to 14 minutes. Slide the entire parchment sheet with the cookies onto a wire rack and let the cookies cool completely. Repeat with the remaining ball of dough and remaining filling, using fresh parchment paper. Chocolate Raisin Pockets will keep at room temperature in an airtight container for 2 to 3 days.

Kids Can Help

My daughter enjoys sealing up the pockets with the tines of a fork.

black and white cookies

Here's a mini version of the New York classic, sized for smaller appetites.

For the cookies

2 cups unbleached all-purpose flour
1 teaspoon baking powder
½ teaspoon baking soda
¼ teaspoon salt
½ cup (1 stick) unsalted butter, softened
¾ cup plus 2 tablespoons granulated sugar
1 large egg
2 teaspoons pure vanilla extract
½ cup full-fat sour cream

For the white icing

1⅓ cups confectioners' sugar
¼ cup heavy cream, plus more if necessary
1 tablespoon fresh lemon juice

For the chocolate icing

4 ounces bittersweet chocolate, finely chopped
¼ cup heavy cream
1 tablespoon plus 1 teaspoon light corn syrup
½ teaspoon pure vanilla extract

1. Make the cookies: Preheat the oven to 350°F. Line baking sheets with parchment paper or spray with nonstick cooking spray.

2. Combine the flour, baking powder, baking soda, and salt in a medium-size bowl.

3. Combine the butter and sugar in a large mixing bowl and cream with an electric mixer on medium speed until well combined, scraping down the sides of the bowl once or twice as necessary.

4. Add the egg and vanilla extract and beat at medium speed until combined. Beginning and ending with the flour mixture, add the flour in 2 additions and the sour cream in 1 addition at low speed until just combined.

5. Drop the dough by heaping tablespoonfuls onto the prepared baking sheets, leaving about 3 inches between each cookie. With moistened palms, flatten the mounds into 1½-inch disks. Bake until the centers are firm and the edges are just light golden, 11 to 14 minutes. Cool for 5 minutes on the baking sheets, then transfer cookies to a wire rack to cool completely.

6. Make the white icing: Whisk together the confectioners' sugar, cream, and lemon juice in a small bowl until smooth. With a small metal spatula, spread white icing on half the surface of each cookie. Let stand 15 minutes to set.

7. Make the chocolate icing: Put 1 inch of water in a small saucepan and bring to a bare simmer. Combine the chocolate, heavy cream, and corn syrup in a stainless steel bowl big enough to fit on top of the saucepan and set it on top of the simmering water, making sure that the water doesn't touch the bottom of the bowl. Heat, whisking occasionally, until the chocolate is completely melted. Remove from the heat and stir in the vanilla extract. If necessary, let the icing stand for a few minutes until thick enough to spread.

8. Spread the chocolate icing on the other half of the cookie. Let stand until set, at least 1 hour. Black and White Cookies will keep at room temperature in an airtight container for up to 2 days.

A Good Excuse to Make Black and White Cookies

Cushion the shock of showing a black-and-white DVD on family movie night by serving these cookies as a snack. Recommended for viewing: *Abbott and Costello Meet Frankenstein*, *Duck Soup*, *King Kong* (1933), *To Kill a Mockingbird*, or *Holiday Inn*.

raisin hermits

Makes about
26 cookies

Recipes for hermits vary, but all contain dried fruit and spices. I've been baking my coffee-spiked version for a long time and never get tired of the richly flavored dough. Raisins are traditional, but chopped apricots or figs are great for a change.

2 cups unbleached all-purpose flour
¾ teaspoon baking soda
¼ teaspoon salt
½ teaspoon ground cinnamon
½ teaspoon ground ginger
¼ teaspoon ground nutmeg
½ cup (1 stick) unsalted butter, softened
1 cup firmly packed light brown sugar
1 large egg
¼ cup strong brewed coffee or espresso, cooled
1 cup raisins
1 cup chopped walnuts

1. Preheat the oven to 375°F. Line baking sheets with parchment paper.

2. Combine the flour, baking soda, salt, cinnamon, ginger, and nutmeg in a medium-size mixing bowl.

3. Cream the butter and brown sugar together in a large mixing bowl with an electric mixer on medium speed until fluffy, 2 to 3 minutes. Add the egg and coffee and beat until smooth. Beat in the flour mixture until just combined. Stir in the raisins and walnuts.

4. Drop the batter by heaping tablespoonfuls onto the lined baking sheets, leaving about 3 inches between each cookie. (Balls of dough may be placed next to each other on parchment paper–lined baking sheets, frozen, transferred to zipper-lock plastic freezer bags, and stored in the freezer for up to 1 month. Frozen cookies may be placed in the oven directly from the freezer and baked as directed.)

5. Bake the cookies until they are golden around the edges but still soft on top, about 10 minutes (a minute or two longer for frozen dough). Let them stand on the baking sheets for 5 minutes, then carefully slide the entire parchment sheet with the cookies from the pan to a wire rack and let them cool completely. Raisin Hermits will keep at room temperature in an airtight container for 2 to 3 days.

ranger cookies

Makes about
30 cookies

Ranger cookies first appeared on my radar when I was writing a book about cereal. Friends and colleagues started telling me about the simple drop cookies their moms used to make, stirring in a cup or two of corn flakes, Wheaties, or Special K. The cereal flakes give these cookies a sturdy structure, making them perfect packing cookies for lunch boxes, picnics, and traveling. Try making your own version, using whichever flaked cereal you prefer, and substituting raisins or other dried fruits and nuts for the chocolate chips.

1 cup unbleached all-purpose flour
½ teaspoon baking soda
¼ teaspoon baking powder
¼ teaspoon salt
½ cup (1 stick) unsalted butter, melted and cooled
½ cup granulated sugar
½ cup firmly packed light brown sugar
1 large egg
1 teaspoon pure vanilla extract
1 cup old-fashioned rolled oats (not instant)
1 cup Special K cereal
1 cup milk chocolate chips
½ cup sweetened flaked coconut

1. Preheat the oven to 350°F.

2. Combine the flour, baking soda, baking powder, and salt in a medium-size mixing bowl.

3. Cream the cooled melted butter, granulated sugar, and brown sugar together in a large mixing bowl with a wooden spoon until smooth. Add the egg and vanilla extract and beat until smooth. Stir in the flour mixture until just incorporated. Stir in the oats and Special K. Stir in the chocolate chips and coconut. Place the bowl in the refrigerator for 10 minutes (or up to 6 hours) to let the dough firm up.

4. Drop the batter by heaping tablespoonfuls onto ungreased baking sheets, leaving about 3 inches between each cookie. (Balls of dough may be placed next to each other on parchment paper–lined baking sheets, frozen, transferred to zipper-lock plastic freezer bags, and stored in the freezer for up to 1 month. Frozen cookies may be placed in the oven directly from the freezer and baked as directed.)

5. Bake the cookies until golden around the edges but still soft on top, 10 to 12 minutes (a minute or two longer for frozen dough). Let the cookies stand on the baking sheet for 5 minutes, then remove them with a metal spatula to a wire rack to cool completely. Ranger Cookies will keep at room temperature in an airtight container for 2 to 3 days.

potato chip cookies

Makes about
14 cookies

Crushed potato chips give these simple cookies richness and crunch. If you like the salty sweetness of treats like chocolate-covered pretzels, try these. This makes a small batch, perfect for when you have just a small amount of potato chips left in the bag, but the recipe can easily be doubled.

½ cup sugar
½ cup (1 stick) unsalted butter, softened
1 teaspoon pure vanilla extract
¾ cup unbleached all-purpose flour
½ cup pecan halves, finely chopped
½ cup crushed potato chips

1. Preheat the oven to 350°F. Line a baking sheet with parchment paper. Pour 2 tablespoons of the sugar into a small bowl; set aside.

2. Cream the butter and the remaining 6 tablespoons of the sugar together in a large mixing bowl until smooth. Stir in the vanilla extract. Stir in the flour, nuts, and potato chips until incorporated.

3. Shape tablespoonfuls of the dough into balls and place on the prepared baking sheet at least 2 inches apart. Grease the bottom of a small juice glass with butter and dip into the sugar in the bowl. Press lightly on a cookie to flatten it and coat it with the sugar. Repeat with the remaining sugar and cookies, regreasing the bottom of the glass as necessary.

4. Bake until the cookies are light golden around the edges, 10 to 12 minutes. Let the cookies stand on the baking sheet for 5 minutes, then remove them with a metal spatula to a wire rack to cool completely. Potato Chip Cookies will keep at room temperature in an airtight container for 2 to 3 days.

Kids Can Help

Most kids love playing with a rolling pin. Put the potato chips into a small zipper-lock plastic bag, and then let your pastry-chefs-in-training roll over the bag until the chips are pulverized.

poppy seed pillows

Makes about 24 cookies

With their sour cream richness, these comforting, cakey cookies are a homey relative to Black and White Cookies (page 178). However, these have poppy seeds and are unfrosted.

2 cups unbleached all-purpose flour
¼ cup poppy seeds
1 teaspoon baking powder
½ teaspoon baking soda
⅛ teaspoon salt
½ cup (1 stick) unsalted butter, softened, plus more for buttering the juice glass
¾ cup sugar
1 large egg
½ teaspoon pure vanilla extract
½ teaspoon grated lemon zest
½ cup full-fat sour cream

1. Preheat the oven to 350°F. Line baking sheets with parchment paper or spray with nonstick cooking spray. Combine the flour, poppy seeds, baking powder, baking soda, and salt in a medium-size bowl.

2. Combine the butter and sugar in a large mixing bowl and cream with an electric mixer on medium speed until well combined, scraping down the sides of the bowl once or twice as necessary.

3. Add the egg, vanilla extract, and lemon zest and beat at medium speed until combined. Beginning and ending with the flour mixture, add the flour in 2 additions and the sour cream in 1 addition at low speed until just combined.

4. Drop the dough by heaping table-spoonfuls onto the prepared baking sheets, leaving about 3 inches between each cookie. Bake until the centers are firm and the edges are just light golden, 11 to 14 minutes. Cool for 5 minutes on the baking sheets, then transfer cookies to a wire rack to cool completely. Poppy Seed Pillows will keep at room temperature in an airtight container for up to 2 days.

madeleines

Makes
12 cookies

Your kids may not write a classic novel because you served them Proust's madeleines, but they will certainly remember these buttery shell-shaped cookies for years to come. Make sure your brown sugar has no lumps before you mix it into the batter. Spray the pan well so you don't have a sticking problem, or, even better, use a nonstick madeleine pan. It's worth the extra money. If you want to try these cookies out before investing in a special madeleine pan, use a mini-muffin tin instead.

2 large eggs
6 tablespoons granulated sugar
2 tablespoons light brown sugar
1 teaspoon pure vanilla extract
⅛ teaspoon salt
1 cup unbleached all-purpose flour
2 teaspoons baking powder
½ cup (1 stick) unsalted butter, melted and cooled
Confectioners' sugar for dusting (optional)

1. Preheat the oven to 375°F. Spray a 12-cavity madeleine pan with nonstick cooking spray.

2. In a large bowl, whisk together the eggs, granulated sugar, brown sugar, vanilla extract, and salt until well blended, about 1 minute.

3. Gently fold in the flour and baking powder with a rubber spatula until just incorporated. Fold in the cooled melted butter.

4. Use a large spoon or small ladle to fill the cavities of the pan ⅔ full. Bake until the madeleines are well risen and golden, 10 to 13 minutes. Remove the pan from the oven and immediately invert onto a wire rack to cool.

5. Serve warm or at room temperature, dusting with confectioners' sugar if desired just before serving. Madeleines are best eaten on the day they are baked.

A Good Excuse to Make Madeleines

Grownups may think of Proust, but little girls will think of another author, Ludwig Bemelmans, when they hear the word "madeleine." Make a batch of these cookies to celebrate his redheaded heroine, Madeline.

kourabiethes

Makes about
24 cookies

I was introduced to these buttery Greek almond cookies by my friend Peg Rosen, who received a batch as a gift from her friend Abigail Carter. Abby learned to make these as a child from an elderly neighbor, so her instructions were sketchy, but Peg helped me figure out specific ingredient quantities and baking times so they come out perfectly, like Abby's, every time.

1 cup (2 sticks) unsalted butter, softened
½ cup confectioners' sugar, plus more for dusting
1 large egg yolk
½ teaspoon baking powder
1 tablespoon brandy
2¼ cups unbleached all-purpose flour
¼ teaspoon salt
½ cup sliced almonds

1. Preheat the oven to 400°F. Line baking sheets with parchment paper.

2. Cream the butter and confectioners' sugar together in a large mixing bowl with an electric mixer on medium speed until fluffy, 2 to 3 minutes. Add the egg yolk and beat until smooth.

3. Place the baking powder in a small bowl and stir in the brandy until smooth. Stir the baking powder mixture into the butter mixture. Stir in the flour and salt until just combined. Stir in the sliced almonds.

4. Scoop up tablespoonfuls of the dough and, with wet hands, roll into 2-inch-long logs. Place each log on the lined baking sheets, shaping it into a crescent and leaving about 2 inches between each cookie.

5. Bake until the cookies are light golden, 13 to 15 minutes. Remove the baking sheets from the oven and place on a wire rack. Dust the hot cookies with confectioners' sugar and cool completely on the baking sheets. Kourabiethes will keep at room temperature in an airtight container for 2 to 3 days.

Kids Can Help

Kids who have had some experience with Play-Doh will be able to roll the dough into logs and shape the logs into crescents.

fregolata

Makes
16 cookies

I first made these cornmeal cookies from Treviso, Italy, in cooking school, and have made them countless times since. They are among my favorite cookies because they are simple to make, yet interesting and unusual. My teacher, the incredibly talented Nick Malgieri, has a special way with Italian cookies, and this recipe is based on his perfect version. Shortbread dough is used two ways—half of it is patted into a tart pan with a removable bottom to make a "crust," and the rest is crumbled on top to form crumbs. The giant baked cookie is then cut into wedges after it has cooled. Serve these as an after-school snack with milk or for dessert with fresh fruit and ice cream.

¾ **cup whole almonds**
½ **cup yellow cornmeal**
1½ **cups unbleached all-purpose flour**
¾ **cup plus 2 tablespoons sugar**
¼ **teaspoon salt**
1 **cup (2 sticks) unsalted butter, melted and cooled**

1. Preheat the oven to 350°F. Spray a 10-inch tart pan with a removable bottom with nonstick cooking spray.

2. Place the almonds in the bowl of a food processor fitted with a metal blade and pulse several times to grind. Take care not to overprocess the nuts. They should be dry, not oily.

3. Combine the ground nuts, cornmeal, flour, sugar, and salt in a large bowl and whisk to blend. Pour in the melted butter. Pick up handfuls of the mixture and rub between your palms until all the ingredients are moistened and the mixture resembles large crumbs.

4. Spoon three-fourths of the mixture into the prepared pan and pat it firmly into an even layer across the bottom of the pan. Scatter the rest of the crumbs over the top, leaving them loose.

5. Bake until the cookie is light golden, about 25 minutes. Transfer the tart pan to a wire rack and let the cookie cool completely in the pan. When cool, remove the sides of the pan and cut the cookie into 16 wedges. Fregolata will keep at room temperature in an airtight container for 3 to 4 days.

teething biscuits

Makes about
20 cookies

These plain, hard, wholesome cookies are great for soothing gum pain in teething babies and are also tasty enough to please big brothers and sisters.

1¾ cups unbleached all-purpose flour
¼ cup whole wheat flour
¼ cup firmly packed light brown sugar
1 teaspoon baking powder
¼ teaspoon salt
1 large egg
⅓ cup milk
2 tablespoons vegetable oil
½ teaspoon pure vanilla extract

1. Preheat the oven to 325°F. Line a baking sheet with parchment paper.

2. Combine the all-purpose flour, wheat flour, brown sugar, baking powder, and salt in a large mixing bowl. Add the egg, milk, vegetable oil, and vanilla extract and mix together with an electric mixer on low speed until just combined.

3. Turn the dough out onto a lightly floured work surface and shape into a flat log about 12 inches long and 2 inches wide. Place it on the lined baking sheet.

4. Bake until the log is firm to the touch, about 30 minutes. Remove from the oven and cool completely on the baking sheet.

5. Transfer the log to a cutting board and cut into ½-inch-thick slices. Lay the slices cut side down on the baking sheet and return them to the oven. Bake them until they are crisp, about 15 minutes. Transfer the sliced cookies to wire racks and let them cool completely. Teething Biscuits will keep at room temperature in an airtight container for 1 to 2 weeks.

Heirlooms of the Future

I've been baking cookies for my kids since they cut their first teeth, and I've included this teething biscuit recipe to prove it. Over the years, they've picked their own favorites from my ever-expanding repertoire of cookies, sometimes surprising me with their choices. Here are their all-time favorites, cookies I predict will achieve heirloom status in their minds. What will your cookie legacy be?

* Stained Glass Star Cookies (page 240): I make these every Christmas, and my girls look forward to them almost as much as they look forward to Santa's visit.

* Cocoa Meringue Cookies (page 91): These bake up soft and chewy on the inside with a light, crackly outer shell. My kids find the pure chocolate and sugar rush irresistible.

* Slice-and-Bake Chocolate Chippers (page 63): These are the cookies my kids ask for every day for their lunch boxes. I just slice a few and bake them when I wake up, so they're nice and fresh for school.

* Pantry Blondies (page 95): My daughter Eve has inherited my love for these bars that are a snap to make, since we always have the ingredients on hand.

jack's biscotti

This classic Italian recipe has been my husband's cookie specialty since he was a college student in Italy. If you are not going to dip them (a tradition in Italy), take them out of the oven on the early side, so that they are still a little yielding.

1 cup whole almonds with skins
2 cups unbleached all-purpose flour
1 cup sugar
½ teaspoon baking powder
Pinch of salt
3 large eggs
2 large egg yolks
1 teaspoon pure vanilla extract

1. Preheat the oven to 350°F.

2. Spread the almonds on a large baking sheet and toast them until fragrant, 6 to 8 minutes. Set them aside to cool. When they are cool, coarsely chop them. Line another large baking sheet with parchment paper.

3. Combine the flour, sugar, baking powder, and salt in a large mixing bowl. Add 2 of the whole eggs, the egg yolks, and vanilla extract and mix together with an electric mixer on low speed until just combined. Mix in the almonds.

4. Turn the dough out onto a lightly floured work surface and divide it in half. Shape each half into a flat log about 12 inches long and 2½ inches wide. Place the logs on the prepared baking sheet several inches apart.

5. Beat the remaining whole egg and brush it over the dough. Bake the logs until they are firm to the touch, about 35 minutes. Remove them from the oven and allow them to cool completely.

6. Reduce the oven temperature to 325°F. Transfer the logs to a cutting board and cut them into 1-inch-thick slices. Lay the slices cut side down on the baking sheet and return them to the oven. Bake until they are crisp, 9 to 12 minutes. Transfer sliced cookies to wire racks and let them cool completely. Jack's Biscotti will keep at room temperature in an airtight container for 2 to 3 weeks.

Biscotti by Any Other Name?

Cookies with a long shelf life have been baked in Europe since the thirteenth century, but they weren't always as sweet and easy to eat as Jack's Biscotti (above) or Teething Biscuits (page 187). Biscuits called hardtack, made with flour and oil, were a staple on sailing ships because they could last for months and even years in storage. Written accounts by sailors over the centuries confirm that they were indeed rock-hard and extremely difficult to chew. Anzac biscuits, the Australian cookies that became well known during World War I because they could last the two months it took to ship them overseas, are descendents of hardtack. Reportedly, they were so hard that soldiers preferred to grind them up and use them as porridge rather than attempt to bite into them.

mandelbrot

Makes about
36 cookies

These traditional German-Jewish cookies are made with almonds and baked twice, much like Italian biscotti. I personally prefer walnuts with the cinnamon-sugar topping, but any other nuts, including almonds, can be substituted. To make these pareve (neutral), use vegetable oil instead of butter.

1¼ cups sugar
½ teaspoon ground cinnamon
2½ cups unbleached all-purpose flour
2 teaspoons baking powder
½ teaspoon salt
5 large eggs
½ cup (1 stick) melted butter or ½ cup
    vegetable oil
1 teaspoon pure vanilla extract
1¼ cups coarsely chopped walnuts

1. Preheat the oven to 350°F. Line baking sheets with parchment paper. Combine ¼ cup sugar and the cinnamon in a small bowl; set aside.

2. Combine the flour, the remaining 1 cup sugar, the baking powder, and salt in a large mixing bowl. In a medium-size bowl, whisk together 4 of the eggs, the butter, and the vanilla extract until smooth. Add the egg mixture to the flour mixture and mix with an electric mixer on low speed until just combined. Mix in the walnuts.

3. Turn the dough out onto a lightly floured work surface and divide it in half. Shape each half into a flat log about 12 inches long and 2 inches wide. Place the logs on the lined baking sheets, several inches apart.

4. Beat the remaining egg and brush it over the dough. Sprinkle each log with the cinnamon-sugar mixture. Bake until the logs are light golden and have spread to about double in width, 25 to 30 minutes. Remove from the oven, place on a wire rack, and cool completely on the baking sheets.

5. Transfer the logs to a cutting board and cut them into ½-inch-thick slices. Lay the slices cut side down on the baking sheet and return them to the oven. Bake them until they are crisp, about 15 minutes longer. Transfer the sliced cookies to wire racks and let them cool completely. Mandelbrot will keep at room temperature in an airtight container for 3 to 4 days.

grandma rose's sour cream icebox cookies

Makes about
60 cookies

These were the first homemade cookies I ever tasted, and the memory of them has stayed with me to this day. In fact, every cousin in my large extended family has the same memory—of my great-grandmother arriving for a visit, toting these light, crisp wafers packed in a recycled Martinson's coffee tin. It wasn't until several years ago that I found the recipe, in my grandmother's handwriting, stuffed into one of my mother's recipe boxes. I was so thrilled to tinker with it and watch as my own children enjoyed the same cookies I had ecstatically gobbled as a child.

3 cups unbleached all-purpose flour
1 tablespoon baking powder
½ teaspoon salt
½ cup (1 stick) unsalted butter, softened
¾ cup plus 3 tablespoons sugar
2 large eggs
½ cup sour cream
1 teaspoon pure vanilla extract
½ teaspoon ground cinnamon

1. Combine the flour, baking powder, and salt in a medium-size mixing bowl.

2. Combine the butter and ¾ cup of the sugar in a large mixing bowl and cream together with an electric mixer on medium-high speed until fluffy, 2 to 3 minutes. Add the eggs, sour cream, and vanilla extract and beat until smooth. Stir in the flour mixture until just incorporated. Refrigerate the dough until firm, about 1 hour.

3. Divide the dough into 2 equal portions. Turn one portion onto a piece of waxed paper and shape it, rolling it inside the paper, into a log about 10 inches long and 2 inches in diameter. Repeat with the remaining dough. Wrap the dough in plastic wrap and freeze for at least 2 hours or up to 24 hours. (Dough logs may be wrapped tightly in plastic wrap and frozen for up to 1 month. Slice and bake directly from the freezer.)

4. Preheat the oven to 350°F. Combine the remaining 3 tablespoons sugar and the cinnamon in a small bowl.

5. Slice the dough into ⅛-inch-thick rounds, rotating the dough often so it doesn't become flattened as you cut. Place the cookies on ungreased baking sheets at least 2 inches apart. Sprinkle with the cinnamon-sugar mixture. Bake them until they are pale golden, 10 to 12 minutes. Let them stand on the baking sheet for 5 minutes, then remove them with a metal spatula to a wire rack to cool completely. Grandma Rose's Sour Cream Icebox Cookies will keep at room temperature in an airtight container for 2 to 3 days.

tom's granny's molasses cookies

**Makes
36 cookies**

My friend Tom Garcia, an excellent cook and baker, told me that his grandmother used to keep a glass jar of these cookies in the kitchen for the many kids in his big extended family. She always put a slice of white bread in the jar to keep the big batch fresh and moist. I've cut down the recipe to make a more manageable number of these spicy, old-fashioned cookies, so you probably won't have to take that precaution. They'll disappear before they dry out.

3 cups unbleached all-purpose flour
1 tablespoon ground cinnamon
1 tablespoon ground ginger
¼ teaspoon salt
½ cup buttermilk
1 teaspoon baking soda
½ teaspoon white vinegar
½ cup vegetable shortening
¾ cup firmly packed light brown sugar
⅔ cup molasses
1 large egg
2 tablespoons granulated sugar
1 teaspoon butter

1. Preheat the oven to 350°F. Line baking sheets with parchment paper or spray with nonstick cooking spray.

2. Combine the flour, cinnamon, ginger, and salt in a large bowl. Combine the buttermilk, baking soda, and vinegar in a glass measuring cup and stir to dissolve the baking soda.

3. Cream the vegetable shortening, brown sugar, and molasses together in a large mixing bowl with a wooden spoon until smooth. Add the egg and beat until smooth. Stir in half the flour mixture until just incorporated. Stir in the buttermilk mixture. Stir in the remaining flour mixture and beat until smooth, scraping down the sides of the bowl once or twice as necessary. Place the bowl in the refrigerator for 15 minutes (or up to 6 hours) to let the dough firm up.

4. Drop tablespoonfuls of dough onto the prepared baking sheets. Place the granulated sugar in a small bowl. Grease the bottom of a juice glass with the butter. Dip the buttered glass in the sugar. Press down on the cookies with the sugar-coated juice glass to flatten them and coat them with sugar, regreasing and redipping the glass in sugar as necessary.

5. Bake the cookies until they are just set, 10 to 12 minutes. Let the cookies stand on the baking sheet for 5 minutes, then remove them with a metal spatula to a wire rack to cool completely. Tom's Granny's Molasses Cookies will keep at room temperature in an airtight container for 2 to 3 days.

EDIBLE ART: rainy day and snow day cookies

There's nothing wrong with mixing and eating a
batch of chocolate chip cookies with your kids to forestall boredom when
it's raining or snowing out. But when you want to create a little more
excitement in the kitchen, you can turn to one of the recipes in this chapter,
which take cookie-dough fun to the next level. These cookie projects are
a lot like art projects for keeping kids busy when they can't go outside to
play. But in my opinion, they have distinct advantages over arts and crafts.
You can't eat a typical art project, for starters. And not only do cookies taste
better than collages and watercolor paintings, but they also don't collect
in giant piles on your counter for months until you must secretly stuff
them in the trash when your kids are not looking so that you can find your
way around the kitchen again.

The first few projects here use the dough from Rolled Sugar Cookies
(page 236), a marvelously versatile recipe. I show you how to decorate
sugar cookies with edible paint (page 196) and confectioners' sugar stencils (page 197), and how to rubber-stamp them with food coloring (page
198). The dough can also be cut into snowman or mitten shapes (pages
199 and 200), in keeping with the snow-day theme.

Giant cookies always delight. There are three versions here to play around
with. The Cookie Puzzle (page 201) will delight kids who like puzzles: Cut
up a large rectangle of cookie dough into puzzle pieces. Once they're baked,
you and your kids can frost and decorate them before putting the pieces
back together. Cookie Pizza (page 202) is always good for a laugh. My kids
choose candy decorations that make their pizza look as realistic as possible:
bright red royal icing for tomato sauce, green sprinkles for basil, slices of
black licorice ropes for olives. The Giant Chocolate Chip Cookie (page 203)
is a great canvas for a special message. It has sometimes supplemented or
even replaced the birthday cake at my older daughter's slumber parties. She
likes to write *Happy Birthday, Rose* herself with frosting.

Transforming cookie dough into flowers (page 204), kitty cats (page
206), or chocolate-flavored moose (page 207) is another option. My
personal favorite in this category are the tiny sugar cookie hamburger buns
sprinkled with sesame seeds and then sandwiched with a peppermint patty
burger and some dyed-green coconut "lettuce" (page 205). For small
children there's Peanut Butter Play-Doh (page 208), an eggless cookie
dough that they can safely snack on while they shape it.

Finally, there are some projects using store-bought cookies and other edible ingredients. They range in simplicity from Chocolate-Coated Pretzel Rods (page 210) that take just a few minutes to dip and decorate with sprinkles, to graham cracker gingerbread houses (page 212), which can take a whole day to construct and embellish.

Oh, and I almost forgot. There's one last recipe, a simple dough for making dog biscuits (page 213). If your kids love your dog as much as my kids love ours, then they'll want to make these treats when they're done making treats for themselves.

Rainy Day Cookie Parties

On rainy days when there's nothing else to do, let your kids invite a few friends over to make some fun cookies. Here are a few tips, learned the hard way, about avoiding total chaos while making cookies with a bunch of children.

* **Keep the guest list small.** Three or four kids is ideal. Six kids in the kitchen at once is living dangerously.
* **Pick an age-appropriate project.** Five-year-olds are going to have trouble putting together Chocolate Pretzel Jewelry Boxes by themselves, but will feel proud of their Chocolate Chip Kitty Cat faces. Nine-year-olds will be able to make beautifully painted cookies, but six-year-olds will be better at stamping them.
* **Be prepared.** Have your dough made, rolled, and cut and your frostings and decorations arranged in small bowls or paper cups before the kids come into the kitchen, so they can get right to the fun part.
* **Have other activities planned** for times when you are cleaning up and the cookies are baking. The fun ends when kids get impatient. Keep them busy with coloring, games, or a short video while they're waiting to eat the cookies.
* **Enjoy, but don't overdo it.** After the kids have tasted some of their cookies, pack up the rest for them to take home to share with their families.

painted cookies

Instead of decorating your sugar cookies after baking them, try using edible paint before you bake them. It's fun and easy and will keep the kids busy on a rainy day. Use paintbrushes reserved for this task, of course. Add the food coloring just a drop at a time and adjust your expectations to account for the color of the egg yolks. (Blue food coloring added to a yolk will produce a pretty green, for example, but it's difficult to get a true blue.) You can make as few or as many paints as you like. I find that four allows for creativity without creating too much mess.

1 recipe dough from Rolled Sugar
   Cookies (page 236), chilled
4 egg yolks
4 teaspoons water
4 shades of liquid food coloring

1. Preheat the oven to 375°F. Line baking sheets with parchment paper.

2. Remove the dough from the refrigerator and knead it 4 or 5 times on a lightly floured work surface to soften it. With a lightly floured rolling pin, roll out the dough ⅛ inch thick. Cut out desired shapes with cookie cutters. Place the cut-out cookies on the lined baking sheets.

3. Place each egg yolk in a separate small bowl. Add a teaspoon of water and a drop of a different shade of food coloring to each and mix to blend. Add another drop of food coloring to each bowl if necessary to achieve the desired color.

4. Use 4 different small, soft artist's paintbrushes to paint the cut-out cookies any way you like.

5. Bake the cookies until they are firm and golden around the edges, about 8 minutes. Slide the entire parchment sheet with the cookies onto wire racks and let the cookies cool completely. Painted Cookies will keep at room temperature in an airtight container for up to 3 days.

stenciled cookies

Makes about
40 cookies

Decorating sugar cookies this way is easy, and it's also a fun way to customize them for any occasion. While your cookie dough is in the refrigerator, you and your children can brainstorm some shapes you'd like to see on top of your cookies—letters and numbers, simple flowers, hearts. (We often use small cookie cutters to trace pumpkins, shamrocks, leaves, and other simple outlines.) Use a large round cutter, at least 3 inches across, to cut the dough, so that you have enough room for a nice-size stencil. For each ¼ cup of confectioners' sugar, you'll need ½ teaspoon of powdered food coloring. For a whole batch of cookies, you'll probably want to mix up more than one color of sugar for decorating, especially if you are using more than one stencil.

1 recipe dough from Rolled Sugar Cookies (page 236), chilled
¼ cup confectioners' sugar per color
½ teaspoon powdered food coloring per color

1. Cut out several 5-inch-square pieces of heavy paper or oaktag. Sketch or trace shapes measuring no more than 2 or 3 inches across onto the paper and cut the shapes out. What's left after you cut the shapes out are your stencils.

2. Combine the confectioners' sugar and powdered food coloring in separate small bowls, making as many different colors as you like.

3. Preheat the oven to 375°F. Line baking sheets with parchment paper.

4. Remove the dough from the refrigerator and knead it 4 or 5 times on a lightly floured work surface to soften it. With a lightly floured rolling pin, roll out the dough ⅛ inch thick. Cut the cookie dough into 3- or 4-inch rounds. Place the cut-out cookies on the lined baking sheets.

5. Place a stencil on top of a cookie. Place a small strainer several inches above the cookie and spoon some of the colored sugar into the strainer. Gently shake the strainer to cover the area of the cookie exposed by the stencil. Set aside the strainer, carefully remove the stencil, and pour the remaining sugar in the strainer back into the bowl.

6. Repeat with the remaining cookies, using different stencils and different colored sugars as desired. When you're done stenciling, place the baking sheets in the refrigerator for 15 minutes.

7. Bake the cookies, one sheet at a time, until they are firm and golden around the edges, 8 to 10 minutes. Slide the entire parchment sheet with the cookies onto wire racks and let the cookies cool completely. Stenciled Cookies will keep at room temperature in an airtight container for up to 3 days.

color-stamped cookies

Makes about
80 small cookies
or 40 larger ones

This is an especially fun project for very small children, who can get frustrated with painting and other types of fine decorating but are capable of using a rubber stamp inked with food coloring. Craft stores have an amazing selection of rubber stamps that can be put to use in the kitchen. Buy a few and dedicate them to cookie projects. (Keep them separate from the rubber stamps you use with ink!) If your kids are small, you should apply the food coloring yourself with a small paintbrush and just let them stamp—this step can get messy with little ones. The colors are vivid, since the food coloring is not diluted. I like to stamp scalloped circles with my kids' initials and then sprinkle the cookies with colored fine sanding sugar, for serving at birthday parties and other special occasions.

1 recipe dough from Rolled Sugar Cookies (page 236), chilled
Liquid, paste, or gel food coloring

1. Preheat the oven to 375°F. Line baking sheets with parchment paper.

2. Remove the dough from the refrigerator and knead it 4 or 5 times on a lightly floured work surface to soften it. With a lightly floured rolling pin, roll out the dough ⅛ inch thick. Cut out desired shapes with cookie cutters. Place the cutout cookies on the lined baking sheets.

3. Use a clean, dry, small paintbrush to coat the raised part of a clean rubber stamp with a thick layer of food coloring. Stamp the unbaked cookies, reapplying the food coloring to the rubber stamp as necessary.

4. Bake the cookies until they are firm and golden around the edges, about 8 minutes. Slide the entire parchment sheets with the cookies onto wire racks and let the cookies cool completely. Color-Stamped Cookies will keep at room temperature in an airtight container for up to 3 days.

snow day snowmen

Makes about twenty 4-inch snowmen

Here's a fun project for a snowy day. Make the dough, refrigerate it while you build a real snowman, and then come back in and warm up by baking snowman-shaped cookies and showering them with fluffy coconut. For Abominable Snowmen, use a large gingerbread man cutter.

1 recipe dough from Rolled Sugar
Cookies (page 236), chilled
8 ounces white chocolate, finely
chopped
2 tablespoons vegetable oil or canola oil
1 tablespoon corn syrup
2 cups sweetened flaked coconut

1. Preheat the oven to 375°F. Line baking sheets with parchment paper.

2. Remove the dough from the refrigerator and knead it 4 or 5 times on a lightly floured work surface to soften it. With a lightly floured rolling pin, roll out the dough ⅛ inch thick. Cut out cookies using a snowman-shaped cutter. Place the cut-out cookies on the lined baking sheets.

3. Bake the cookies until they are firm and golden around the edges, about 8 minutes. Slide the entire parchment sheet with the cookies onto wire racks and let the cookies cool completely.

4. Put 1 inch of water in the bottom of a double boiler or medium-size saucepan and bring to a bare simmer. Combine the chocolate, vegetable oil, and corn syrup in the top of the double boiler or in a stainless-steel bowl set on top of the simmering water, making sure that the water doesn't touch the bottom of the bowl. Heat, whisking occasionally, until the chocolate is completely melted and blended with the oil and syrup.

5. Use a small offset spatula to spread some chocolate glaze over each cookie. Place the glazed cookies on rimmed baking sheets and heavily cover them with the coconut. Let the glaze harden, about 2 hours. Snow Day Snowmen will keep at room temperature in an airtight container for 3 to 4 days. Separate them with layers of waxed paper to prevent sticking.

snow day cookie mittens

Instead of using a cookie cutter, trace your child's hand (or hands if you want to make pairs of mittens) on a piece of cardboard to use as a template for these mitten-shaped cookies. Then decorate them with stripes of icing to look like real mittens. The yield above is approximate—the actual yield will depend on the size of your child's hand.

1 recipe dough from Rolled Sugar Cookies (page 236), chilled
1 recipe Royal Icing (page 237)
Food colorings of your choice
Sprinkles, sanding sugar, and/or other sugar decors

1. Have your child place his or her hand on a piece of heavy cardboard, four fingers together and thumb sticking out, and draw around it to make a mitten shape. Cut out the mitten with scissors.

2. Preheat the oven to 375°F. Line baking sheets with parchment paper.

3. Remove the dough from the refrigerator and knead it 4 or 5 times on a lightly floured work surface to soften it. With a lightly floured rolling pin, roll out the dough ⅛ inch thick. Place the cardboard mitten on top of the dough and use a sharp paring knife to cut out the mitten shapes. Place the cut-out cookies on the lined baking sheets.

4. Bake the cookies until they are firm and golden around the edges, about 8 minutes. Slide the entire parchment sheet with the cookies onto wire racks and let the cookies cool completely.

5. Divide the icing into several smaller bowls and stir in food colorings to color. Spread the icing on the cookies and decorate with sprinkles, sanding sugar, and/or other sugar decors as desired. Snow Day Cookie Mittens will keep at room temperature in an airtight container for 3 to 4 days. Separate them with layers of waxed paper to prevent sticking.

cookie puzzle

Makes 1 large puzzle, with 6 to 8 cookie pieces

This is a fun project to make and to eat. You roll cookie dough into a rectangle and cut it into uneven shapes. After you bake and cool the puzzle, you can decorate the individual pieces and put the puzzle back together to serve. Don't refrigerate the dough after you mix it. Freshly mixed dough is easier to roll into a large sheet.

½ recipe dough from Rolled Sugar Cookies (page 236), freshly mixed and not refrigerated
½ recipe Royal Icing (page 237)
Food coloring (optional)
Sprinkles and/or colored sugar (optional)

1. Preheat the oven to 375°F.

2. Lightly flour a piece of parchment paper. With a lightly floured rolling pin, roll the dough into a rectangle measuring about 9 inches x 12 inches. Trim with a sharp paring knife so that it is an exact 8 x 10-inch rectangle.

3. Use a sharp paring knife to cut the rectangle into 6 or 8 abstract puzzle pieces and gently move the pieces at least ½ inch away from each other on the parchment. Slide the cookie pieces, still on the parchment, onto a rimless baking sheet. Bake until the edges have begun to turn golden, 9 to 12 minutes. Remove from the oven, slide the cookie pieces, still on the parchment, onto a wire rack, and cool completely.

4. Divide the icing into separate bowls and color with food coloring, if you are using it. Spread each cookie shape with frosting, not quite to the edges. Sprinkle the pieces with sprinkles or colored sugar, if you are using it. Before serving, reassemble the puzzle on a platter. Leftovers will keep at room temperature in an airtight container for 3 to 4 days.

cookie pizza

Makes 1 pizza
to serve 8 to 10

No matter how many times we make a cookie pizza at my house, we always wind up laughing as we decorate it. It's entertaining in the extreme to come up with sweet versions of typical pizza garnishes. Have your decorations ready to go before you spread the "sauce" on the pizza, because the icing will harden quickly.

1 cup unbleached all-purpose flour
½ teaspoon baking powder
¼ teaspoon salt
½ cup (1 stick) unsalted butter, softened
¼ cup granulated sugar
¼ cup firmly packed light brown sugar
1 large egg
1 teaspoon pure vanilla extract
1 cup Royal Icing (page 237)
Red food coloring
Candy "toppings" (see box below)

1. Preheat the oven to 375°F. Spray the bottom and sides of a 9-inch springform pan with nonstick cooking spray.

2. Combine the flour, baking powder, and salt in a small bowl. Cream the butter, granulated sugar, and brown sugar together in a large mixing bowl with an electric mixer until smooth. Add the egg and vanilla extract and beat until smooth. Stir in the flour mixture until a dough forms.

3. Turn the dough out into the springform pan and, with wet hands, press it into an even layer on the bottom of the pan. Bake until golden, 12 to 14 minutes. Remove from the oven onto a wire rack, and cool completely in the pan.

4. Release the cookie from the sides of the springform pan. Place ½ cup of the royal icing in a small bowl and stir in several drops of red food coloring. Spread the "tomato sauce" over the cooled cookie, leaving a 1-inch border unfrosted for the "crust." Place the remaining ½ cup white icing in a pastry bag fitted with a small plain tip, or in a small zipper-lock plastic bag with a small hole cut into one corner. Squirt the white icing over the red icing to look like melted cheese.

5. Working quickly before the icing hardens, arrange the candy toppings on top of the pizza. Let the icing dry before cutting into 8 or 10 wedges. Cookie Pizza will keep, wrapped in plastic wrap at room temperature, for 2 to 3 days.

Cookie Pizza Toppings

Choose from the following to garnish your cookie pizza:

* Olives: black licorice ropes sliced into ¼-inch-thick circles
* Anchovies: Swedish fish
* Pepperoni: circles of red fruit leather
* Peppers: strips of green fruit leather
* Parsley or basil: green sprinkles

giant chocolate chip cookie

Makes 1 large cookie to serve 12 to 14

One giant chocolate chip cookie just begs to be decorated with frosting and sprinkles. It's a great medium for any message: *Get Well, Congratulations, Happy Pre-K Graduation.* I've even made this for a birthday party when one of my children had taken a temporary dislike to cake. You can make your own royal icing or frosting for decorating this, or just buy some tubes of ready-made icing at the store.

1 cup unbleached all-purpose flour
½ teaspoon baking soda
½ teaspoon salt
6 tablespoons unsalted butter, melted and cooled slightly
½ cup granulated sugar
¼ cup firmly packed light brown sugar
1 large egg
1 teaspoon pure vanilla extract
1 cup semisweet mini chocolate chips
1 cup Royal Icing (page 237), tinted any color you like, or 2 tubes of store-bought icing
Sprinkles or nonpareils

1. Preheat the oven to 350°F. Line a 10-inch round cake pan with heavy-duty aluminum foil, making sure that the foil is tucked along all the edges of the pan and that there is at least 1 inch overhanging the top of the pan on all sides.

2. Combine the flour, baking soda, and salt in a medium-size mixing bowl. Cream the cooled melted butter, granulated sugar, and brown sugar together in a large mixing bowl with a wooden spoon until smooth. Add the egg and vanilla extract and beat until smooth. Stir in the flour mixture until just incorporated. Stir in the chocolate chips.

3. Use a small offset spatula to spread the dough in an even layer on the bottom of the pan. Bake until the cookie is golden around the edges and just firm in the center, 15 to 18 minutes. Remove the pan to a wire rack and let the cookie cool completely.

4. Carefully lift the foil containing the cookie from the pan. Peel the foil off the cookie and transfer the cookie to a serving platter. Decorate with frosting and sprinkles as desired. Cut into wedges and serve. Leftovers will keep at room temperature in an airtight container for up to 2 days.

sugar cookie flowers

When April showers keep you indoors, mix a batch of sugar cookie dough, color it in pretty springtime hues, and shape it into flower cookies. Spring is on the way.

2 cups unbleached all-purpose flour
1 teaspoon baking powder
½ teaspoon salt
1 cup (2 sticks) unsalted butter, softened
1 cup granulated sugar
2 large eggs
1½ teaspoons pure vanilla extract
Pink and blue food coloring (or other colors of your choice)
Pink and blue sanding sugars (or other colors of your choice)

1. Preheat the oven to 375°F. Line baking sheets with parchment paper.

2. Combine the flour, baking powder, and salt in a small bowl. Cream the butter and sugar together in a large mixing bowl with an electric mixer until smooth. Add the eggs and vanilla extract and beat until smooth. Beat in the flour mixture until a dough forms.

3. Divide the dough equally between 2 bowls. Stir a few drops of food coloring into each portion of dough until uniformly colored.

4. To make flowers, measure out level ½ teaspoonfuls of dough and roll into balls. Roll the pink balls in pink sugar and the blue balls in blue sugar. Place a ball of one color on a prepared baking sheet and arrange 6 balls in the other color around it. Repeat with the remaining dough so that you have about 10 flowers with pink petals and blue centers, and 10 flowers with blue petals and pink centers.

5. Bake until the edges of the cookies are just golden, 10 to 12 minutes. Slide the entire parchment sheet with the cookies onto a wire rack and let the cookies cool completely. Sugar Cookie Flowers will keep at room temperature in an airtight container for 2 to 3 days.

hamburger cookies

Puffy little sugar cookies make perfect buns for peppermint patty "hamburgers." Although there are several steps, these really aren't that complicated, and kids will love to help make the condiments and assemble the burgers.

For the buns
1 cup unbleached all-purpose flour
½ teaspoon baking powder
¼ teaspoon salt
½ cup (1 stick) unsalted butter, softened
¼ cup granulated sugar
¼ cup firmly packed light brown sugar
1 large egg
1 teaspoon pure vanilla extract
1 tablespoon sesame seeds

For the ketchup and special sauce
3 tablespoons unsalted butter
¾ cup confectioners' sugar
Red food coloring

For the lettuce
6 tablespoons sweetened flaked coconut
Green food coloring

24 mini peppermint patties

1. Preheat the oven to 375°F. Line baking sheets with parchment paper.

2. Make the buns: Combine the flour, baking powder, and salt in a small bowl. Cream the butter, granulated sugar, and brown sugar together in a large mixing bowl with an electric mixer until smooth. Add the egg and vanilla extract and beat until smooth. Beat in the flour mixture until a dough forms.

3. Measure out level teaspoonfuls of dough and roll into balls. Place the balls on the prepared baking sheets, 2 inches apart. Sprinkle half of the dough balls with sesame seeds. Bake until the edges of the cookies are just golden, about 5 minutes. Slide the entire parchment sheet with the cookies onto wire racks and let the cookies cool completely.

4. Make the ketchup and special sauce: Combine the butter and confectioners' sugar in a small bowl and stir with a spoon until smooth. Place half of the mixture in another small bowl and stir in some red food coloring to make ketchup.

5. Make the lettuce: Combine the coconut and green food coloring in a small bowl and stir until the coconut is green.

6. To assemble the burgers: Arrange the cookies without sesame seeds flat sides up. Dab a little "ketchup" on each cookie, sprinkle with "lettuce," and place a peppermint patty on top. Spread a little "special sauce" on the flat sides of the sesame seed cookies and place them, frosting side down, on top of the peppermint patties. Hamburger Cookies will keep in an airtight container at room temperature for 1 to 2 days.

chocolate chip kitty cats

Younger kids especially will love to transform rounds of chocolate chip cookie dough into little calico cat faces.

1 cup unbleached all-purpose flour
¼ teaspoon baking powder
¼ teaspoon salt
5 tablespoons unsalted butter, softened
¼ cup firmly packed light brown sugar
2 tablespoons granulated sugar
1 large egg
½ teaspoon pure vanilla extract
1 cup semisweet chocolate chips
48 pecan halves
72 plain M&M's
Ninety-six 2½-inch thin pretzel sticks

1. Combine the flour, baking powder, and salt in a medium-size mixing bowl.

2. Combine the butter, brown sugar, and granulated sugar in a large mixing bowl and cream together with an electric mixer on medium-high speed until fluffy, 2 to 3 minutes. Add the egg and vanilla extract and beat until smooth. Stir in the flour mixture until just incorporated. Stir in the chocolate chips.

3. Turn the dough onto a piece of waxed paper and shape it, rolling it inside the paper, into a log about 8 inches long and 2 inches in diameter. Wrap the dough in plastic wrap and refrigerate it for at least 2 hours or up to 24 hours. (The dough log may be wrapped tightly in plastic wrap and frozen for up to 1 month. Slice and bake directly from the freezer.)

4. Preheat the oven to 350°F. Slice the dough into ⅓-inch-thick rounds, rotating the dough often so it doesn't become flattened as you cut. Place the cookies on ungreased baking sheets 3 inches apart.

5. For ears, press 2 pecan halves onto the top of each cookie, hanging over the edge of the cookie. Press 3 M&M's into each cookie for the eyes and nose. For whiskers, place 2 pretzel sticks on each side of the nose, pressing them in slightly.

6. Bake the cookies until they are pale golden around the edges but still soft on top, 13 to 15 minutes (a minute or two longer for frozen dough). Let them stand on the baking sheet for 5 minutes, then remove them with a metal spatula to a wire rack to cool completely. Chocolate Chip Kitty Cats will keep at room temperature in an airtight container for 2 to 3 days.

chocolate moose cookies

Makes
32 cookies

These moose-shaped chocolate cookies have pretzel-twist antlers and M&M eyes. To change them into reindeer for Christmas, use red M&M's for noses. For the most realistic-looking moose heads, round out the corners of the dough triangles with your fingertip and pinch the triangle slightly an inch or so above the tip. For super-chocolatey moose, you can dip their antlers into melted white or dark chocolate once the cookies have cooled. Let the chocolate-dipped cookies stand on parchment paper until the chocolate is set, about 2 hours.

3¼ cups unbleached all-purpose flour
⅓ cup unsweetened natural cocoa
powder
2 teaspoons cream of tartar
1 teaspoon baking soda
¼ teaspoon salt
1 cup (2 sticks) unsalted butter,
softened
1½ cups sugar
3 large eggs
1 teaspoon pure vanilla extract
64 mini pretzel twists
96 peanut M&M's

1. Combine the flour, cocoa powder, cream of tartar, baking soda, and salt in a small bowl. Cream the butter and sugar together in a large mixing bowl with an electric mixer. Add the eggs and vanilla extract and beat until smooth. Stir in the flour mixture until a dough forms.

2. Divide the dough into 4 equal balls, wrap each tightly in plastic wrap, and refrigerate until firm, at least 2 hours and up to 1 day. (The dough can be frozen for up to 1 month; defrost it in the refrigerator before use.)

3. Preheat the oven to 375°F. Line a baking sheet with parchment paper.

4. Remove one ball from the refrigerator and knead it 4 or 5 times on a lightly floured work surface to soften it. With a lightly floured rolling pin, roll out the dough into an 8-inch circle. Use a cake pan or plate to trim it so that it is perfectly round. Cut the circle into 8 wedges.

5. Place each wedge on the lined baking sheet at least 2 inches apart. Pinch it slightly a little bit below the center to create the snout. Round out each corner of the triangle with the tip of your finger. Lightly press a pretzel twist into each of the upper corners for antlers. Press 2 M&M's into the triangle for eyes. Press another M&M into the triangle about 1 inch from the point for a nose.

6. Bake the cookies until the edges are just firm, 8 to 10 minutes. Slide the entire parchment sheet with the cookies onto a wire rack and let the cookies cool completely. Repeat with the remaining dough balls. Chocolate Moose Cookies will keep at room temperature in an airtight container for up to 3 days.

peanut butter play-doh

This is a great no-bake recipe for preschoolers and kindergartners, who love to play with and eat cookie dough. Have them shape and sculpt it as they would real Play-Doh, and then let them decorate their sculptures with chocolate-covered raisins, M&M's, little jelly beans, or whatever else their hearts desire. It's entirely safe to eat raw (assuming no one is allergic to milk or peanut butter!), since there are no eggs in the dough. Be sure to use regular commercial peanut butter here, not natural.

1⅓ to 1½ cups powdered milk
½ cup creamy peanut butter
½ cup honey
M&M's, chocolate-covered peanuts or raisins, or small jelly beans for decorating

1. Combine 1⅓ cups of the powdered milk, the peanut butter, and honey in the bowl of an electric mixer and mix on medium-low until smooth.

2. Pinch off a piece of the dough and test it by playing with it. If it is too sticky to form a sturdy shape, stir in more powdered milk, teaspoon by teaspoon, until it is the consistency of real Play-Doh. Mold and decorate with M&M's, chocolate-covered peanuts or raisins, and/or small jelly beans, as desired. Peanut Butter Play-Doh will keep, wrapped in plastic wrap and refrigerated, for up to 1 week.

cookie pretzels

Makes 16 cookies Twisting chocolate cookie dough into pretzel shapes makes for a fun way to spend time together in the kitchen. Coarse sanding sugar—white or in any color you like—makes pretty "salt."

2¼ cups unbleached all-purpose flour
1 teaspoon baking powder
¼ teaspoon salt
6 tablespoons unsalted butter, softened
½ cup granulated sugar
2 eggs
1 teaspoon pure vanilla extract
2 ounces semisweet or bittersweet chocolate, melted and cooled
½ cup coarse sanding sugar

1. Combine the flour, baking powder, and salt in a small bowl. Cream the butter and sugar together in a large mixing bowl with an electric mixer until smooth. Add the eggs and vanilla extract and beat until smooth. Add the chocolate and stir until incorporated. Cover the bowl tightly with plastic wrap and refrigerate the dough until firm, at least 2 hours and up to 1 day.

2. Preheat the oven to 375°F. Line baking sheets with parchment paper. Pour the sanding sugar onto a rimmed baking sheet.

3. Scrape the dough onto a lightly floured work surface and divide it into 4 equal portions. Lightly drape 3 portions in plastic wrap. Divide the fourth portion into 4 equal pieces. Roll each piece into a 9-inch rope. Gently roll the rope in the sanding sugar so it is well coated. Transfer the rope to a lined baking sheet and twist into a pretzel shape by crossing the left side of the strip to the middle, forming a loop, and then folding the right side up and over the first loop. Repeat with the remaining 3 ropes, placing the pretzels 2 inches apart on the baking sheets.

4. Repeat with the remaining dough portions until all of the pretzels have been shaped. (Pretzels may be placed next to each other on parchment paper–lined baking sheets, frozen, transferred to zipper-lock plastic freezer bags, and stored in the freezer for up to 1 month. Frozen cookies may be placed in the oven directly from the freezer and baked as directed.)

5. Bake until firm, 11 to 13 minutes (a minute or two longer for frozen dough). Transfer to a wire rack to cool completely. Cookie Pretzels will keep at room temperature in an airtight container for 2 to 3 days.

chocolate-coated pretzel rods

Makes 12 rods

This isn't really a cookie project, but it's close enough. Dipping pretzel rods into chocolate and decorating them with sprinkles is lots of fun and easy for even little kids to do.

8 ounces semisweet, milk, or white chocolate
1 teaspoon vegetable oil
6 tablespoons nonpareils or sprinkles
16 pretzel rods

1. Put 1 inch of water in the bottom of a double boiler or medium-size saucepan and bring to a bare simmer. Place the chopped chocolate and oil in the top of the double boiler or in a stainless-steel bowl set on top of the simmering water, making sure that the water doesn't touch the bottom of the bowl. Heat, whisking occasionally, until the chocolate is completely melted. Remove from the heat.

2. Line a baking sheet with parchment or waxed paper. Place the nonpareils or sprinkles in a shallow bowl. Working over the bowl, smooth the chocolate over three-fourths of one of the pretzel rods, scraping the excess back into the bowl. Sprinkle the nonpareils lightly over the chocolate. Set the pretzel rod on the prepared baking sheet and repeat with the remaining pretzel rods.

3. Refrigerate until the chocolate is firm, about 30 minutes. Chocolate-Coated Pretzel Rods will keep at room temperature in an airtight container for up to 1 week.

chocolate marshmallow cookies

Makes 12 cookies

Packaged chocolate marshmallow cookies never taste as good as they look. These sort-of-homemade approximations do. So make a batch with your kids when you are looking for a no-bake cookie project for a rainy day. Chocoholics can substitute chocolate wafer cookies for the wheatmeal biscuits.

12 Carr's Wheatmeal Biscuits
1½ cups Marshmallow Fluff
8 ounces best-quality bittersweet chocolate, finely chopped
2 tablespoons vegetable oil

1. Place the biscuits on a wire rack set over a rimmed baking sheet. Top each biscuit with a rounded heaping tablespoonful of Marshmallow Fluff. Place the baking sheet in the freezer for 10 minutes to allow the marshmallow to firm up.

2. Combine the chocolate and oil in a microwave-safe bowl. Melt the chocolate in the microwave, taking care not to let it burn. Stir until smooth.

3. Spoon some chocolate over each biscuit to coat the biscuit and marshmallow completely. Return the baking sheet to the freezer for another 10 minutes, until the chocolate is set. Refrigerate for up to 6 hours, until ready to serve. Chocolate Marshmallow Cookies are best eaten on the day they are made.

chocolate pretzel jewelry boxes

Makes 3 small boxes Fill these fun-to-make boxes with jelly bean or other candy "jewels." The recipe can easily be doubled for larger groups of kids.

4 ounces semisweet chocolate, finely chopped
½ teaspoon vegetable oil
6 cups thin pretzel sticks
3 large jelly beans, plus more for filling the boxes

1. Put 1 inch of water in the bottom of a double boiler or medium-size saucepan and bring to a bare simmer. Place the chopped chocolate and oil in the top of the double boiler or in a stainless-steel bowl set on top of the simmering water, making sure that the water doesn't touch the bottom of the bowl. Heat, whisking occasionally, until the chocolate is completely melted. Remove from the heat and let cool to lukewarm.

2. Line a rimmed baking sheet with parchment or waxed paper. Dip the ends of a pretzel in the chocolate and place on the parchment. Repeat, placing about 12 pretzels side by side, glued together with chocolate, to create a square base for each box. Repeat to form the cover for your box. Dip a large jelly bean or other large round hard candy halfway into the chocolate and place in the center of your box top (this will be the knob).

3. Build the sides of each box by dipping the ends of the pretzels into the chocolate and stacking them first on 2 parallel sides of the box bottom and then on the other 2 parallel sides of the box bottom, repeating until your box is a couple of inches tall (this will take about 5 or 6 pretzels on each side).

4. Place the baking sheet in the refrigerator until the chocolate is set, about 2 hours. Carefully peel the boxes from the parchment paper. Fill with jelly beans. Carefully peel the box tops from the parchment paper and set them on top of the boxes. Chocolate Pretzel Jewelry Boxes will keep, wrapped in plastic wrap at room temperature, for up to 3 days.

graham cracker cookie house

Makes 1 house I make these for every occasion (I even did a red, white, and blue one decorated with red licorice bits, starlight mints, and blue jelly beans for Memorial Day weekend) and for no reason at all. Of course, Christmas is a natural, especially if you don't want to commit to a real gingerbread house. (If you do, see page 244.) Save your leftover Halloween candy for decorating this, and get together enough supplies so that each of your kids can make a house. If you are very brave, you can even do this project with a small group at a birthday or holiday party. For younger children, you might want to assemble the houses ahead of time and just let them decorate.

1 recipe Royal Icing (page 237)
7 whole graham crackers, plus a few
    extras in case of breakage
Candy decorations, such as
    peppermints, jelly beans, gummy
    bears, Life Savers, gumdrops,
    M&M's, and Smarties

1. Scrape the icing into a pastry bag fitted with a small, plain tip. Squeeze a small dollop of icing (about the size of a quarter) onto the bottom of one of the whole graham crackers and place the graham cracker, icing side down, on an 8- or 9-inch round cardboard cake circle.

2. Snap one of the graham crackers in half. Pipe a thin line of icing all around the edge of the graham cracker sitting on the cardboard. Position one of the graham cracker halves upright along a short edge and one of the whole graham crackers upright along a long edge to form two walls. Repeat with one whole graham cracker and one graham cracker half so that your house now has 4 walls. Place juice glasses against each of the walls to hold them in position. Let stand for 15 minutes to let the icing set.

3. For the roof, pipe a thin line of icing along the long edges of two whole graham crackers and place them on top of the house so that the bottom edges run along the long walls and the top edges meet at a point. Let stand another 15 minutes.

4. Snap the remaining graham cracker in half and use a sharp serrated knife to trim each half into a triangle with three equal sides. Pipe a thin line of icing along the edges of each triangle and insert into the spaces at each end of the house. Let stand another 15 minutes to dry.

5. Decorate your house as desired, affixing the candy decorations of your choice with the remaining icing.

homemade dog biscuits

Makes about twenty 3-inch dog bones

My daughter Eve loves to pamper our pet with special treats, so I developed this recipe just for her and Trixie, our faithful and patient bichon frise.

2 cups whole wheat flour
½ cup yellow cornmeal
6 tablespoons vegetable oil
1 cup chicken or beef broth

1. Preheat the oven to 350°F. Line a baking sheet with parchment paper.

2. Combine the flour and cornmeal in a large mixing bowl. Add the oil and broth and stir until the mixture is crumbly and comes together when you squeeze some in your hand.

3. Turn the mixture out onto a lightly floured work surface and knead until it becomes a stiff dough. With a lightly floured rolling pin, roll out the dough to a ½-inch thickness. Use a bone-shaped cookie cutter to cut the dough. Place the biscuits on the prepared baking sheet. Reroll the scraps and cut more biscuits until you have used all the dough.

4. Bake the biscuits until they are golden and firm, 20 to 25 minutes. Place the baking sheets on wire racks and cool completely on the baking sheets. Homemade Dog Biscuits will keep at room temperature in an airtight container for up to 2 weeks.

celebrating with cookies: RECIPES FOR HOLIDAYS throughout the year

ON PLATE, CLOCKWISE FROM TOP LEFT: Red, White, and Blue Sables; Stained Glass Star Cookies; Hamantaschen

I don't need an excuse to bake, although I try to
have some good ones ready for my husband when I walk in the door with
10 pounds of butter, 20 pounds of flour, and 20 pounds of sugar from the
local warehouse club. For me, there's no occasion too small—the dog's
birthday, the third day of school, the beginning of the new television
season—for dedicating a batch of freshly baked cookies. So when a real
holiday rolls around, I will without question be in the kitchen, baking
some cookies in observance.

The fact is, although I love everyday cookies, I love holiday cookies even
more. Holiday cookies are not only sweet and delicious, but they also help
bring families and friends together in celebration. They provide a sense of
tradition and a feeling of security, year in and year out. This chapter contains
recipes that I reserve for holidays. They are special because they are designed
specifically to celebrate a certain day. I wouldn't make Valentine's Day Linzer
Hearts (page 221) on Halloween, and I wouldn't make Double Chocolate
Mummy Cookies (page 232) on Presidents' Day. When there's a holiday
coming up on the calendar, my kids have learned to anticipate a particular
treat. Thanksgiving is next week? Then they know they'll be eating Thanksgiving Maple Leaves (page 233). Ten more shopping days till Christmas?
They can find me in the kitchen mixing dough for Stained Glass Star Cookies
(page 240). Baking holiday cookies not just in December but throughout
the year fosters a joyful attitude toward everyday life. There's always another
holiday celebration around the bend, another sweet treat to look forward
to, another way to enjoy each others' company as we talk about what Easter
or Passover or Chinese New Year or Mardi Gras means.

I hope you'll use some of the following recipes to mark special days
throughout the year, or choose your own favorites and dedicate them to
certain days, creating your own family traditions in the process.

deep-fried new year's cookies

Makes about
18 puffed cookies

Deep-fried balls of dough rolled in cinnamon sugar are a New Year's Day tradition in many parts of Italy. Serve these doughnut-like treats for breakfast—that is, if your kids won't be sleeping late on New Year's Day. They also make a festive dessert.

½ cup plus 1 tablespoon sugar
1 teaspoon ground cinnamon
1 cup warm water (105° to 110°F)
1 package (2¼ teaspoons) active dry yeast
1½ cups unbleached all-purpose flour
½ teaspoon salt
4 cups vegetable oil or canola oil for frying

1. Combine ½ cup of the sugar and the cinnamon in a small bowl and set aside. Pour the warm water into a large mixing bowl and sprinkle with the yeast. Let stand 5 minutes to dissolve. Stir in the flour, salt, and remaining 1 tablespoon sugar until a very wet dough forms. Cover the bowl with plastic wrap and let it rise at room temperature until it has puffed up and doubled in size, 45 minutes to 1 hour.

2. Heat the oil in a large, deep pot to 365°F. Dip a soup spoon into the hot oil and then use the oil-coated spoon to scoop up a heaping spoonful of dough. Use another soup spoon to scrape the dough into the pot. Repeat with as many spoonfuls as will fit comfortably in the pot without touching each other. Fry, turning once, until the cookies are golden, 1 to 1½ minutes. Remove with a slotted spoon and let drain on a paper towel–lined rimmed baking sheet.

3. Spread the cinnamon sugar on another rimmed baking sheet. When the cookies have all been fried but are still warm, transfer them to this sheet and roll them in the sugar to coat. Serve warm. Deep-Fried New Year's Cookies are best eaten soon after they are made.

chinese new year fortune cookies

Makes about
10 cookies

Chinese New Year is a good excuse to make these delicate cookies. I won't lie to you—these are tricky to shape, and the first time you try it you might lose a few. You can only bake a couple at a time, because you have to shape them as soon as they come out of the oven, while they're still hot. If you wait even a few seconds too long, the cookies will crack down the center before you can fold and bend them. I recommend practicing your folding technique on a paper circle, so you understand the geometry of the cookies. Write up fortunes that suit your family to put inside. We never tire of my dad's favorite: "Help, I'm being held prisoner in a fortune cookie factory!"

½ cup unbleached all-purpose flour
½ cup plus 1 tablespoon sugar
Pinch of salt
¼ cup (½ stick) unsalted butter, softened
½ teaspoon pure vanilla extract
1 large egg white

1. Preheat the oven to 300°F. Use a small bowl to trace 2 circles, 4 inches in diameter each, on a piece of parchment paper. Repeat with 8 more pieces of parchment paper. Place 2 of the pieces of parchment paper on 2 baking sheets.

2. Place the flour, sugar, and salt in a medium-size bowl. Whisk to combine.

3. Cream the butter and vanilla extract together in a large mixing bowl with an electric mixer on medium-high speed until fluffy. Stir in half the flour mixture. Add the egg white and beat until all ingredients are moistened. Beat in the remaining flour mixture until a rough dough forms. Scrape down the sides of the bowl. Turn the mixer to medium-high and beat until the batter is very smooth, scraping down the sides of the bowl once, about 2 minutes.

4. Spoon a level tablespoon of batter into the center of each circle on one of the parchment-lined baking sheets. Use a small offset spatula to spread the dough in an even layer to the edges of the circle. Place in the oven and bake until golden and just set, 8 to 10 minutes.

5. Remove the baking sheet from the oven. Working quickly, slide a large offset spatula under one of the cookies and place it on a clean kitchen towel. Fold the cookie in half and pinch the top edges together to form a semicircle. Insert an index finger into each side of the cookie. Press your thumbs into the outside of the fold and pull your index fingers downward to form a fortune cookie shape. Let the fortune cookie cool on the towel and repeat with the warm cookie remaining on the parchment. Repeat the whole process, of baking and folding the cookies, using fresh parchment and a cooled cookie sheet, until all of the batter is used up.

6. Write fortunes on strips of paper with nontoxic ink. Thread the fortunes through the cooled cookies. Chinese New Year Fortune Cookies will keep at room temperature in an airtight container for 2 to 3 days.

Fortunes

Here are my favorite fortunes, some serious and some silly. And you can always come up with your own, customizing to surprise your family.

* A horse may be forced to drink, but a pencil must be lead.
* A member of your family will do something that will make you proud.
* A truly wise man never plays leapfrog with a unicorn.
* Beware of all enterprises that require new clothes.
* Clones are people two.
* Don't bite my finger, look where it's pointing.
* Don't panic.
* Drop the vase and it will become a Ming of the past.
* If at first you don't succeed, you're doing about average.
* If it screams, it's not food.
* Many are cold, but few are frozen.
* Pay no attention to the man behind the curtain.
* Sorry, the Cookie Monster got here first.
* You are just in time to be too late.
* Help! I'm being held prisoner in a fortune cookie factory.

mardi gras praline cookies

**Makes about
24 large cookies**

I made these candy-topped cookies last Mardi Gras and served them after a big pot of not-too-spicy gumbo for the kids. To make it a party, give everyone a string of Mardi Gras beads. Be sure to sift the confectioners' sugar for a smooth glaze. If you like a darker praline with more molasses flavor, you can use dark brown sugar instead of light brown in the glaze.

1¼ cups pecan halves
1⅔ cups unbleached all-purpose flour
1½ teaspoons baking powder
1 teaspoon salt
½ cup (1 stick) unsalted butter, melted
  and slightly cooled
2 cups firmly packed light brown sugar
½ cup granulated sugar
1 large egg
1 teaspoon pure vanilla extract
½ cup plus 2 tablespoons heavy cream
1 cup confectioners' sugar

1. Preheat the oven to 350°F. Spread the pecans on a rimmed baking sheet and toast until fragrant, 8 to 10 minutes. Let cool completely. Coarsely chop and set aside.

2. Combine the flour, baking powder, and salt in a medium-size bowl. Set aside.

3. Cream the cooled melted butter, 1 cup of the brown sugar, and the granulated sugar together in a large mixing bowl with a wooden spoon until smooth. Add the egg and vanilla extract and beat until smooth. Stir in the flour mixture until just incorporated. Place the bowl in the refrigerator for 10 minutes (or up to 6 hours) to let the dough firm up.

4. Drop the batter by heaping tablespoon-fuls onto ungreased baking sheets, leaving about 3 inches between each cookie. (Balls of dough may be placed next to each other on parchment paper–lined baking sheets, frozen, transferred to zipper-lock plastic freezer bags, and stored in the freezer for up to 1 month. Frozen cookies may be placed in the oven directly from the freezer and baked as directed.) Bake the cookies until golden around the edges but still soft on top, 12 to 14 minutes (a minute or two longer for frozen dough). Let the cookies stand on the baking sheet for 5 minutes, then remove them with a metal spatula to a wire rack to cool completely.

5. Place a rimmed baking sheet under the wire rack. In a small saucepan, combine the remaining 1 cup light brown sugar with the heavy cream. Bring to a boil over medium heat. Turn down the heat and simmer, stirring constantly, for 3 minutes. Remove from the heat and whisk in the confectioners' sugar. Stir in the pecan pieces.

6. Spoon a scant tablespoon of the pecan mixture onto each cookie. Let stand until the praline is set, about 1 hour. Mardi Gras Praline Cookies will keep at room temperature in an airtight container for 2 to 3 days.

valentine's day linzer hearts

Makes about 20 cookies

These are absolutely delicious, in addition to being beautiful.

1 cup blanched whole almonds
⅔ cup granulated sugar
1 cup (2 sticks) unsalted butter, softened
1 large egg yolk
1 teaspoon vanilla extract
2⅔ cups unbleached all-purpose flour
¼ teaspoon salt
¼ cup seedless raspberry jam
Confectioners' sugar for sprinkling

1. Place the almonds and ⅓ cup of the sugar in a food processor and process until almonds are just finely ground. Do not overprocess, or the mixture will become oily.

2. Cream the butter and the remaining ⅓ cup of sugar together in a large mixing bowl with an electric mixer on medium-high speed until fluffy. Add the egg yolk and vanilla extract and beat until incorporated. Add the flour, salt, and almond mixture and mix on low speed until the dough comes together in a ball.

3. Press the dough into three ½-inch-thick disks, wrap each in plastic wrap, and refrigerate for at least 2 hours and up to 2 days. (The dough can be wrapped tightly in plastic wrap and frozen for up to 1 month; defrost it in the refrigerator before use.)

4. Preheat the oven to 350°F. Line baking sheets with parchment paper.

5. Remove one of the dough disks from the refrigerator and knead it 4 or 5 times on a lightly floured work surface to soften it. With a lightly floured rolling pin, roll out the dough a scant ¼ inch thick. Use a 2½- to 3-inch heart-shaped cutter to cut out as many hearts as you can. Use a 1-inch heart-shaped cutter to cut a smaller heart out of the center of half of the larger hearts.

6. Place the cookies on the lined baking sheets and bake until pale golden, 10 to 12 minutes. Slide the entire parchment sheet with the cookies onto a wire rack and let the cookies cool completely. Repeat with the remaining disks of dough, using fresh parchment paper.

7. To assemble the cookies, use a small offset spatula to spread about ½ teaspoon of jam on the uncut-out hearts to within ¼ inch of the edges of the cookie. Lightly sift some confectioners' sugar over the cut-out hearts. Place a cut-out heart on top of a jam-covered heart. Valentine's Day Linzer Hearts will keep at room temperature in an airtight container for up to 2 days.

A Good Excuse to Make Valentine's Day Linzer Hearts

This is one of my all-time favorite cookie recipes, and I use it throughout the year. Heart-shaped cookies express love and gratitude no matter what the date, so make these to bring to a friend on her birthday or to thank someone for a special favor. These pretty cookies are delicate, so don't try to mail them. Carry them by hand so you can say "I love you" or "Thanks" in person.

presidents' day cherry-almond thumbprints

Makes about 24 cookies

George Washington's birthday (and his famous admission that it was he who cut down the cherry tree) is a good excuse to make one of my favorite thumbprint combinations: rich almond-flavored dough with a center of cherry preserves.

1½ cups blanched whole almonds
2 cups unbleached all-purpose flour
½ teaspoon salt
1 cup (2 sticks) unsalted butter, melted and cooled slightly
½ cup firmly packed light brown sugar
6 tablespoons granulated sugar
1 large egg
1 teaspoon pure almond extract
½ cup best-quality cherry preserves

1. Preheat the oven to 325°F. Line baking sheets with parchment paper.

2. Place the nuts in a food processor and finely chop. Don't overprocess; the nuts should look dry, not oily. Combine the flour, salt, and ground nuts in a medium-size mixing bowl.

3. Cream the cooled melted butter, brown sugar, and granulated sugar together in a large mixing bowl with an electric mixer on medium speed until smooth. Add the egg and almond extract and beat until smooth. Stir in the flour-nut mixture until just combined.

4. Scoop up a heaping tablespoonful of dough and roll it between your palms to form a ball. Place the balls on the lined baking sheets, leaving about 3 inches between each cookie. Press each cookie with the back of a small measuring spoon to make a well or "thumbprint." If the edges crack when you make the thumbprint, just press them back together. (Shaped cookies may be placed next to each other on parchment paper–lined baking sheets, frozen, transferred to zipper-lock plastic freezer bags, and stored in the freezer for up to 1 month. Frozen cookies may be placed in the oven directly from the freezer and baked as directed.) Bake the cookies until they are lightly colored, 20 to 22 minutes (a minute or two longer for frozen dough). Let them stand on the baking sheets for 5 minutes, then carefully slide the entire parchment sheet with the cookies from the pan to a wire rack and let cool completely.

5. Carefully fill each cookie indentation with about 1 teaspoon preserves. Presidents' Day Cherry-Almond Thumbprints will keep at room temperature in an airtight container, with layers separated by waxed paper, for 2 to 3 days.

abraham lincoln stovepipe hats

**Makes about
40 cookies**

Homemade graham-cracker rounds are topped with a marshmallow and covered with chocolate. They may look like stovepipe hats, but they taste like s'mores.

1½ cups unbleached all-purpose flour
½ cup whole wheat flour
½ teaspoon baking powder
¼ teaspoon baking soda
Pinch of salt
¼ cup (½ stick) unsalted butter, melted
    and cooled
½ cup firmly packed light brown sugar
1 teaspoon pure vanilla extract
6 tablespoons whole or low-fat milk
12 ounces bittersweet or semisweet
    chocolate, finely chopped
3 tablespoons vegetable oil
2 tablespoons light corn syrup
About 40 marshmallows

1. Combine the all-purpose flour, whole wheat flour, baking powder, baking soda, and salt in a medium-size mixing bowl.

2. Cream the butter and brown sugar together in a large mixing bowl with an electric mixer on medium speed until smooth. Add the vanilla extract and milk and beat until smooth. Add the flour mixture and stir until the dough comes together.

3. Divide the dough into 2 equal-size disks, wrap in plastic wrap, and refrigerate for at least 2 hours and up to 2 days.

4. Preheat the oven to 350°F. Line baking sheets with parchment paper.

5. On a lightly floured work surface with a lightly floured rolling pin, roll one disk of dough out to a ⅛-inch thickness. Cut the dough into 2-inch circles with a

biscuit cutter or juice glass. Repeat with the remaining disk. Re-roll the scraps and cut more circles. Transfer the circles to the lined baking sheets. Bake until lightly colored, about 10 minutes. Let them stand on the baking sheets for 5 minutes, then carefully slide the entire parchment sheet with the cookies from the pan to a wire rack and let cool completely.

6. Put 1 inch of water in the bottom of a double boiler or medium-size saucepan and bring to a bare simmer. Combine the chocolate, vegetable oil, and corn syrup in the top of the double boiler or in a stainless-steel bowl set on top of the simmering water, making sure that the water doesn't touch the bottom of the bowl. Heat, whisking occasionally, until the chocolate and oil are completely melted.

7. Place a rimmed baking sheet under the wire rack of cookies, spacing the cookies at least 1 inch apart. Place a marshmallow on top of each cookie. Spoon some of the chocolate mixture on top of each marshmallow so that it runs down the sides. Use a small offset spatula to cover the marshmallow and cookie "brim" with chocolate. Let the cookies stand until the glaze has hardened, about 2 hours. Abraham Lincoln Stovepipe Hats will keep at room temperature in an airtight container for 2 to 3 days.

st. patrick's day mini soda breads

Makes about
14 biscuits

Soda bread is traditional for St. Patrick's Day, and these soda bread biscuits sandwiched with raspberry preserves are a sweet way to honor the tradition.

1½ cups unbleached all-purpose flour
¾ teaspoon baking soda
¾ teaspoon baking powder
½ teaspoon salt
¼ cup (½ stick) unsalted butter, softened
1½ teaspoons caraway seeds
1 egg yolk
½ cup buttermilk
2 tablespoons honey
¼ cup raspberry preserves

1. Preheat the oven to 350°F. Line a baking sheet with parchment paper or spray it with nonstick cooking spray.

2. Combine the flour, baking soda, baking powder, and salt in a large mixing bowl. Add the butter and beat with an electric mixer mix on low speed until the mixture resembles coarse meal. Stir in the caraway seeds.

3. Whisk together the egg yolk, buttermilk, and honey in a small bowl. Add the egg mixture to the flour mixture and stir just until the dry ingredients are moistened. Do not overmix.

4. Turn out the clumps of dough onto a lightly floured work surface and gently knead once or twice until the dough comes together. With one or two passes of a lightly floured rolling pin, gently roll the dough out ½ inch thick. Dip a 1½-inch biscuit cutter into some flour and cut as many rounds as you can from the dough. Transfer the rounds to the prepared baking sheet. Gently pat the scraps together and cut out more rounds with the remaining dough.

5. Bake until the rounds have risen and are light golden, 10 to 12 minutes. Transfer to a wire rack and let cool for 5 minutes. Split each one in half, spread each bottom half with ½ teaspoon of the preserves, and serve warm. St. Patrick's Day Mini Soda Breads are best eaten on the day they are made.

hamantaschen

Makes about
16 cookies

These traditional Purim treats are supposed to resemble the tricornered hat of the villain Haman. Canned lekvar (sweetened prune puree) and poppy seed filling are shelved with matzoh meal and other kosher products in the supermarket.

1½ cups unbleached all-purpose flour
¾ teaspoon baking powder
⅛ teaspoon salt
1 tablespoon unsalted butter, softened
1 tablespoon vegetable shortening
½ cup sugar, plus more for sprinkling
2 large eggs
½ teaspoon lemon zest
1 teaspoon pure vanilla extract
½ cup canned lekvar or poppy seed
    filling

1. Combine the flour, baking powder, and salt in a medium-size bowl.

2. Cream the butter, shortening, and sugar together in a large mixing bowl with an electric mixer on medium-high speed until fluffy. Add 1 of the eggs, the lemon zest, and vanilla extract and beat until incorporated, scraping down the sides of the bowl as necessary. Add the flour mixture and mix on low speed until the dough comes together in a ball.

3. Shape the dough into a disk, wrap in plastic wrap, and refrigerate for at least 2 hours and up to 2 days. (The dough can be wrapped tightly in plastic wrap and frozen for up to 1 month; defrost it in the refrigerator before use.)

4. Preheat the oven to 350°F. Line baking sheets with parchment paper.

5. Remove the dough from the refrigerator and knead it 4 or 5 times on a lightly floured work surface to soften it. With a

lightly floured rolling pin, roll out the dough ⅛ inch thick. Use a 3-inch round biscuit cutter to cut out as many rounds as possible. Re-roll scraps until all the dough is used. Place the rounds on the lined baking sheets.

6. Lightly beat the remaining egg. Brush each round with some of the egg. Place a rounded teaspoon of lekvar or poppy seed filling in the center of each round. Draw 3 edges of the dough together in the center to form a triangle. Pinch the seams together to seal. Brush the sealed cookies with some more of the egg. Sprinkle each cookie with sugar.

7. Bake until golden, 15 to 18 minutes. Slide the entire parchment sheet with the cookies onto wire racks and let the cookies cool completely. Hamantaschen will keep at room temperature in an airtight container for up to 2 days.

A Good Excuse to Make Hamantaschen

If you don't celebrate Purim, put these cookies to nontraditional use on Presidents' Day and call them George Washington Hats. Show your kids how to fold a dough round into a tricorn hat and then let them do the rest of the filling and folding.

passover macaroons

Makes about
24 cookies

Passover desserts tend toward dry and tasteless variations on sponge cake, so when I started making these chewy, flavorful macaroons for our large family seder, everyone rejoiced. Sweetened flaked coconut is too sweet to be the primary ingredient. I use unsweetened coconut, which is available at natural foods stores and most supermarkets. To make chocolate macaroons, simply add 4 ounces of melted and cooled bittersweet or semisweet chocolate to the mixture and stir to combine.

¾ cup sugar
2½ cups unsweetened dried coconut
2 large egg whites
1 teaspoon pure vanilla extract
⅛ teaspoon salt

1. Preheat the oven to 375°F. Line baking sheets with parchment paper.

2. Combine the sugar, coconut, egg whites, vanilla extract, and salt in a medium-size mixing bowl and mix with a rubber spatula.

3. Drop the batter by heaping tablespoonfuls onto the lined baking sheets, leaving about 1½ inches between each cookie.

4. Bake until golden, 10 to 12 minutes. Slide the entire parchment sheet with the cookies onto a wire rack and let cool completely. Carefully peel them off the parchment paper. Passover Macaroons will keep at room temperature in an airtight container for up to 1 week.

bird's nest cookies with easter eggs

Makes about 24 cookies

I have a special weakness for cookies that look like something other than cookies, so I love these. Here butter cookie dough is rolled in coconut and shaped into little bird's nests. To finish the nests off, candy-coated chocolate eggs are placed in their centers before serving. Just try to find a cuter classroom treat for an Easter/spring party.

1¼ cups sweetened flaked coconut
2 cups unbleached all-purpose flour
½ teaspoon baking powder
½ teaspoon salt
1 cup (2 sticks) unsalted butter, softened
½ cup sugar
1 large egg
1 teaspoon pure vanilla extract
½ teaspoon coconut extract (optional)
About 60 small milk chocolate eggs with sugar shells, such as Cadbury Mini Eggs

1. Preheat the oven to 350°F. Spread the coconut out in an even layer on a rimmed baking sheet. Toast until pale golden, stirring once or twice to promote even cooking, 8 to 10 minutes. Remove from the oven and cool completely on the baking sheet.

2. Line baking sheets with parchment paper. Combine the flour, baking powder, and salt in a medium-size bowl.

3. Cream the butter and sugar together in a large mixing bowl with an electric mixer until smooth. Add the egg, vanilla extract, and coconut extract, if you are using it, and beat until smooth. Stir in the flour mixture until just incorporated.

4. Shape the dough into 1¼-inch balls. Roll the balls in the toasted coconut so that they are completely coated. Place the balls 3 inches apart on the lined baking sheets. With your thumb, make an indentation in the center of each ball large enough to hold 2 or 3 chocolate eggs. Shape the sides of the cookies with your thumb and index finger so that they stand up and have nice bird's nest shapes, if necessary.

5. Bake until golden, 10 to 12 minutes. Remove from the oven and let cool completely on the baking sheets. You may store the cooled cookies at room temperature in an airtight container for up to 2 days. Just before serving, place 2 to 3 milk chocolate eggs in the indentation of each cookie.

matzoh bark

Makes about
24 pieces

You can buy chocolate-covered matzoh around Passover, but making this chocolate-caramel-nut confection yourself is simple and delicious.

4 whole plain unsalted matzoh breads
1 cup (2 sticks) unsalted butter
1 cup firmly packed light brown sugar
1 cup semisweet chocolate chips
¾ cup coarsely chopped walnuts

1. Preheat the oven to 350°F. Line a rimmed baking sheet with heavy-duty aluminum foil. Place the matzoh bread in a single layer on top of the foil, breaking them where necessary and rearranging the pieces so that all the foil is covered.

2. Combine the butter and brown sugar in a small heavy saucepan and cook over medium heat until the mixture comes to a boil. Lower the heat and simmer, stirring constantly with a wooden spoon, for 3 minutes.

3. Pour the hot sugar mixture over the matzoh, spreading it in an even layer with a small offset spatula if necessary. Bake until the matzoh is golden and the sugar is bubbling, 10 to 12 minutes.

4. Sprinkle the chocolate chips and walnuts over the caramel and refrigerate until the caramel and chocolate are set, about 2 hours. Break it into about 24 pieces. Matzoh Bark will keep at room temperature in an airtight container, in layers separated with waxed paper to prevent sticking, for up to 1 week.

Mother's Day and Father's Day Cookies

I've wracked my brain trying to come up with a recipe for each of these holidays. Something shaped like a golf ball or a tie for dad? Too stereotypical. A bouquet of tulip-shaped cookies on lollipop sticks for mom? Sounds kind of complicated for kids to make alone, without having Mom to help and clean up the mess at the end of the day.

So instead, I've gone through these recipes and come up with the easiest, least messy recipes imaginable. If your kids want to help you make Dad a batch of cookies, or they want to bake for you for a change, have them choose from the following list, help them shop, and then sit back and let them do most of the work (and cleaning up) all by themselves. They'll feel great, and you will, too.

* Slice-and-Bake Sugar Cookies (page 58)
* Lemon–Cream Cheese Meltaways (page 75)
* Flourless Peanut Butter Cookies (page 81)
* Almond Joy Cookies (page 84)
* Homemade Milk Chocolate Crunch (page 87)
* Scottish Shortbread (page 88)
* After-Dinner Microwave Brownies (page 104)
* Seven-Layer Bars (page 127)

red, white, and blue sables

**Makes
54 small cookies**

These buttery cookies are a nice addition to a Memorial Day, Independence Day, or Labor Day dessert spread. Make sure to chop the cherries or cranberries and the blueberries very finely for the best red, white, and blue coloring. If you'd like to give the cookies some sparkle, brush each long rectangle of dough with egg white and roll in sanding sugar before slicing.

¾ cup (1½ sticks) unsalted butter, softened
⅓ cup sugar
1 large egg, separated
1 teaspoon pure vanilla extract
1½ cups unbleached all-purpose flour
¼ teaspoon salt
¼ cup dried cherries or cranberries, finely chopped
¼ cup dried blueberries, finely chopped

1. Cream the butter and sugar together in a large mixing bowl with an electric mixer on medium-high speed until fluffy. Add the egg yolk and vanilla extract and beat until incorporated, scraping down the sides of the bowl as necessary. Add the flour and salt and mix on low speed until the dough comes together in a ball.

2. Divide the dough into 3 equal-size balls. Return one ball to the mixer and mix in the dried cherries. Remove it from the mixer and shape into a disk. Return the second ball to the mixer and mix in the blueberries until incorporated. Remove it from the mixer and shape into a disk. Shape the remaining ball into a disk. Wrap all 3 disks in plastic wrap and refrigerate for at least 2 hours and up to 2 days.

3. Remove the disks of dough from the refrigerator. Kneading once or twice to soften the dough, roll each disk out on a lightly floured work surface into a 2½ x 10-inch rectangle, about ⅓-inch thick.

4. Use a pastry brush to brush the top surface of the cherry dough with some of the egg white. Slide the vanilla dough on top of the cherry dough. Brush the top of the vanilla dough with the remaining egg white, and slide the blueberry dough on top of the vanilla dough. Press down lightly on top of the dough with a cookie sheet to make the layers adhere.

5. Trim the dough into an even 2 x 9-inch rectangle. Cut the rectangle lengthwise into two 1-inch lengths. Wrap each length in plastic wrap. Refrigerate until firm, at least 2 hours and up to 2 days. (The dough can be wrapped tightly in plastic wrap and frozen for up to 1 month; defrost it in the refrigerator before use.)

6. Preheat the oven to 350°F. Line baking sheets with parchment paper.

7. Slice each skinny rectangle into twenty-seven ⅓-inch-thick cookies, rotating the rectangle often so you don't squash the dough. Arrange the cookies on the lined baking sheets at least 1 inch apart. Bake until they are dry and firm to the touch, 10 to 12 minutes. Slide the entire parchment sheet with the cookies onto a wire rack and let the cookies cool completely. Red, White, and Blue Sables will keep at room temperature in an airtight container for 3 to 4 days.

halloween pumpkin cookies with caramel glaze

Makes about 36 cookies

They're not shaped like pumpkins, but these moist, cakey cookies are made with pumpkin puree, so they're perfect for school Halloween parties and Thanksgiving snacking.

For the cookies
2 cups unbleached all-purpose flour
1 teaspoon baking powder
½ teaspoon baking soda
½ teaspoon salt
1 teaspoon ground cinnamon
½ teaspoon ground ginger
½ teaspoon ground nutmeg
½ cup (1 stick) unsalted butter, softened
1 cup firmly packed light brown sugar
2 large eggs
1 cup canned pumpkin puree
2 teaspoons pure vanilla extract

For the glaze
½ cup heavy cream
½ cup firmly packed light brown sugar
Pinch of salt
6 tablespoons light corn syrup
¼ cup (½ stick) unsalted butter
1 teaspoon pure vanilla extract

1. Preheat the oven to 375°F.

2. Make the cookies: Combine the flour, baking powder, baking soda, salt, cinnamon, ginger, and nutmeg in a medium-size bowl.

3. Cream the butter and brown sugar together in a large mixing bowl with an electric mixer until smooth. Add the eggs, pumpkin puree, and vanilla extract and beat until smooth. Stir in the flour mixture until just incorporated.

4. Drop the batter by heaping tablespoonfuls onto ungreased baking sheets, leaving about 3 inches between each cookie. Bake the cookies until golden, 10 to 12 minutes. Let the cookies stand on the baking sheet for 5 minutes, then remove them with a metal spatula to a wire rack to cool completely.

5. Make the glaze: Combine the cream, brown sugar, salt, corn syrup, and butter in a heavy, medium-size saucepan and cook over medium heat, stirring occasionally, until the sugar is dissolved and the butter is melted. Bring to a boil, turn down the heat, and let simmer for 5 minutes without stirring. Transfer the glaze to a heatproof bowl, stir in the vanilla extract, and let cool until thickened, about an hour.

6. Place a parchment paper–lined rimmed baking sheet under the cookies on the wire rack. Spoon some of the glaze over each cookie, picking up each cookie and working over the bowl to let any excess drip back into the bowl. Place the cookies back on the rack and let stand until the glaze is firm, about 1 hour. Halloween Pumpkin Cookies with Caramel Glaze are best eaten on the day they are made, though they will keep at room temperature in an airtight container for 1 to 2 days.

pepita oatmeal cookies

Makes about 30 cookies

These fruit- and seed-filled oatmeal cookies are a nice, wholesome contrast to all of that Halloween candy, but they won't make your kids feel sugar-deprived. I like dried cranberries with the pumpkin seeds, but raisins or dried cherries also work well.

1 cup unbleached all-purpose flour
½ teaspoon baking powder
¼ teaspoon baking soda
½ teaspoon ground cinnamon
¼ teaspoon salt
½ cup (1 stick) unsalted butter, melted and cooled
½ cup granulated sugar
½ cup firmly packed dark brown sugar
2 tablespoons honey
1 large egg
1 teaspoon pure vanilla extract
1½ cups old-fashioned rolled oats (not instant)
½ cup dried cranberries
½ cup unsalted pepitas (hulled green pumpkin seeds)
½ cup unsweetened dried coconut

1. Preheat the oven to 350°F.

2. Combine the flour, baking powder, baking soda, cinnamon, and salt in a medium-size mixing bowl.

3. Cream the cooled melted butter, granulated sugar, brown sugar, and honey together in a large mixing bowl with a wooden spoon until smooth. Add the egg and vanilla extract and beat until smooth. Stir in the flour mixture until just incor-porated. Stir in the oats, cranberries, pepitas, and coconut. Place the bowl in the refrigerator for 10 minutes (or up to 6 hours) to let the dough firm up.

4. Drop the batter by heaping tablespoon-fuls onto ungreased baking sheets, leaving about 3 inches between each cookie. (Balls of dough may be placed next to each other on parchment paper–lined baking sheets, frozen, transferred to zipper-lock plastic freezer bags, and stored in the freezer for up to 1 month. Frozen cookies may be placed in the oven directly from the freezer and baked as directed.)

5. Bake the cookies until golden around the edges but still soft on top, 10 to 12 minutes (a minute or two longer for frozen dough). Let the cookies stand on the baking sheet for 5 minutes, then remove them with a metal spatula to a wire rack to cool completely. Pepita Oatmeal Cookies will keep at room temperature in an airtight container for 2 to 3 days.

double chocolate mummy cookies

Makes about
25 cookies

No need to go out and buy expensive white chocolate for these Halloween treats. White chocolate chips work very well here.

2½ cups unbleached all-purpose flour
½ cup unsweetened natural cocoa
    powder
½ teaspoon salt
¼ teaspoon baking soda
6 tablespoons unsalted butter, softened
1 cup sugar
2 large eggs
1 teaspoon pure vanilla extract
One 12-ounce bag white chocolate chips
1 tablespoon vegetable oil
About 50 mini semisweet chocolate
    chips for decorating

1. Preheat the oven to 350°F. Line baking sheets with parchment paper.

2. Combine the flour, cocoa powder, salt, and baking soda in a medium-size mixing bowl.

3. Cream the butter and sugar together in a large mixing bowl with an electric mixer on medium-high speed until well combined. Add the eggs and vanilla extract and beat until smooth. Stir in the flour mixture until the dough comes together.

4. Scoop up a tablespoonful of dough and roll it between your palms to form a 2½-inch-long carrot shape for the body of the mummy. Flatten the body slightly with your fingertips. Scoop up a scant teaspoonful of dough and roll it between your palms into a ball to form the head of the mummy. Press the head into the wide end of the body. Place on a prepared

baking sheet. Repeat with the remaining dough.

5. Bake the cookies until firm to the touch, 12 to 14 minutes. Remove from the oven and let cool completely on the cookie sheets.

6. Put 1 inch of water in the bottom of a double boiler or medium-size saucepan and bring to a bare simmer. Combine the white chocolate chips and vegetable oil in the top of the double boiler or in a stainless-steel bowl set on top of the simmering water, making sure that the water doesn't touch the bottom of the bowl. Heat, whisking occasionally, until the chocolate is completely melted.

7. Place a cookie on a wide spatula. Hold the spatula over the bowl of white chocolate and spoon some of the white chocolate over the cookie, just to coat it. Slide the cookie back onto the parchment-lined baking sheet and repeat with the remaining cookies.

8. When the white chocolate has begun to harden but is not completely set, use a toothpick to score horizontal lines across each mummy body and head to create "bandages." Place two mini chocolate chips on the heads for eyes. Let set completely, at least 2 hours, before serving. Double Chocolate Mummy Cookies will keep at room temperature in an airtight container for 2 to 3 days.

thanksgiving maple leaves

Makes about 36 large cookies

These pretty, delicate cookies have become a tradition at our house on Thanksgiving, served alongside apple tart and pumpkin cheesecake at the end of a large family dinner. I guess I could cut these out in turkey shapes for the holiday, but I love it when the shape of a cookie reflects its flavor. And turkey-flavored cookies—well, I wouldn't know how to make those, anyway. I use a large leaf cutter that I bought at Williams-Sonoma years ago. Your yield will, of course, depend on the size of your cookie cutter.

1 cup (2 sticks) unsalted butter, softened
1 cup granulated sugar
1 large egg, separated
½ cup pure maple syrup
¼ teaspoon maple extract
3 cups unbleached all-purpose flour
½ teaspoon salt
¼ cup turbinado sugar (often called sugar in the raw)

1. Cream the butter and granulated sugar together in a large mixing bowl with an electric mixer on medium-high speed until fluffy. Add the egg yolk, maple syrup, and maple extract and beat until incorporated, scraping down the sides of the bowl as necessary. Add the flour and salt and mix on low speed until the dough comes together in a ball.

2. Divide the dough into 3 equal-size balls. Wrap each ball in plastic wrap and refrigerate it for at least 2 hours and up to 2 days. (The dough can be wrapped tightly in plastic wrap and frozen for up to 1 month; defrost it in the refrigerator before use.)

3. Preheat the oven to 350°F. Line baking sheets with parchment paper.

4. Remove one ball from the refrigerator and knead it 4 or 5 times on a lightly floured work surface to soften it. With a lightly floured rolling pin, roll out the dough ⅛ inch thick. Cut it into maple leaf shapes with a cookie cutter. Refrigerate the scraps. Place cookies on the prepared baking sheets. Repeat with the remaining balls of dough and then with the chilled scraps.

5. Lightly beat the egg white. Brush each cookie with some of the beaten egg white and sprinkle liberally with the turbinado sugar.

6. Bake the cookies until they are firm and golden around the edges, about 8 minutes. Slide the entire parchment sheet with the cookies onto a wire rack and let the cookies cool completely. Thanksgiving Maple Leaves will keep at room temperature in an airtight container for several days.

traditional hanukkah rugelach

We celebrate Hanukkah and Christmas in my house, and since the first night of Hanukkah usually comes first, these are the first of the year-end holiday cookies to come out of my oven. They help build excitement for all of the cookies to come. Walnuts and raisins are traditional, but other nuts and dried fruits may be substituted. Just make sure to chop everything in small pieces, so the dough triangles can be rolled up with ease.

For the cream cheese dough
- 2 cups unbleached all-purpose flour
- 1½ tablespoons sugar
- ¼ teaspoon salt
- One 8-ounce package chilled cream cheese, cut into 8 pieces
- 1 cup (2 sticks) chilled unsalted butter, cut into 16 pieces

For the raisin-walnut filling
- ½ cup sugar
- 1 teaspoon ground cinnamon
- 1¼ cups walnuts
- ⅔ cup apricot preserves
- 1¼ cups golden raisins

For the glaze
- ⅓ cup heavy cream

1. Make the dough: Combine the flour, sugar, and salt in a food processor and pulse to combine. Add the cream cheese and butter and pulse until the mixture resembles coarse meal (do not overprocess). Turn the mixture out onto a lightly floured work surface and press it into a ball. Divide the ball into 4 equal-size pieces and shape each piece into a 4-inch disk. Wrap each disk in plastic wrap and refrigerate it for at least 2 hours and up to 2 days. (The dough can be frozen for up to 1 month; defrost it in the refrigerator before use.)

2. Preheat the oven to 375°F. Line baking sheets with parchment paper.

3. Make the filling: Combine the sugar and cinnamon in a small bowl. Place the walnuts in a food processor and process until finely chopped. Transfer the chopped walnuts to a medium-size mixing bowl. Place the preserves in the food processor and process until any large chunks are broken up. Transfer to another small bowl.

4. Remove one dough disk from the refrigerator and, with a lightly floured rolling pin, roll out the dough into a 9-inch circle on a lightly floured work surface. Using a 9-inch plate or pie plate as a guide, trim the edges to make a neat circle.

5. Spread 2½ tablespoons of the preserves over the dough. Sprinkle with 5 table-spoons of the raisins. Sprinkle with 2 tablespoons of the cinnamon sugar. Sprinkle with 5 tablespoons of the walnuts. Pat the filling firmly with your fingertips to secure it to the dough. Cut the dough circle into 8 wedges. Roll each wedge into a crescent (starting with the wide end of each wedge) and place it on a prepared baking sheet. Repeat with the remaining dough disks. Place the baking sheets in the freezer for at least 30 minutes. (Rolled rugelach can be wrapped tightly in plastic wrap and frozen for up to 1 month. Place the rugelach in the oven directly from the freezer.)

6. Brush the frozen rugelach with the heavy cream and bake until they are golden, 24 to 25 minutes. Transfer them to wire racks with a metal spatula and let cool completely. Traditional Hanukkah Rugelach will keep at room temperature in an airtight container for 2 to 3 days.

Kids Can Help

These cookies aren't difficult to make, but there are quite a few steps. Enlist your kids to help and the project will be more fun and less work. Sprinkling on the filling ingredients and rolling up the dough triangles into crescents are good jobs for children ages seven and up.

Other Holiday Cookie Ideas for Your Consideration

Any cookie can be a holiday cookie if you designate it as such and then bake it faithfully every year when that holiday rolls around. But some cookies just shout out to be made on certain days. Here are some suggestions for holiday/cookie match-ups:

* **Valentine's Day:** Peanut Butter Kisses (page 131)
* **George Washington's Birthday:** Black Forest Brownies (page 107), Chocolate-Cherry-Pistachio Swirls (page 65)
* **May Day:** Sugar Cookie Flowers (page 204)
* **Fourth of July:** Hamburger Cookies (page 205), S'mores Brownies (page 108)
* **Bastille Day:** Madeleines (page 184)
* **Columbus Day:** Cookie Pizza (page 202)
* **Thanksgiving:** Gingery Pumpkin Bars with Milk Chocolate Glaze (page 116), Pecan Pie Squares (page 123)
* **Christmas:** Chocolate Chip Gingerbread Bars (page 115), Snow Day Snowmen (page 199)

rolled sugar cookies

This is the recipe I turn to throughout the year when I want to celebrate any holiday at all with cookies. I just choose the appropriate cookie shapes (pumpkins, candy canes, hearts, bunnies), color royal icing in matching hues (orange for pumpkins, red and white for candy canes, pink for hearts, any pastel for bunnies), and decorate with colored sugar and sprinkles to match. One batch of cookies will make enough for a classroom of kids. You can decorate them yourself, or if you want to be a hero you can bring in the cookies, icing, and sprinkles and let the kids do it themselves.

1 cup (2 sticks) unsalted butter, softened
½ cup granulated sugar
1 large egg yolk
1 teaspoon pure vanilla extract
2¼ cups unbleached all-purpose flour
¼ teaspoon salt
Royal Icing (recipe follows) for decoration
Colored sugar or sprinkles for decoration

1. Cream the butter and sugar together in a large mixing bowl with an electric mixer on medium-high speed until fluffy. Add the egg yolk and vanilla extract and beat until incorporated, scraping down the sides of the bowl as necessary. Add the flour and salt and mix on low speed until the dough comes together in a ball.

2. Divide the dough into 3 equal-size balls. Wrap each ball in plastic wrap and refrigerate for at least 2 hours and up to 2 days. (The dough can be wrapped tightly in plastic wrap and frozen for up to 1 month; defrost it in the refrigerator before use.)

3. Preheat the oven to 375°F. Line baking sheets with parchment paper.

4. Remove one ball from the refrigerator and knead it 4 or 5 times on a lightly floured work surface to soften it. With a lightly floured rolling pin, roll out the dough ⅛ inch thick. Cut it into the desired shapes and place on the lined baking sheets. Refrigerate the scraps.

5. Bake the cookies until they are firm and golden around the edges, about 8 minutes. Slide the entire parchment sheet with the cookies onto a wire rack and let the cookies cool completely. Repeat with the remaining balls of dough and then with the chilled scraps, using fresh parchment paper each time. Decorate the cookies with the icing and colored sugar or sprinkles as desired. Rolled Sugar Cookies will keep at room temperature in an airtight container for several days.

royal icing

Makes about 3 cups, enough to decorate 1 batch
of Rolled Sugar Cookies

This sweet, pure-white icing is a dream to
pipe and spread. Meringue powder or
powdered egg whites give it its fluffy
texture and shine and don't present the
health hazards of raw egg whites. Divide a
batch into separate portions and color each
one with a drop of food coloring, if you'd
like to decorate your cookies in a few
different colors. Royal icing hardens
quickly when exposed to air, so be sure to
press a sheet of plastic wrap directly on
top of the surface of icing that you aren't
planning on using immediately, to keep it
soft and spreadable.

A Good Excuse to Make Rolled Sugar Cookies

Your kitchen drawer is overflowing with
old cookie cutters that you haven't used
in recent memory. Choose just one
seasonal cutter, maybe a pumpkin for
Halloween, and challenge yourself or
your kids to decorate this one shape in as
many different ways as possible, using
frosting, sprinkles, and sugar decors, in
honor of the season. Then do it again next
month with a Christmas tree shape, and
the next month with a heart, and so on.
Before you know it, you'll be putting most
of your cutters to use and developing a
holiday cookie tradition at the same time.

**2 tablespoons meringue powder or
   powdered egg whites**
¼ cup water
2 cups confectioners' sugar
Food coloring (optional)

1. Combine the meringue powder and
water in a medium-size mixing bowl.
With an electric mixer fitted with the
whisk attachment, beat the mixture on
high speed until soft peaks form. Add the
confectioners' sugar and beat until the
icing is shiny and smooth, 3 to 5 minutes.

2. Divide the icing among small bowls
and stir in a drop or two of food coloring
in each bowl, if you are using it. Use
immediately, or cover the surface of each
bowl of icing with plastic wrap (otherwise the icing will begin to harden) and
refrigerate until you are ready to use it, up
to 1 day. Spread the icing on the cookies
with a small offset spatula or craft stick, or
place it in a pastry bag fitted with a small,
plain tip and pipe it decoratively onto the
cookies.

sparkling candy canes

Use a food processor, or place the candies in a zipper-lock plastic bag and roll over with a rolling pin, to crush the candies finely. A sprinkling of green or silver nonpareils instead of the crushed peppermint is pretty, too.

1 cup (2 sticks) unsalted butter, softened
1 cup confectioners' sugar
1 large egg
1 teaspoon pure vanilla extract
2½ cups unbleached all-purpose flour
½ teaspoon salt
Red food coloring
¼ cup crushed peppermint candies (about 10 candies)
¼ cup granulated sugar
1 large egg white, lightly beaten

1. Cream the butter and confectioners' sugar together in a large mixing bowl with an electric mixer on medium-high speed until fluffy. Add the egg and vanilla extract and beat until incorporated, scraping down the sides of the bowl as necessary. Add the flour and salt and mix on low speed until the dough comes together in a ball.

2. Remove half of the dough from the mixer and set aside. Add several drops of red food coloring to the remaining dough and mix until it is uniformly red. Shape each portion of dough into a ball, wrap in plastic wrap, and refrigerate until firm, at least 2 hours and up to 1 day.

3. Preheat the oven to 350°F. Line baking sheets with parchment paper.

4. On a lightly floured work surface, roll 1 level teaspoon of the white dough into a 5-inch-long rope. Roll 1 level teaspoon of the red dough into a 5-inch rope. Twist the ropes together and place on a prepared baking sheet. Curve one end down to create a cane shape. Repeat with the remaining dough, placing the cookies about 2 inches apart on the baking sheets.

5. Combine the crushed peppermint candy and the granulated sugar in a small bowl. Lightly brush the cookies with the egg white and sprinkle with the crushed candy mixture. Bake until the white parts of the cookies are just coloring, 10 to 12 minutes. Remove to a wire rack to cool completely. Sparkling Candy Canes will keep at room temperature in an airtight container for 2 to 3 days.

Kids Can Help

Kids ages eight and up with well-developed fine motor skills will be able to twist and shape the dough.

corn flake christmas wreaths

Makes about 16 wreaths

This idea comes from Dede Wilson, whose book *A Baker's Field Guide to Christmas Cookies* (The Harvard Common Press, 2003) is a must for anyone interested in some seriously fun holiday baking. Kids make these cookies almost without help, but Mom should stir in the food coloring to avoid the semipermanent staining of little fingers and the permanent staining of fabrics and countertops. Mini red M&M's make cute holly berries for chocolate lovers, and cinnamon Red Hots are good for people who like some spice.

10 ounces white chocolate, finely chopped
½ teaspoon green food coloring
2½ cups corn flakes
About 80 red mini M&M's or cinnamon Red Hots

1. Line a baking sheet with parchment paper.

2. Put 1 inch of water in the bottom of a double boiler or medium-size saucepan and bring to a bare simmer. Place the white chocolate in the top of the double boiler or in a stainless-steel bowl set on top of the simmering water, making sure that the water doesn't touch the bottom of the bowl. Heat, whisking occasionally, until the chocolate is completely melted.

3. Remove from the heat and stir in the food coloring. When the chocolate is a uniform green, stir in the corn flakes.

4. Drop heaping tablespoonfuls of the corn flake mixture onto the prepared baking sheet. Using the handle of a wooden spoon, make a ½-inch hole in the center of each cookie, spreading the cookies to about 3 inches in diameter.

Repeat with the remaining mounds, working quickly before the chocolate hardens. Apply 5 M&M's or cinnamon Red Hots to the wreaths while the chocolate is still sticky.

5. Place the baking sheet in the refrigerator until the chocolate is completely cooled, about 30 minutes. Corn Flake Christmas Wreaths will keep at room temperature in an airtight container (separate layers with sheets of parchment or waxed paper to prevent sticking) for 4 to 5 days.

A Good Excuse to Make Sparkling Candy Canes, Corn Flake Christmas Wreaths, and Stained Glass Star Cookies

Santa Claus is coming to town, and he prefers fun, colorful cookies in seasonal shapes to plain old oatmeal or chocolate chip cookies, say my children. So make some of these novelty cookies just for him.

stained glass star cookies

These are my family's hands-down holiday favorite. Over the years I've experimented with different shapes and flavors of candy, and everyone in my house agrees that the stars filled with butterscotch are the prettiest and most delicious. They are a bit of a project, so I spread out the work, making the dough one day, rolling and cutting the cookies the next, then freezing the cookies until I want to bake them. This way I can make just a couple for Santa's reindeer and save the rest for New Year's Eve. I have a set of nesting star-shaped cookie cutters, and I use the largest and smallest of the set for these cookies. Star cutters in large and small sizes can be purchased separately at any cookware shop. The delicate cookies shatter easily and are difficult to transport, so I keep them at home and serve them to anyone who drops by, and as an extra treat alongside other holiday desserts on Hanukkah, Christmas Eve, Christmas, and New Year's Eve.

1 cup (2 sticks) unsalted butter, softened
¾ cup sugar
1 large egg yolk
1 teaspoon pure vanilla extract
2¼ cups unbleached all-purpose flour
¾ cup (about 6 ounces) butterscotch candies

1. Cream the butter and ½ cup of the sugar together in a large mixing bowl with an electric mixer on medium-high speed until fluffy. Add the egg yolk and vanilla extract and beat until incorporated, scraping down the sides of the bowl as necessary. Add the flour and mix on low speed until the dough comes together in a ball.

2. Divide the dough into 3 equal-size balls. Wrap each ball in plastic wrap and refrigerate it for at least 2 hours and up to 2 days. (The dough can be wrapped tightly in plastic wrap and frozen for up to 1 month; defrost it in the refrigerator before use.)

3. Preheat the oven to 375°F. Line baking sheets with parchment paper.

4. Place the butterscotch candies in a food processor fitted with a metal blade and process until they are finely ground. Transfer the ground candy to a small bowl.

5. Remove one ball of dough from the refrigerator and knead it 4 or 5 times on a lightly floured work surface to soften it. With a lightly floured rolling pin, roll out the dough to ⅛ inch thick. Use a star-shaped cookie cutter measuring about 3 inches across to cut the dough into star shapes. Use a star-shaped cookie cutter measuring about 1¼ inches across to make a star cut in the center of each cookie, making a cut-out area for the crushed candy. Transfer the cookies to the prepared baking sheets. Refrigerate the scraps. (Cut-out cookies can be frozen on a baking sheet, layers of them separated by parchment paper and the baking sheet tightly wrapped in plastic, for up to 1 month. Remove them from the freezer, place them in single layers on parchment paper–lined baking sheets, and proceed directly to the next step in the recipe.)

6. Using a very small measuring spoon, carefully fill each small star cutout with the candy so that the candy is resting on the parchment paper and is level with the dough. Sprinkle the cookies with some of the remaining ¼ cup sugar. Bake the cookies until they are firm and golden around the edges, about 8 minutes (a minute or two longer for frozen dough). Let them cool completely on the baking sheets. Repeat with the remaining dough balls and then the chilled scraps, using fresh parchment each time. Stained Glass Star Cookies will keep at room temperature in an airtight container for several days.

pine nut cookies

Makes about
18 cookies

This traditional Italian cookie is one of my husband, Jack Bishop's, Christmas specialties. He makes them by the dozens to give to friends and family and to serve on Christmas Eve alongside a big bowl of clementines. The recipe is adapted from his *Complete Italian Vegetarian Cookbook* (Houghton Mifflin, 1997).

1 cup pine nuts
1⅔ cups blanched slivered almonds
1⅓ cups granulated sugar
2 large egg whites
¼ cup confectioners' sugar

1. Preheat the oven to 375°F. Line baking sheets with parchment paper or spray them with nonstick cooking spray. Place the pine nuts in a shallow bowl.

2. Place the almonds and granulated sugar in the work bowl of a food processor and grind finely. Add the egg whites and process until smooth. Scrape the dough into a large bowl.

3. With wet hands, scoop a rounded tablespoonful of the dough up and shape it into a ball. Roll the ball in the pine nuts to coat all over. Place the ball on a prepared baking sheet. Repeat with the remaining dough, placing the cookies at least 2 inches apart on the sheets.

4. Bake until the cookies are light golden, 13 to 15 minutes. Do not let the nuts turn dark brown or they will be bitter. Let the cookies cool completely on the baking sheets. Sift confectioners' sugar over their tops. Pine Nut Cookies will keep at room temperature in an airtight container for up to 2 days.

snowball cookies

I wind up making multiple batches of these tender pecan shortbread balls, otherwise known as Mexican wedding cakes, at Christmas time, because they are simple and classic and look so seasonal covered in snowy white confectioners' sugar. Walnuts may be substituted for the pecans if you like.

1½ cups pecan halves
2¼ cups unbleached all-purpose flour
1 teaspoon salt
1 cup (2 sticks) unsalted butter, softened
½ cup granulated sugar
1½ teaspoons water
1½ teaspoons pure vanilla extract
½ cup confectioners' sugar

1. Preheat the oven to 325°F. Spread the pecan halves out in a single layer on a rimmed baking sheet and toast until fragrant, 8 to 10 minutes. Remove from the oven and let cool completely.

2. Place the nuts in a food processor and process until they are finely chopped. Combine the chopped nuts, flour, and salt in a medium-size mixing bowl and set aside.

3. Cream the butter and granulated sugar together in a large mixing bowl with an electric mixer on medium-high speed until fluffy, 2 to 3 minutes. Beat the water and vanilla extract into the butter mixture. Stir in the nut-flour mixture until just combined.

4. Scoop up rounded tablespoonfuls of dough and roll them between your palms to form balls. Place the balls on ungreased baking sheets, leaving 1½ inches between each cookie. Bake the cookies until they are cooked through but not dry, about 20 minutes. Remove the cookies with a metal spatula to a wire rack to cool.

5. Place the confectioners' sugar in a shallow bowl. When the cookies are completely cooled, roll each one in sugar to coat heavily. Snowball Cookies will keep at room temperature in an airtight container for 2 to 3 days.

Kids Can Help

Let your children roll the cooled cookies in the confectioners' sugar, since they probably have good experience rolling real snowballs.

durable gingerbread men

Makes about
eighteen 5-inch
gingerbread men

This is the cookie dough I use to make my gingerbread house, but it is also great for making gingerbread men that can be decorated and hung on a Christmas tree. Raisins, cinnamon Red Hots, or chocolate chips can be placed on the cookies before baking to form eyes. Use Royal Icing (page 237) to draw on frills and to glue on additional candy if desired.

½ **cup vegetable shortening**
½ **cup sugar**
1 **teaspoon baking powder**
½ **teaspoon baking soda**
½ **teaspoon salt**
1 **teaspoon ground ginger**
½ **teaspoon ground cinnamon**
¼ **teaspoon ground cloves**
½ **cup dark (not light or blackstrap) molasses**
1 **large egg**
1 **tablespoon white vinegar**
2½ **cups unbleached all-purpose flour**
Raisins, chocolate chips, and/or cinnamon Red Hots for eyes and buttons
Royal Icing (page 237, optional)

1. Combine the shortening and sugar in a large mixing bowl with an electric mixer on medium-high speed until well combined.

2. Add the baking powder, baking soda, salt, ginger, cinnamon, and cloves and beat until incorporated.

3. Add the molasses, egg, and white vinegar and beat until smooth, scraping down the sides of the bowl once or twice as necessary.

4. Add the flour, 1 cup at a time, and stir until incorporated. Scrape the dough onto a sheet of plastic wrap and press into a rough square. Wrap tightly and refrigerate for at least 3 hours and up to 3 days.

5. Preheat the oven to 375°F. Line a baking sheet with parchment paper.

6. Cut away one-fourth of the dough, and rewrap the rest in plastic wrap. With a lightly floured rolling pin, roll out the dough on a lightly floured work surface to a ¼-inch thickness. Cut the dough into gingerbread people and place the cookies on the prepared baking sheet. Refrigerate the scraps. Make the eyes, nose, mouth, and buttons by pressing raisins, chocolate chips, and/or Red Hots into the cookies. If you are making these as ornaments, cut out a hole at the top of each cookie with a drinking straw.

7. Bake the cookies until they are firm, 8 to 10 minutes. Slide the entire parchment sheet with the cookies onto a wire rack and let the cookies cool completely. Repeat with the remaining dough and then with the chilled scraps, using fresh parchment paper each time. Decorate with the icing as desired. Durable Gingerbread Men will keep at room temperature in an airtight container for 7 to 10 days.

candy-covered gingerbread house

Makes
1 gingerbread house

It's much more fun to decorate a gingerbread house than to bake and assemble the gingerbread. So I've designed a simple, modestly sized house and focused on covering it with candy. My children were delighted with it, and yours will be, too. In the event your family wants to eat your creation after all your hard work, be sure to do so within 1 week.

2 recipes dough from Durable
    Gingerbread Men (page 243), chilled
2 recipes Thicker Royal Icing (page
    247)
Six 2½-inch square pieces of a paper
    lace doily
1 roll pink bubble gum "tape"
5 packages Necco Wafers
About 45 pastel-colored Jordan almonds
About 50 small brown jelly beans
1 Smartie
1 licorice Scottie dog
About 40 candy spearmint leaves
8 green rock candy lollipops
8 large white gumdrops
About 40 pink wintergreen candies
About thirty-two 3 x ½-inch chocolate-
    covered cookies

1. Enlarge the patterns on pieces of thin cardboard or sturdy paper (old file folders are good for this project). Preheat the oven to 375°F.

2. Lightly flour a piece of parchment paper and roll out about one-fourth of the dough onto the parchment so that it is ¼ inch thick. Place the pattern for the front of the house onto the dough and cut around the pattern with a sharp knife. Cut away the door opening and set aside the door piece. Cut away the windows. Remove the scraps from the parchment, wrap in plastic wrap, and refrigerate until ready to re-roll.

3. Slide the parchment onto a rimless baking sheet. Place the door piece next to the house front piece on the baking sheet, at least 1 inch away from it. With the back of a knife, score the door vertically every ½ inch to create the illusion of boards. Bake for about 10 minutes, then remove the door piece to a wire rack with a spatula. Continue to bake the house front until the edges are lightly browned and the center is firm, an additional 2 to 4 minutes. Remove from the oven and let cool on the pan for 5 minutes. Slide the parchment onto a wire rack and let cool completely. Repeat the rolling and baking with the back piece, side pieces, and roof pieces. When the pieces are cool, transfer them to parchment paper–lined baking sheets and tightly cover the sheets in plastic until ready to assemble, up to 1 week.

4. Assemble the house: Choose a large board or tray on which to display your house. (I use a large overturned oval platter that's 15 inches wide and 22 inches long.) Fit a pastry bag with a #10 tip and fill with icing. Keep the rest of the icing in a bowl, pressing a piece of plastic wrap against the surface to prevent it from drying out. Pipe icing along the bottom edge of the front of the house. Position it where you want it to stand on the board and place a heavy mug or tumbler on

Use these patterns to prepare the walls and roof of the house.

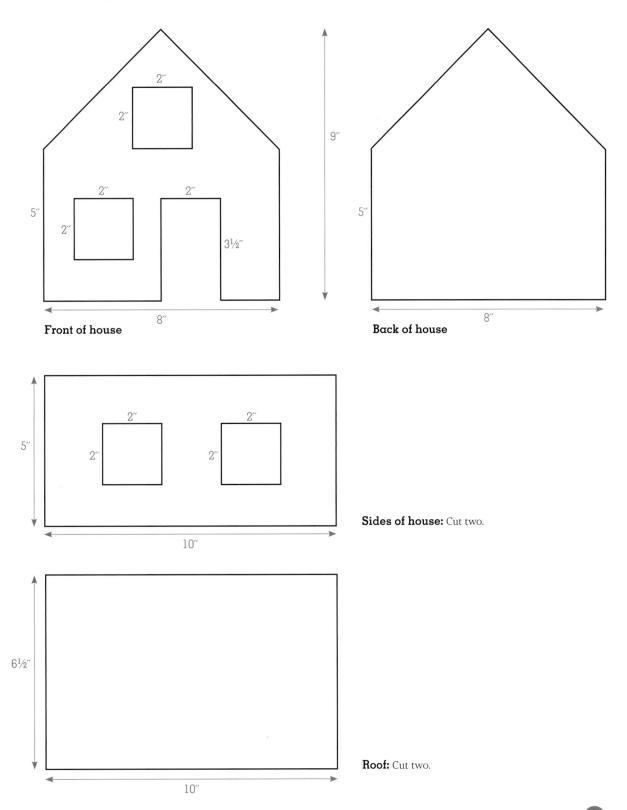

Front of house

Back of house

Sides of house: Cut two.

Roof: Cut two.

either side to help it stand upright until the icing dries. Pipe icing along the bottom edge and front edge of one of the sides and attach the side to the front so that it is flush against the back of the front piece. Repeat with the other side and then with the back, adding more mugs for support as necessary. Glue six 2½-inch square pieces of a paper lace doily to the inside of each window with a dab of icing on each corner, for curtains. For support, insert straight pins through the front wall into each side wall, and through the back wall into each side wall. Wrap the tip of the pastry bag with plastic wrap and refrigerate until ready to continue. Let the house stand until the icing is dry, about 1 hour. Remove the pins.

5. Attach the roof: Pipe icing along the top edges of the sides and along either side edge of one roof piece. Position the roof piece on top of the house, lining it up so its top edge runs from point to point of the front and back of the house. Secure the roof piece by inserting a straight pin through the front and back of the house and into the roof at the peak and at the eaves. Repeat with the second roof piece. Let stand until icing is dry, about 1 hour. Remove the straight pins.

6. Decorate the house: Cut twelve 2-inch pieces of bubble gum tape. Dab the back of each piece with frosting and attach one piece to either side of each window to make shutters.

7. Shingle the roof with the Necco Wafers: Squeeze a little bit of icing on the Neccos, one at a time, and apply a row of Neccos along the bottom edge of one side of the roof. Apply another row above this one, overlapping the second row slightly over the first row. Continue until you

reach the peak of the roof, making about 11 rows in total. Repeat with the other side of the roof.

8. Trim the roof: Squeeze a little bit of icing onto the larger end of a Jordan almond and place it upright at one end of the peak of the roof. Repeat with more Jordan almonds to create a line of upright almonds along the roof's peak. Squeeze a little bit of icing along the back of an almond and apply it to the edge where the front of the house meets one side. Repeat, placing almonds upward along this edge so they form a line from the bottom to the top. Repeat with the remaining three corners of the house.

9. Pipe icicles: Place the tip of the pastry bag against the corner bottom edge of the roof. Squeeze a little icing out of the bag, then stop squeezing as you pull it downward into a small point. (This is not difficult, but you might practice along the edge of an empty box or the top edge of a pot before beginning on the house.) Pipe icicles along the side eaves and along the front and back edges of the roof.

10. Landscape the house: Use a large offset spatula to spread a thin layer of icing in front of the house and to the edge of your board or platter, to resemble a snow-covered yard. Make a slightly winding path extending from the doorway with the jelly beans, about 5 beans wide (the length will depend on the size of the platter and how far you've positioned the front of your house from the edge). Pipe some icing along the left-hand side of the door and stand the door up, so it's slightly ajar, at the doorway of the house. Squeeze a small amount of icing on the Smartie and fix it to the door as the doorknob. Pipe a little icing on the feet of the licorice Scottie and stand it in front of the partially opened door. Pipe a little icing on the bottom of some spearmint leaves and place these "bushes" along either side of the door.

11. Spread some icing in a thin layer on one side of the house to the edge of the platter. Place spearmint leaf bushes against this side of the house as described above. Repeat with the back of the house and the other side, so the bushes surround the house.

12. Insert the ends of the rock candy lollipops into the round tops of the gumdrops. Squeeze some icing on the flat bottoms of the gumdrops and position the trees around the house and along the walkway.

13. Construct the fence: Begin on one side of the jelly bean path, and place the pink wintergreen candies at 3-inch intervals around the house, fixing them to the "snow" with a dot of icing, until you reach the other side of the jelly bean path. Pipe dots of icing onto the tops of the candies and then place the ends of the chocolate cookie "logs" on top of the dots. Repeat with another layer of candies and cookies to create a fence. Let the decorated and landscaped house stand overnight before moving.

thicker royal icing

Makes about 6½ cups, enough to assemble and decorate 1 gingerbread house

This is thicker and less runny than regular Royal Icing (page 237), making it more suitable for gluing together the pieces of a gingerbread house. One batch is more than enough to both put together the house and decorate it. You will need a second batch to spread on the surface around the house to look like snow. Make the batches one at a time, and cover with plastic to prevent the icing from drying out while you work.

3 tablespoons meringue powder or
    powdered egg whites
½ cup warm water
4½ cups confectioners' sugar (one
    16-ounce package)

1. Combine the meringue powder and water in a medium-size mixing bowl. With an electric mixer fitted with the whisk attachment, beat the mixture on high speed until soft peaks form. Add the confectioners' sugar and beat until the icing is shiny, smooth, and increased in volume, 6 to 8 minutes. If the icing is too stiff to pipe or spread, add another tablespoon or two of water and whip until the proper consistency is achieved.

2. Use immediately, or cover the surface of each bowl of icing with plastic wrap (otherwise the icing will begin to harden) and refrigerate until you are ready to use it, up to 1 day.

from mom with love: a few ideas for COOKIES IN A JAR

Confetti Cookies, Cranberry-Oatmeal Cookies

Cookies are meant for sharing with family, friends, neighbors, schoolmates, teachers. In earlier chapters, I presented cookie recipes to share on ordinary days, snow days, and holidays. I've shown you what I do when I'm desperate for cookies to share with my kids, and how I avoid desperation by keeping slice-and-bake cookie dough of all kinds in the freezer to share with whomever stops by. In this chapter I'll show you one last way I share cookies. Here are a few recipes for homemade cookie mixes to give to someone, someone who in turn can bake a fresh batch at his or her leisure.

Cookies in a jar are simply the dry ingredients of a cookie recipe, packed up nicely and ready to be mixed with wet ingredients to make cookie dough. If you are the lucky recipient of a jar of homemade cookie mix, all you have to do is dump the contents into a large bowl, stir in some melted butter and an egg or two, and *voilà*: cookie dough. I had seen these recipes around, but because I was always baking cookies and giving them away, I didn't feel the need to make another kind of cookie gift. A case of 1-quart mason jars in my local 5&10 attracted my eye one day, and all of a sudden I felt the need. The jars were so pretty and old-fashioned. Then I saw the bolts of gingham fabric in every color right next to the jars, and that was it. I bought the jars and some gingham to slip between the lids and the rims as decoration, and I was ready to go.

The following recipes represent the range of possibilities for cookies in a jar. Simple drop and bar cookies work best, because eventually all their ingredients get mixed together, anyway. You can't premix ingredients for a recipe that has different layers (Raspberry–Cream Cheese Brownies, for example) or one that must be mixed in stages, with the butter and sugar creamed together first and then the flour mixed in second (such as Rolled Sugar Cookies). For the convenience of the recipient, a mix that requires the addition of only a few ingredients (butter, eggs, vanilla extract) to complete it is best. Other add-on ingredients that can't be packed in the jar ideally should be packed alongside it in a box or basket, as with the 8-ounce jar of applesauce needed to bake Applesauce Bars for Teacher (page 253).

If you invest in a case of mason jars, you may want to branch out from the recipes in this chapter. Many of the chocolate chip and oatmeal cookies in chapter 1 and the blondies in chapter 4 adapt easily to this format, because they call for melted, not softened, butter. If you do adapt some other recipes, practice your division facts with your fourth-grader before you begin, because you may have to adjust quantities to wind up with 4 cups of cookie mix, the amount you will need to fill the jar.

Tips for Packing Cookies

It's fun to give cookie mixes in a jar, but cookies fresh from your oven are also a wonderful, if more perishable, gift. Most of the cookies in this book are sturdy enough to travel to a friend's house, packed in a tin or an airtight plastic container. But if you want to mail your cookies, you'll need to take precautions so that they arrive fresh and intact.

* Choose cookie recipes that will keep for several days. Thick, sturdy drop cookies and hard biscotti are better choices than delicate rolled cookies. Bar cookies fit well into square containers, but be sure to separate brownie and blondie layers with waxed paper so that the bars don't stick to each other. Avoid recipes with soft frostings or fillings that might smear or ooze during travel.

* Pack your cookies in a sturdy tin or plastic container (a cardboard container doesn't keep cookies as fresh and may exhibit grease stains by the time it arrives), filling the container so that the cookies can't slide around, but not overfilling it so that the cookies get squashed.

* Pack the cookie container in a box that's 2 or 3 inches larger all around. Fill the bottom of the larger box with a 2- or 3-inch layer of packing peanuts or bubble wrap (I recycle packing material that comes to me with merchandise I've ordered by mail). Surround the cookie container's sides and top with more packing peanuts or folded layers of bubble wrap so that it is secure inside the larger box.

* It's not necessary to mail your package overnight, but spring for Priority Mail so that your cookies are still fresh when they arrive.

cranberry-oatmeal cookies in a jar

Makes about 24 cookies

Like making jams and jellies in the summer and putting them in the cupboard so that they're there when you need them in the dead of winter, putting together cookie mixes in pretty containers means that you're always prepared when you need a last-minute hostess or thank-you gift. This recipe is my standby, because it's simple enough so that even a noncook will have success with it, but a little bit more special than run-of-the-mill chocolate chip or oatmeal cookies. I put the ingredients in an old-fashioned 1-quart glass mason jar and wrap it in a cute new kitchen towel. A wooden spoon (I keep a fresh supply ready) and a homey recipe card with instructions for making the cookies (I type this out and print it) complete the package.

¾ **cup unbleached all-purpose flour**
½ **teaspoon baking soda**
¼ **teaspoon salt**
¼ **teaspoon ground cinnamon**
1½ **cups old-fashioned rolled oats (not instant)**
½ **cup dried cranberries**
½ **cup firmly packed light brown sugar**
¼ **cup granulated sugar**
¾ **cup white chocolate chips**

Whisk together the flour, baking soda, salt, and cinnamon in a small bowl. Spoon the mixture into the bottom of a clean, wide-mouth 1-quart jar. Gently tap the jar on the counter to even out the flour. Spoon the oats into the jar and tap the jar on the counter to even out the oats. Spoon in the cranberries and press with the back of a spoon to compact the mixture. Spoon in the brown sugar and then the granulated sugar, and press with the spoon again to compact. Spoon in the white chocolate chips. Seal the jar tightly. It will be filled to the top. (Cranberry-Oatmeal Cookies in a Jar will keep for several weeks in a cool, dry pantry.)

On a recipe card, write or type the following:

R E C I P E

Cranberry-Oatmeal Cookies with White Chocolate Chips

Preheat the oven to 350°F. Pour the contents of this jar into a large bowl and stir to combine. Stir in 1 stick of melted unsalted butter, 1 large egg, and ½ teaspoon vanilla extract. Drop tablespoonfuls of dough onto ungreased baking sheets, 3 inches apart. Bake until the edges of the cookies are golden and the tops are set, 11 to 13 minutes. Cool on wire racks.

applesauce bars for teacher

Makes 16 bars

Put together the ingredients for these wholesome cookies when the school year is just getting underway. Pack the jar, along with an 8-ounce jar of applesauce for the recipe and a shiny red apple for teacher, in a little bushel basket lined with a gingham napkin.

2 cups unbleached all-purpose flour
¾ teaspoon baking soda
¼ teaspoon salt
½ teaspoon ground cinnamon
¼ teaspoon ground cloves
¾ cup coarsely chopped walnuts
½ cup firmly packed light brown sugar
¼ cup granulated sugar
¾ cup raisins

Whisk together the flour, baking soda, salt, cinnamon, and cloves in a small bowl. Spoon the mixture into the bottom of a clean, wide-mouth 1-quart jar. Spoon the nuts on top of the flour mixture. Spoon the brown sugar and then the granulated sugar on top of the nuts. Press down on the mixture with the back of the spoon to pack it down. Spoon the raisins into the jar. Seal the jar tightly. It will be filled to the top. (Applesauce Bars for Teacher will keep for several weeks in a cool, dry pantry.)

On a recipe card, write or type the following:

RECIPE

Applesauce Bars

Preheat the oven to 350°F. Spray an 8-inch square baking pan with nonstick cooking spray. Pour the contents of this jar into a large bowl and stir to combine. Stir in 1 stick of melted unsalted butter, 1 large egg, one 8-ounce jar applesauce, and ½ teaspoon vanilla extract. Scrape the batter into the pan. Bake until a cake tester comes out dry, 30 to 35 minutes. Let cool completely in the pan. Cut into 16 squares.

get-well sand art brownies

When your child's best friend is under the weather and can't come over to play, make this version of cookies in a jar. Layering the ingredients is just like doing sand art, and it'll keep your own kid busy. The friend who is home sick will have fun mixing the brownie batter. Pack the jar in a cardboard box along with some inexpensive craft supplies and kits (I like the $1 craft kits that you can pick up at Michael's or A. C. Moore stores), and let your child decorate the box with markers and stickers.

⅓ cup unbleached all-purpose flour
½ teaspoon baking soda
¼ teaspoon salt
¾ cup unsweetened natural cocoa powder, sifted
½ cup semisweet chocolate chips
½ cup firmly packed light brown sugar
½ cup granulated sugar
½ cup chopped walnuts or pecans
¾ cup white chocolate chips

Spoon the flour, baking soda, and salt into the bottom of a clean, wide-mouth 1-quart jar. Spoon the cocoa powder on top of the flour. Pour in the semisweet chocolate chips. Spoon in first the brown sugar and then the granulated sugar. Sprinkle on the nuts and then top with the white chocolate chips. Seal the jar. (Get-Well Sand Art Brownies will keep for several weeks in a cool, dry pantry.)

On a recipe card, write or type the following:

RECIPE

Sand Art Brownies

Preheat the oven to 350°F. Line an 8-inch square baking pan with aluminum foil so that it is tucked into all the corners of the pan and overhangs the top edges by 1 inch. Pour the contents of this jar into a large bowl and stir to combine. Stir in 10 tablespoons (1 stick plus 2 tablespoons) melted unsalted butter, 2 large eggs, and 1 teaspoon vanilla extract. Scrape the batter into the pan. Bake until just set, 25 to 30 minutes. Let cool completely in the pan. Lift the foil from the pan and place the brownies on a cutting board. Cut into 16 squares.

confetti cookies in a jar

Makes about 32 cookies

This is the gift I like to bring to new neighbors to welcome them to town. The simple sugar cookie dough is sure to please the new kids on the block, whatever their tastes. The multicolored baking bits make them celebratory.

1 cup M&M's Mini Baking Bits
2 cups unbleached all-purpose flour
1 teaspoon baking powder
½ teaspoon salt
½ cup firmly packed light brown sugar
½ cup granulated sugar

Spoon ⅓ cup of the baking bits into a clean, wide-mouth 1-quart jar. Whisk together the flour, baking powder, and salt in a small bowl. Spoon the mixture into the jar. Gently tap the jar on the counter to even out the flour. Spoon another ⅓ cup baking bits on top of the flour. Spoon the light brown sugar and then the granulated sugar into the jar. Spoon the remaining ⅓ cup baking bits into the jar. Seal the jar tightly. It will be filled to the top. (Confetti Cookies in a Jar will keep for several weeks in a cool, dry pantry.)

On a recipe card, write or type the following:

RECIPE

Confetti Cookies

Preheat the oven to 350°F. Pour the contents of this jar into a large bowl and stir to combine. Stir in 2 sticks of melted unsalted butter, 2 large eggs, and 1½ teaspoons vanilla extract. Refrigerate the dough for 15 minutes to firm up. Drop tablespoonfuls of dough onto ungreased baking sheets, 3 inches apart. Bake until the edges of the cookies are golden and the tops are set, 13 to 15 minutes. Cool on wire racks.

Kids Can Help

After they help spoon the ingredients for these cookies into a jar, let your kids make confetti out of colored paper (cut or tear it into tiny pieces) and put some inside an envelope with a few neighborhood essentials. Include brochures or a list of phone numbers for the local kid-friendly attractions like the bowling alley or the paint-your-own-pottery place, take-out menus from the best pizza and Chinese restaurants, and so forth, to give along with the jar.

self-reliance mocha cookies

Your baby is all grown up and living in a college dorm. Send him this package, complete with mixing bowl, measuring cups and spoons, baking sheet, and kitchen timer so he can make his own darn cookies now. The self-reliance part is that he has to go out and buy the perishable ingredients he will need—butter and eggs—and, of course, bake the cookies himself. I developed this particular recipe while remembering how much coffee I drank when I first left home. But you can adapt almost any of your child's favorite cookie recipes to pack in a jar. Just follow the model below.

1 cup unbleached all-purpose flour
3 tablespoons unsweetened natural
   cocoa powder
1 teaspoon baking soda
½ teaspoon salt
1½ tablespoons instant espresso
   powder
1 cup chopped walnuts or pecans
⅔ cup firmly packed light brown sugar
¼ cup granulated sugar
1 cup semisweet chocolate chips

Combine the flour, cocoa powder, baking soda, salt, and espresso powder in a medium-size bowl. Spoon the mixture into the bottom of a clean, wide-mouth 1-quart jar. Spoon the nuts on top of the flour mixture. Spoon in the brown sugar and then the granulated sugar on top of the brown sugar. Pour in the chocolate chips. Seal the jar tightly. It will be filled to the top. (Self-Reliance Mocha Cookies will keep for several weeks in a cool, dry pantry.)

On a recipe card, write or type the following:

RECIPE

Mocha Cookies

Preheat the oven to 325°F. Pour the contents of this jar into a large bowl and stir to combine. Stir in 1 stick of melted unsalted butter, 1 large egg, and 1 teaspoon vanilla extract. Drop tablespoonfuls of dough onto aluminum foil– or parchment paper–lined baking sheets, 3 inches apart. Bake until the edges and the tops of the cookies are just firm, 10 to 12 minutes. Cool the cookies completely on the baking sheets (they're very soft when warm).

resources

Every cookie in this book can be made with ingredients and equipment from the supermarket and your local cookware shop. But sometimes it's fun to look farther afield for good deals and unusual items. To stock my kitchen with bulk parchment paper, heirloom cookie cutters, and hard-to-find candies, I regularly turn to the following places:

CopperGifts.com
1-620-421-0654
www.coppergifts.com

Beautiful copper cookie cutters aren't a necessity, but once you have a couple of them, you'll find yourself longing for more. This Web site sells almost 700 different handcrafted cookie cutters in every shape imaginable, including palm trees, cleats, whales, and paw prints. These make great gifts, along with a batch of cookies.

Hometown Favorites
1445 Miller Store Road
Virginia Beach, VA 23455
888-694-2656
www.hometownfavorites.com

This site stocks an amazing array of hard-to-find candies, for all of your baking needs and well beyond. Take a look at the retro products they stock from the '60s, '70s, and '80s. You can order a boxed selection from your favorite decade to introduce your kids to some memorable candies from your own childhood.

King Arthur Flour
The Baker's Catalogue
58 Billings Farm Road
White River Junction, VT 05001
800-343-3002
www.bakerscatalogue.com

This is where I go to order sanding sugar in rainbow colors, meringue powder in large containers, pastry bags and tips, and parchment paper in bulk. It is also a great source for bulk chocolate and the highest-quality cocoa powder. Look for small cookie scoops, seasonal cookie cutters, and decorations, too.

The Vermont Country Store
P.O. Box 6999
Rutland, VT 05702-6999
802-362-8460
www.vermontcountrystore.com

It's fun to browse this site for small quantities of old-fashioned candies to decorate a gingerbread house. While you're at it, take a look at the nostalgic kitchenware, dish cloths, and table linens.

measurement equivalents

Please note that all conversions are approximate.

Liquid Conversions

U.S.	Metric
1 tsp	5 ml
1 tbs	15 ml
2 tbs	30 ml
3 tbs	45 ml
$^1/_4$ cup	60 ml
$^1/_3$ cup	75 ml
$^1/_3$ cup + 1 tbs	90 ml
$^1/_3$ cup + 2 tbs	100 ml
$^1/_2$ cup	120 ml
$^2/_3$ cup	150 ml
$^3/_4$ cup	180 ml
$^3/_4$ cup + 2 tbs	200 ml
1 cup	240 ml
1 cup + 2 tbs	275 ml
$1^1/_4$ cups	300 ml
$1^1/_3$ cups	325 ml
$1^1/_2$ cups	350 ml
$1^2/_3$ cups	375 ml
$1^3/_4$ cups	400 ml
$1^3/_4$ cups + 2 tbs	450 ml
2 cups (1 pint)	475 ml
$2^1/_2$ cups	600 ml
3 cups	720 ml
4 cups (1 quart)	945 ml (1,000 ml is 1 liter)

Weight Conversions

U.S./U.K.	Metric
$^1/_2$ oz	14 g
1 oz	28 g
$1^1/_2$ oz	43 g
2 oz	57 g
$2^1/_2$ oz	71 g
3 oz	85 g
$3^1/_2$ oz	100 g
4 oz	113 g
5 oz	142 g
6 oz	170 g
7 oz	200 g
8 oz	227 g
9 oz	255 g
10 oz	284 g
11 oz	312 g
12 oz	340 g
13 oz	368 g
14 oz	400 g
15 oz	425 g
1 lb	454 g

Oven Temperature Conversions

°F	Gas Mark	°C
250	$^1/_2$	120
275	1	140
300	2	150
325	3	165
350	4	180
375	5	190
400	6	200
425	7	220
450	8	230
475	9	240
500	10	260
550	Broil	290

index

28- Coffee Heath bar crunch
30- Mexican Choc. Chip (pepitas)
31- Favorite Jumble Choc. Chip
67- Pecan Sandies (no garnish)
84- Almond Joy Cookies
165- Whoopie Pies
112- Congo Bars